Over 200 Delicious Recipes Under 400 Calories

GREAT TASTE - LOW FAT

TIME
LIFE®
BOOKS

ALEXANDRIA, VIRGINIA

First printing. Printed in U.S.A.

TIME-LIFE is a trademark of Time Warner Inc. U.S.A.

ISBN 0-7835-5254-8

CIP data available upon application.
Librarian, Time-Life Books
2000 Duke Street
Alexandria, VA 22314

TABLE OF CONTENTS

Lemon Chicken with Roast Potatoes and Garlic

page 149

Old-Fashioned Orange Buttermilk Cake

page 427

INTRODUCTION

This *Great Taste~Low Fat* cookbook is designed to take the work and worry out of everyday low-calorie cooking; to provide delicious, fresh, and filling recipes for family and friends; to use quick, streamlined methods and available ingredients; and, within every recipe, to keep the percentage of calories from fat under 30 percent.

The challenge we took on for *Great Taste~Low Fat* was a complex one: to create tasty, low-calorie, satisfying, and easy recipes using only ingredients that are readily available nationwide. Our creative and experienced chefs rose to the task by drawing on both their culinary expertise and old-fashioned common sense to streamline the recipes and make use of every bit of flavor.

In each of the recipes we retain the key flavors and texture of the classic or high-calorie dish by using just enough of the essential ingredients to provide the desired effect. Our chefs were also delighted to be able to include ingredients that go beyond traditional low-calorie fare, such as Canadian bacon and reduced-fat sour cream—we use just enough to add flavor, but not a lot of fat.

And finally, we made certain that the recipes are perfectly proportioned: When we say that a recipe serves four, we mean it. The portions are *hefty*.

SECRETS OF LOW-CALORIE COOKING

The "Secrets of Low-Calorie Cooking" chapter sets the stage for the rest of the book by explaining the tricks we have used to add flavor and body to low-calorie dishes, as well as the simple techniques used in cooking them.

First and foremost, we strive to heighten and brighten the flavors in a dish by relying on an array of intensely flavored ingredients, from herbs and spices to a variety of canned tomato products. We also look to time-honored thickeners (such as cornstarch) and the many reduced-fat and nonfat dairy products available in supermarkets to add body and a sense of mouth-watering creaminess to dishes.

The cooking techniques we use are really quite simple. For example, meat, chicken, and fish are often dredged in flour and quickly cooked to seal in their juices. Vegetables may be cooked until they are caramelized, which adds an incredible depth of flavor without adding calories. And cutting the ingredients into small pieces exposes more surface area, allowing faster cooking and greater absorption of flavor.

Quick cooking not only helps retain the juices and flavors of ingredients, it also helps the harried cook fit these recipes into a weekday schedule. The vast majority of the recipes in this book take under 45 minutes to prepare and those that do take more than one hour are generally baked dishes that do not require much attention. And for those nights when time is in especially short supply, we have included a chapter of recipes that take under 25 minutes to prepare, called Extra-Quick.

We also encourage the sensible use of frozen and canned foods, and on page 11 of the "Secrets" chapter, we offer some helpful information on those things you can do to stock up on home-made convenience foods, such as frozen pre-chopped vegetables and precooked beans or rice.

VARIETY IS THE KEY

One of the keys to success in maintaining a healthful, low-calorie diet is variety. There should never be a feeling that you are eating the same dull, uninspired food each day. In this book, we have made a special effort to provide creatively different recipes. In the Pasta chapter, for example, try Chicken-Fried Pasta. Or try one of the hearty main courses in the poultry, meat, and seafood chapters, such as Broiled Orange Chicken with Basil, Barbecued Beef Stew, or Southern-Style Shrimp Boil. If you choose one of the quick main dishes, such as Salsa-Marinated Chicken, you'll also have time to prepare a side dish: Try the Herbed Parmesan Oven Fries. And for special occasions, you can offer your family one of the delicious, low-fat desserts—such as Zesty Lemon Squares or Fallen Chocolate Mousse Cake—with a clear conscience.

CONTRIBUTING EDITORS

Sandra Rose Gluck, a New York City chef, has years of experience creating delicious low-calorie recipes that are quick to prepare. Her secret for satisfying results is to always aim for great taste and variety. By combining readily available, fresh ingredients with simple cooking techniques, Sandra has created the perfect recipes for today's busy lifestyles.

Grace Young has been the director of a major test kitchen specializing in low-fat and health-related cookbooks for over 12 years. Grace oversees the development, taste testing, and nutritional analysis of every recipe in this book. Her goal is simple: take the work and worry out of low-calorie cooking so that you can enjoy delicious, healthy meals every day.

Kate Slate has been a food editor for almost 20 years, and has published thousands of recipes in cookbooks and magazines. As the Editorial Director of this book, Kate combined simple, easy to follow directions with practical cooking tips. The result is guaranteed to make your low-calorie cooking as rewarding and fun as it is foolproof.

NUTRITION

Every recipe in *Great Taste-Low Fat* provides per-serving values for the nutrients listed in the chart at right. The daily intakes listed in the chart are based on those recommended by the USDA and presume a nonsedentary lifestyle. The nutritional emphasis in this book is not only on controlling calories, but on reducing total fat grams. Research has shown that dietary fat metabolizes more easily into body fat than do carbohydrates and protein. In order to control the amount of fat in a given recipe and in your diet in general, no more than 30 percent of the calories should come from fat.

Nutrient	Women	Men
Fat	<65 g	<80 g
Calories	2000	2500
Saturated fat	<20 g	<25 g
Carbohydrate	300 g	375 g
Protein	50 g	65 g
Cholesterol	<300 mg	<300 mg
Sodium	<2400 mg	<2400 mg

These recommended daily intakes are averages used by the Food and Drug Administration and are consistent with the labeling on all food products. Although the values for cholesterol and sodium are the same for all adults, the other intake values vary depending on gender, ideal weight, and activity level. Check with a physician or nutritionist for your own daily intake values.

SECRETS OF LOW-CALORIE COOKING

THE LOW-CALORIE KITCHEN

To get started cooking the low-calorie way, you need only a few pieces of cooking equipment and a handful of pantry staples:

• **Equipment:** A nonstick skillet, which eliminates or minimizes the need for fat in cooking, is essential to making low-calorie dishes. A nonstick Dutch oven is also convenient to have for cooking in quantity. Choose pans that are sturdy but not too heavy to lift and maneuver comfortably. Be sure lids are snug fitting and handles securely attached. Nonstick skillets with ridges let you cook meats over high heat while the fat drains away from the food. A rack for roasting or broiling accomplishes the same result.

• **Reduced-Fat Dairy Products:** A whole range of new nonfat, low-fat, and reduced-fat dairy products make possible sensible versions of formerly fatty dishes, such as cheesecake. Many of the sauces, soups, and stews in this book also use reduced-fat dairy products to create a satisfying creamy richness, or pleasing "mouth feel." For most cooking purposes, a reduced-fat or "light" dairy product is the best choice. Nonfat dairy products should be used judiciously, since flavor and texture may be lacking, and cooking may cause them to separate and possibly curdle. An exception is nonfat yogurt, which can usually be successfully substituted for regular yogurt.

To use nonfat yogurt for creamier stews and sauces, mix it first with a little flour to stabilize it, then stir it into the dish toward the end of cooking. Reduced-fat sour cream may be stirred into a cooked dish, but only at the end of cooking, off the heat. Evaporated skimmed milk lends noticeable body to soups, stews, and sauces. Buttermilk, a low-fat dairy product made by adding lactic acid cultures to skim milk, gives tang to salad dressings, biscuits, and cakes. It can also be used as a marinade for oven-fried chicken before the dry coating is added. Reduced-fat cheeses are good in such dishes as dips and under-the-skin poultry stuffings.

• **Other Thickeners:** Besides dairy products that act as thickeners, there are several basic pantry items that can be used to thicken sauces. Flour makes an opaque sauce, while cornstarch creates a clear one, and requires less cooking than flour. Tomato paste adds thickness, sweetness, and color.

FLAVOR ENHANCERS

In low-calorie cooking, highly flavored ingredients are used to replace the flavor-carrying qualities of fat. In addition to a wide variety of canned tomato products (see page 8), the following essential flavorings are used in this book:

• Herbs and spices add flavor and fragrance to any dish. Use fresh herbs when available, and add them at the end of the cooking time.

• Acidic ingredients, such as citrus juices and vinegars, give a pleasantly complex sharpness.

• Citrus zest (see box at right).

• Sweet ingredients. Dried fruits, brown sugar, honey, and maple syrup soften the acidity in a tart dish.

• Salty ingredients. Soy sauce, Parmesan cheese, and olives lift the flavors in a recipe. They are always used in moderation.

• Flavorful oils. Using olive oil or sesame oil for cooking adds a subtle intensity.

• Nuts, especially toasted, are used in small amounts for an appealing crunch and flavor.

• Wines and spirits add a deep, earthy bite.

• Onion-flavored ingredients, such as garlic, shallots, and scallions, form an important flavor base in most recipes. Cooking tames their pungency.

• Hot peppers and their derivatives give mild dishes a welcome bit of fire.

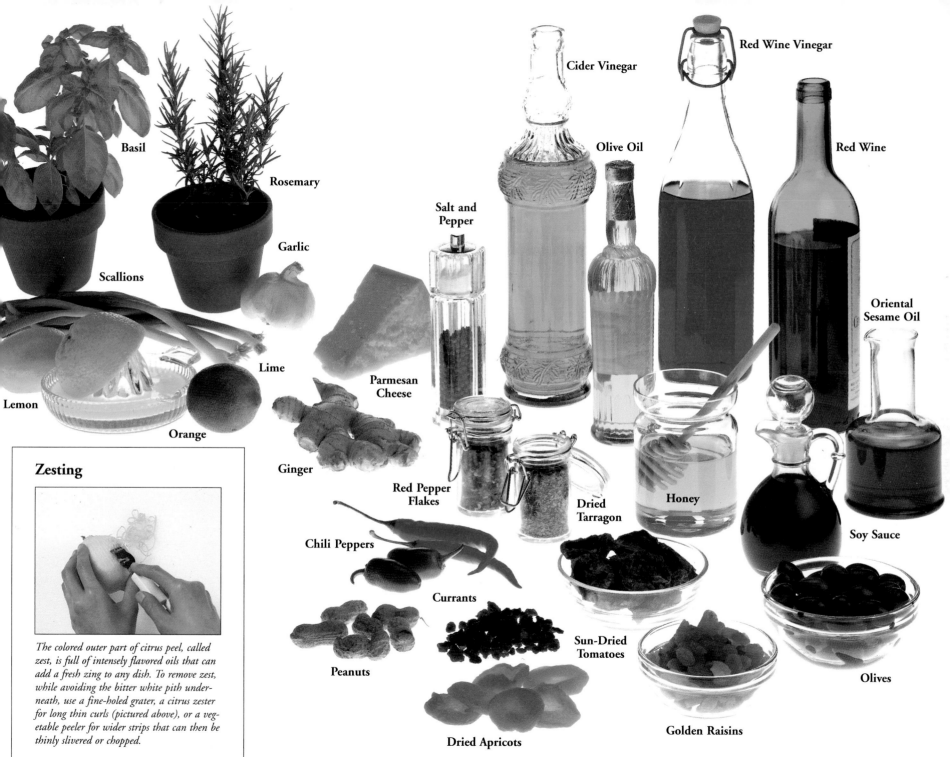

Basil

Rosemary

Garlic

Scallions

Lime

Lemon

Orange

Ginger

Parmesan Cheese

Salt and Pepper

Cider Vinegar

Olive Oil

Red Wine Vinegar

Red Wine

Oriental Sesame Oil

Red Pepper Flakes

Dried Tarragon

Honey

Soy Sauce

Chili Peppers

Currants

Sun-Dried Tomatoes

Olives

Peanuts

Dried Apricots

Golden Raisins

Zesting

The colored outer part of citrus peel, called zest, is full of intensely flavored oils that can add a fresh zing to any dish. To remove zest, while avoiding the bitter white pith underneath, use a fine-holed grater, a citrus zester for long thin curls (pictured above), or a vegetable peeler for wider strips that can then be thinly slivered or chopped.

A WORLD OF TOMATOES

Tomatoes add flavor, body, and texture to many low-calorie dishes.

• Beefsteak tomatoes. Use this meaty, seasonal variety for lightly cooked dishes.

• Plum tomatoes, a year-round, reliably tasty choice for salads, baked pastas, and long-simmering sauces.

• Cherry tomatoes, used in salads and stir-fries to add a delicate sweetness.

• Sun-dried tomatoes, used in small amounts for their intensely tangy-sweet flavor. Add a few to a regular tomato sauce to deepen the flavor.

• Canned no-salt-added stewed tomatoes. Mildly sweet and cooked with other vegetables for flavor, they need little additional cooking or seasoning.

• Canned crushed tomatoes, often used as a thick, flavorful base for a slow-simmered sauce.

• Canned no-salt-added tomato sauce, for a fine quick sauce. Combine with other tomato products or fresh tomatoes for added body.

• Canned no-salt-added tomato paste, used for both thickening and flavor. Taste as you add since its sweetness can overwhelm a sauce.

If a recipe calls for chopped fresh tomatoes, especially for a long-simmering sauce, you may prefer to peel them to avoid having bits of tomato peel floating about. With or without the skin, the flavor of the finished dish will not be affected. But peeling the tomatoes will create a smoother, more refined sauce. Peeling is simply a matter of blanching the tomatoes in boiling water, which loosens the skins for easy removal. If you are serving the sauce with pasta, you can cook the pasta in the same pot to streamline preparation. However, in dishes such as salads, leaving the skin on is desirable because the skin helps the tomatoes hold their shape.

Blanching and Peeling Tomatoes

Drop the tomatoes into a large pot of boiling water just until the skins begin to wrinkle slightly. This will take anywhere from 10 to 30 seconds, but no longer. With a slotted spoon, transfer the tomatoes to a cutting board. When cool enough to handle, peel the tomatoes, using a paring knife. The skins should slip off easily. If you wish to seed the tomatoes, cut each tomato in half crosswise, and squeeze through a sieve set over a bowl to catch the juices, or simply scoop out the seeds with a spoon.

LOW-FAT COOKING TECHNIQUES

Our cooking techniques not only reduce calories and fat in the recipes, but offer ways to intensify the flavor to compensate for the lowered fat in the dish. For example, caramelizing means to cook meats and vegetables, especially onions, until the natural sugars have deeply browned, creating a rich base for pan-cooked preparations. Reducing or boiling off liquid in a mixture causes the flavors to become concentrated and mingle together deliciously in the pan. In another easy method, browning poultry or meat after it is dredged in flour seals in the juices and heightens the flavor of the finished sauté, stew, or braise.

Caramelizing

To caramelize, cook the ingredients in a nonstick skillet, with little or no fat, over low to medium-low heat, until browned and meltingly tender. Stir occasionally to prevent sticking. Caramelizing will take a minimum of eight minutes or so.

Reducing

Reducing or cooking off liquid is a simple method for concentrating flavors. Add desired liquid to the browned ingredients in the nonstick skillet, bring to a boil over medium to medium-high heat, and continue to cook off the liquid until reduced by half or totally reduced, according to the recipe. Stir the mixture occasionally with a plastic spatula or wooden spoon. Never use a metal spatula, which could scratch the specially treated nonstick surface of the pan.

Dredging, an old-fashioned culinary technique, is still very much at home in contemporary low-calorie cooking. Coating thin pieces of meat, such as skinless, boneless chicken breasts or cutlets, with a small amount of seasoned flour (or, for a mildly crunchy coating, cornmeal or bread crumbs) produces a tasty coating, lending textural contrast as well as sealing in flavor and moisture. A quick pre-browning of the coated food intensifies the flavor of the coating, adding to the complexity of the finished dish. If creating a pan sauce is part of the recipe, the browned bits of flour from the coating left in the bottom of the skillet will help thicken the sauce.

Dredging

Before dredging, pat the poultry or meat thoroughly dry with paper towels. Spread flour on a plate or sheet of waxed paper, then press the meat into the flour to coat all sides. Shake off any excess flour to ensure an attractive, evenly browned crust.

Browning

In a nonstick skillet, cook the coated meat over medium heat until lightly browned and crisp on both sides, turning once halfway through cooking time. Take care not to overcrowd the pan or the meat will steam instead of brown.

Skimming Fat

When simmering soup or stock, or preparing a sauce, from time to time lay a double thickness of paper towels on top to blot up fat. Or, to degrease a finished sauce, let it stand for a few minutes, then skim fat from the top with a wide, flat spoon.

TECHNIQUES FOR QUICK AND EVEN COOKING

For sautéing and stir-frying, foods that are to be cooked together should be of a uniform size. For speedy cooking, the pieces should be either small or thin—or both.

For sautéing, this means that meat and poultry are sliced thin, and sometimes pounded to flatten the meat into a thin cutlet or scallop. (Fish steaks and fillets, and shrimp and scallops, are already just right for pan-cooking.) Vegetables for a sauté may be sliced, diced, or julienne-cut.

For stir-frying, the ingredients are usually cut quite small: Meat, poultry, and thick cuts of fish may be cut into cubes or strips. Thin vegetables such as bell peppers are cut into strips or squares, while solid vegetables like sweet potatoes or carrots may be sliced or julienned. Cutting vegetables crosswise on a diagonal exposes more surface area for quicker cooking.

Our recipes call for lean cuts of meat that are cut very thin and cooked quickly. The quick-cooking keeps the meat juicy, and cutting it into small pieces tenderizes it by shortening the meat fibers. Chilling the meat before cutting it firms up the texture, making it easier to slice: Fifteen minutes in the freezer will do the trick.

Pounding

A boneless chicken breast half is naturally thicker at one side. To even it out a bit, place the chicken breast between two sheets of plastic wrap or waxed paper. Pound the thicker side lightly with the flat side of a meat pounder or small skillet.

To make quick-cooking cutlets from boneless pork chops, place the chops between two sheets of plastic wrap or waxed paper and with the flat side of a meat pounder or small skillet, pound the chops to a ¼- to ⅛-inch thickness.

Diagonal Slicing

Cutting long, slender vegetables—especially hard vegetables that require longer cooking times, such as carrots and parsnips—on the diagonal exposes more surface area to the heat for quicker cooking; it also gives the slices an appealing oval shape.

Cutting Chicken Strips

This is how to cut the chicken when the recipe calls for "chicken breasts cut crosswise into ½-inch-wide strips" (crosswise means across the grain). For easier cutting, chill the chicken breasts in the freezer for about 15 minutes first.

Cutting Beef Strips

To cut the very thin strips of meat called for in our stir-fry recipes, first chill the steak in the freezer for about 15 minutes to make it firmer. Then with a long, sharp knife, cut the steak in half horizontally, using a careful sawing motion.

Separate the two pieces of meat and return them briefly to the freezer, if necessary, to refirm them. Then cut each piece crosswise (across the grain) into thin strips; our recipes call for strips that are either ⅛ or ¼ inch thick.

A WELL-STOCKED FREEZER

Store-bought frozen foods are great timesavers for busy cooks, but choices are limited. Set aside some time on a weekend and fill your freezer with healthy staples tailored to your family's tastes. When freezing foods, make sure they are wrapped well and be sure to label and date each package. Here are some suggestions and storage guidelines:

• **Beans.** Many people prefer dried beans to canned: Home-cooked beans are lower in sodium and have a firmer texture than canned. It's easy to cook a big batch of beans and freeze them in amounts suited to the recipes you'll be using. Soak the beans in water overnight, or, to save time, quick-soak them: Place the beans in a large pot with cold water to cover by 2 inches. Bring to a boil and simmer for 2 minutes, then cover and let stand for 1 hour. Drain, add fresh water, and cook the beans according to the directions on the bag. Drain and cool the cooked beans, then store them in freezer bags or plastic containers for up to 6 months. To reheat frozen beans, place them in a pan with ¼ cup water per 1 cup beans. Cover, bring to a simmer over low heat, and cook until heated through.

• **Rice.** Brown rice takes 45 minutes to cook, but it can be made ahead and frozen. To reheat rice, steam the rice in a double boiler or steamer or microwave it on high power for 3 to 5 minutes. Frozen rice will keep for at least 6 months.

• **Onions.** You can buy pre-chopped onions, but it's simple (and less expensive) to lay in your own supply of this frequently used ingredient. Peel the onions, chop them by hand or in a food processor, and seal in large or small bags. Cut-up leeks and scallions can be frozen the same way. Frozen raw onions will keep for 6 months or longer, but the flavor will fade with time. Onions that have been frozen should be used only for cooking.

• **Bell peppers.** Diced bell peppers also freeze well. Wash, stem, and seed the peppers, then dice them or cut them into squares, as your recipes require. Package, seal, and freeze for up to 6 months. Peppers that have been frozen should be used only for cooking.

PASTA

Left, Vegetable Lasagna (p. 29).
Above, Chicken-Fried Pasta (p. 25).

Beef Lasagna

SERVES: 8
WORKING TIME: 35 MINUTES
TOTAL TIME: 55 MINUTES

Our updated lasagna is just as sumptuous and satisfying as the Italian original. We've kept the fat within reasonable limits by using part-skim mozzarella. For fuller flavor, we've sprinkled in orange juice concentrate and cinnamon. You may assemble the lasagna a day ahead and refrigerate it, and heat just before serving. Be sure to let lasagna stand for about ten minutes before cutting.

12 lasagna noodles (12 ounces)
2 teaspoons olive oil
2 large onions, chopped
3 cloves garlic, minced
8 ounces extra-lean ground beef
28-ounce can crushed tomatoes
¼ cup thawed frozen orange juice concentrate
¼ cup chopped fresh basil
¾ teaspoon salt
½ teaspoon cinnamon
¼ teaspoon freshly ground black pepper
¼ cup flour
2½ cups low-fat (1%) milk
8 ounces shredded part-skim mozzarella cheese (about 2 cups)
½ cup grated Parmesan cheese

1. Heat a large pot of water to boiling, and cook the noodles until almost tender. Drain. Transfer to a bowl of cold water to prevent sticking. Meanwhile, in a large nonstick skillet, heat the oil until hot but not smoking over medium heat. Add the onions and garlic and cook, stirring frequently, until the onions are softened, about 7 minutes. Add the beef and cook, stirring frequently, until no longer pink, about 4 minutes. Add the tomatoes, juice concentrate, basil, ½ teaspoon of the salt, the cinnamon, and pepper. Cook until the meat sauce is slightly thickened, about 5 minutes. Set aside.

2. Preheat the oven to 450°. Place the flour in a medium saucepan over medium heat, and gradually whisk in the milk. Bring to a boil and add the remaining ¼ teaspoon salt. Cook, whisking frequently, until the white sauce is slightly thickened, about 4 minutes.

3. In a 13 x 9-inch baking dish, spread ¼ cup of the meat sauce. Lay 3 noodles on top and spoon one-quarter of the remaining meat sauce, one-third of the white sauce, and ½ cup of the mozzarella over. Repeat twice with the remaining noodles, meat sauce, white sauce, and mozzarella. Lay the remaining noodles on top. Spread the remaining meat sauce over, sprinkle the remaining ½ cup mozzarella and the Parmesan on top, and bake for 15 minutes, or until the cheese has melted and the top is lightly golden.

Suggested accompaniment: Chocolate ice milk with chocolate shavings.

FAT: 9G/21%
CALORIES: 387
SATURATED FAT: 4.5G
CARBOHYDRATE: 52G
PROTEIN: 25G
CHOLESTEROL: 37MG
SODIUM: 642MG

RADIATORE SALAD WITH ROASTED RED PEPPERS

SERVES: 4
WORKING TIME: 20 MINUTES
TOTAL TIME: 30 MINUTES

3 red bell peppers, each cut in half

3 cloves garlic, peeled

1 pound tomatoes

8 ounces radiatore pasta

3 tablespoons red wine vinegar

3 tablespoons chopped fresh mint

2 tablespoons olive oil

1 teaspoon salt

¼ teaspoon freshly ground black pepper

1 zucchini, quartered lengthwise and cut into thin slices

1. Preheat the broiler. Place the pepper halves, cut-sides down, on the broiler rack. Broil the peppers 4 inches from the heat for 10 minutes, or until the skin is charred. Transfer the pepper halves to a small bowl, cover with plastic wrap, and let stand for 5 minutes. Transfer the peppers to a cutting board, remove the skin and any seeds, and cut into thick slices. Set aside.

2. Meanwhile, heat a large pot of water to boiling, and blanch the garlic in the boiling water for 3 minutes. Reserve the boiling water for the tomatoes and, with a slotted spoon, transfer the garlic to a cutting board. Blanch the tomatoes in the reserved boiling water for 30 seconds. Reserve the boiling water again and, with a slotted spoon, transfer the tomatoes to a cutting board. Using a paring knife, peel the tomatoes and coarsely chop. Mince the garlic. Set the tomatoes and garlic aside.

3. Cook the radiatore in the reserved boiling water until just tender. Drain well.

4. In a large serving bowl, whisk together the vinegar, mint, oil, salt, and black pepper. Stir in the roasted peppers, garlic, tomatoes, and zucchini. Add the radiatore and toss to combine. Serve immediately, or cover and refrigerate for up to 4 hours. If chilled, bring to room temperature before serving.

Suggested accompaniment: A fresh fruit salad in a lemon-sugar syrup.

FAT: 8G/23%
CALORIES: 320
SATURATED FAT: 1.1G
CARBOHYDRATE: 54G
PROTEIN: 9G
CHOLESTEROL: 0MG
SODIUM: 567MG

This summery salad relies on the best tomatoes, zucchini, and red bell peppers for its garden-fresh flavor. Cook's trick: Blanching the garlic sweetens its taste. The mint adds a lovely fragrance but if unavailable, you may use fresh basil or flat-leaf Italian parsley. Rotini, ruote, elbows, or ziti would all be good substitutes for the radiatore.

FUSILLI ALLA PUTTANESCA

SERVES: 4
WORKING TIME: 20 MINUTES
TOTAL TIME: 25 MINUTES

1 tablespoon olive oil

1 large red onion, diced

4 cloves garlic, minced

1 rib celery, thinly sliced

14½-ounce can no-salt-added stewed tomatoes

2 tablespoons no-salt-added tomato paste

½ teaspoon red pepper flakes

½ teaspoon salt

¼ teaspoon dried oregano

¼ teaspoon dried rosemary

⅓ cup pitted green olives, halved

6⅛-ounce can water-packed tuna, drained and flaked

3 tablespoons chopped fresh parsley

8 ounces long fusilli pasta

1. Start heating a large pot of water to boiling for the pasta. In a large nonstick skillet, heat the oil until hot but not smoking over medium heat. Add the onion and garlic and cook, stirring frequently, until the onion has softened, about 7 minutes. Stir in the celery and cook until the celery is crisp-tender, about 3 minutes.

2. Add the tomatoes, breaking them up with the back of a spoon. Stir in the tomato paste, pepper flakes, salt, oregano, and rosemary until well combined. Add the olives and bring to a boil over high heat. Reduce to a simmer, cover partially, and cook until the flavors are blended and the sauce is slightly thickened, about 5 minutes. Stir in the tuna and cook until the tuna is heated through, about 2 minutes longer. Stir in the parsley.

3. Meanwhile, cook the fusilli in the boiling water until just tender. Drain well. Transfer the tuna mixture to a large bowl, add the fusilli, toss to combine, and serve.

Suggested accompaniments: Red wine, a salad of Boston lettuce and radicchio with sliced red onion in a citrus vinaigrette, and a finale of angel food cake.

Italy's well-loved puttanesca sauce is quickly prepared from ingredients usually on hand, and has become a standard favorite in this country as well. Our version replaces the traditional anchovies with fat-slashing water-packed tuna. Canned salmon would also be at home in this dish.

FAT: 6G/15%
CALORIES: 366
SATURATED FAT: .8G
CARBOHYDRATE: 56G
PROTEIN: 22G
CHOLESTEROL: 17MG
SODIUM: 731MG

We've
used tender fresh clams
for this classic for
better flavor and
texture—be careful not
to overcook them or
they will be rubbery.
Our sauce is
surprisingly low in fat
since it calls for tangy
buttermilk, accented
with hot cayenne
pepper. Spinach
linguine is nice to use
because the thick
strands soak up the
sauce and colorfully
show off the clams.

SPINACH LINGUINE WITH CLAM SAUCE

SERVES: 4
WORKING TIME: 25 MINUTES
TOTAL TIME: 35 MINUTES

1 tablespoon olive oil

3 cloves garlic, minced

3 shallots, minced

⅔ cup dry white wine

½ cup reduced-sodium chicken broth, defatted

½ teaspoon dried oregano

2 dozen littleneck or other small hard-shell clams, well scrubbed

2 teaspoons cornstarch

⅓ cup buttermilk

¼ cup chopped fresh parsley

⅛ teaspoon cayenne pepper

8 ounces spinach linguine

1. Start heating a large pot of water to boiling for the pasta. In a large nonstick skillet, heat the oil until hot but not smoking over medium heat. Add the garlic and shallots and cook, stirring frequently, until the garlic is softened, about 3 minutes. Stir in the wine, broth, and oregano. Increase the heat to medium-high and bring to a boil.

2. Add the clams, cover, and cook just until the clams are opened, about 5 minutes. With a slotted spoon, transfer the opened clams to a bowl; discard any that do not open. Reserve the clam liquid. When cool enough to handle, remove the clams from their shells (see tip). Discard the shells and coarsely chop the clams.

3. Strain the reserved clam liquid through a cheesecloth-lined sieve set over a bowl, return to the cooking pot, and bring to a boil over medium-high heat. In a cup, combine the cornstarch and 2 tablespoons of water, stir to blend, and stir into the clam liquid. Cook, stirring constantly, until the mixture is slightly thickened, about 1 minute. Remove from the heat. Stir in the buttermilk, parsley, cayenne, and clams until well combined.

4. Meanwhile, cook the linguine in the boiling water until just tender. Transfer the clam sauce to a large bowl, add the linguine, and toss to combine. Spoon the pasta mixture into 4 shallow bowls and serve.

Suggested accompaniments: Crusty baguette, and dried fruits steeped in sherry for dessert.

FAT: 5G/13%
CALORIES: 334
SATURATED FAT: .7G
CARBOHYDRATE: 49G
PROTEIN: 16G
CHOLESTEROL: 19MG
SODIUM: 157MG

TIP

To prepare fresh clams, cook them just until the shells open. Unopened clams will be spoiled, so they must be discarded. When cool enough to handle, spread the shells apart and use a fork to cut the clam muscle from the shell.

CHICKEN AND POTATOES WITH PENNE

SERVES: 4
WORKING TIME: 15 MINUTES
TOTAL TIME: 25 MINUTES

Combining potatoes and pasta is a traditional northern Italian touch that adds both heartiness and texture to this fresh-tasting dish.

6 ounces penne or other tubular pasta

2 teaspoons olive oil

1 ounce Canadian bacon, diced

1 large onion, diced

½ pound all-purpose potatoes, peeled and cut into ½-inch dice

1 pound skinless, boneless chicken breasts, cut into 1-inch chunks

½ pound mushrooms, thinly sliced

2 tablespoons fresh lemon juice

¾ teaspoon salt

½ teaspoon dried rosemary

1 cup chopped plum tomatoes

1. In a large pot of boiling water, cook the pasta until just tender. Drain, return the pasta to the cooking pot, and cover to keep warm.

2. Meanwhile, in a large nonstick skillet, heat the oil until hot but not smoking over medium heat. Add the bacon and onion and cook, stirring frequently, until the onion begins to soften, about 5 minutes. Stir in the potatoes, cover, and cook for 5 minutes.

3. Stir in the chicken, mushrooms, lemon juice, salt, rosemary, and ½ cup of water. Bring to a boil over medium-high heat, reduce to a simmer, cover, and cook until the chicken is cooked through and the potatoes are tender, adding a little more water if the mixture seems dry, about 8 minutes longer.

4. Stir in the tomatoes, pour the sauce over the pasta, and toss to combine. Spoon the chicken-pasta mixture onto 4 plates and serve.

Suggested accompaniment: Thinly sliced navel oranges sprinkled with orange liqueur for dessert.

FAT: 5G/12%
CALORIES: 386
SATURATED FAT: 1G
CARBOHYDRATE: 48G
PROTEIN: 36G
CHOLESTEROL: 69MG
SODIUM: 597MG

FAJITA-STYLE FETTUCCINE

SERVES: 4
WORKING TIME: 25 MINUTES
TOTAL TIME: 25 MINUTES

8 ounces fettuccine

¾ pound skinless, boneless chicken breasts, cut into ¼-inch-wide strips

3 cloves garlic, minced

1 red bell pepper, slivered

1 medium red onion, slivered

⅓ cup fresh lemon juice

¼ cup chopped fresh cilantro or parsley

2 teaspoons cornstarch

1 teaspoon dried oregano

1 teaspoon dried basil

½ teaspoon ground cumin

½ teaspoon freshly ground black pepper

¼ teaspoon salt

1 tablespoon olive oil

⅓ cup reduced-sodium chicken broth, defatted

1. In a large pot of boiling water, cook the pasta until just tender. Drain.

2. Meanwhile, in a medium bowl, combine the chicken, garlic, bell pepper, onion, lemon juice, 2 tablespoons of the cilantro, the cornstarch, oregano, basil, cumin, black pepper, and salt and toss gently to coat thoroughly.

3. In a large nonstick skillet, heat the oil until hot but not smoking over medium-high heat. Add the chicken mixture and cook, stirring frequently, until the chicken is cooked through and the vegetables are tender, about 5 minutes.

4. Add the broth and cook, stirring constantly, until the mixture just comes to a simmer, about 1 minute longer. Remove from the heat. Stir in the remaining 2 tablespoons cilantro. Place the pasta on 4 plates, spoon the chicken and vegetables on top, and serve.

Suggested accompaniments: Hearts of romaine lettuce with a nonfat blue cheese dressing. For dessert, lemon ice sprinkled with toasted coconut.

FAT: 7G/17%
CALORIES: 381
SATURATED FAT: 1.2G
CARBOHYDRATE: 50G
PROTEIN: 29G
CHOLESTEROL: 103MG
SODIUM: 262MG

For a new twist on the original Texas fajita, we've substituted chicken for skirt steak, and pasta for tortillas.

CHICKEN-FRIED PASTA

SERVES: 4
WORKING TIME: 20 MINUTES
TOTAL TIME: 30 MINUTES

S*tir-frying the cooked bow-ties with the chicken and vegetables creates a slightly crisp pasta, which is then accented by a final sprinkle of vinegar and soy sauce in this exquisitely flavorful recipe. Store tightly wrapped fresh, unpeeled ginger in the refrigerator for up to a week or in the freezer for up to two months.*

6 ounces bow-tie pasta

2 teaspoons peanut oil

1 pound skinless, boneless chicken thighs, cut into 2-inch chunks

4 cloves garlic, minced

2 teaspoons minced fresh ginger

½ teaspoon salt

2 leeks, cut into 2-inch julienne strips

2 carrots, cut into 2-inch julienne strips

½ cup frozen peas

2 tablespoons rice wine vinegar or cider vinegar

2 teaspoons reduced-sodium soy sauce

1. In a large pot of boiling water, cook the pasta until just tender. Drain, rinse under cold water, and drain again.

2. Meanwhile, in a large nonstick skillet, heat the oil until hot but not smoking over medium heat. Add the chicken and cook, stirring frequently, until lightly browned, about 5 minutes. Stir in the garlic, ginger, and salt and cook, stirring frequently, until fragrant, about 1 minute. Add the leeks and carrots and cook until the chicken is almost cooked through and the vegetables are tender, about 3 minutes.

3. Add the pasta and the peas and cook, stirring frequently, until the chicken is cooked through and the pasta is slightly crisp, about 3 minutes longer. Sprinkle with the vinegar and soy sauce. Spoon the chicken-pasta mixture onto 4 plates and serve.

Suggested accompaniments: Sesame bread sticks, and an orange and cucumber salad drizzled with a chive-flavored buttermilk dressing.

FAT: 8G/19%
CALORIES: 384
SATURATED FAT: 1.6G
CARBOHYDRATE: 48G
PROTEIN: 30G
CHOLESTEROL: 94MG
SODIUM: 520MG

MIXED SEAFOOD PASTA

SERVES: 4
WORKING TIME: 20 MINUTES
TOTAL TIME: 35 MINUTES

Fresh herbs and clam juice add a flavor boost to this dish—an assortment of vegetables and seafood that invites variation. You might try scallops or clams with haddock, orange roughy, halibut, cod, or any other mild white fish, and in any combination that strikes your fancy. Be sure to have lemon wedges on hand to serve alongside.

1 tablespoon olive oil

1 leek, halved lengthwise and cut into ½-inch-thick slices

1 red bell pepper, diced

1 zucchini, quartered lengthwise, cut into thin slices

1 rib celery, thinly sliced

1 cup bottled clam juice

¼ cup fresh lemon juice

½ teaspoon dried oregano

¼ teaspoon salt

¼ teaspoon hot pepper sauce

⅛ teaspoon red pepper flakes

9 ounces medium shrimp, shelled, deveined, and cut lengthwise in half

½ pound flounder fillets, any visible bones removed, cut into 1¼-inch chunks

1 teaspoon cornstarch

3 tablespoons chopped fresh parsley (optional)

2 tablespoons chopped fresh basil

8 ounces penne pasta

1. Start heating a large pot of water to boiling for the pasta. In a large nonstick skillet, heat the oil until hot but not smoking over medium heat. Add the leek and cook, stirring occasionally, until softened, about 4 minutes. Stir in the bell pepper, zucchini, and celery and cook until the vegetables are almost tender, about 4 minutes.

2. Add the clam juice, lemon juice, oregano, salt, pepper sauce, and pepper flakes and bring to a boil over high heat. Reduce to a simmer, add the shrimp and flounder, and cook just until the seafood is just opaque, about 3 minutes. With a slotted spoon, transfer the seafood mixture to a large bowl.

3. In a cup, combine the cornstarch and 1 tablespoon of water and stir to blend. Bring the broth mixture to a boil over medium-high heat, stir in the cornstarch mixture, and cook, stirring constantly, until the sauce is slightly thickened, about 1 minute longer. Stir in the parsley and basil and pour the sauce over the seafood mixture.

4. Meanwhile, cook the penne in the boiling water until just tender. Drain well. Add the penne to the seafood mixture and toss to combine. Spoon the seafood pasta into 4 shallow bowls and serve.

Suggested accompaniments: Shredded Belgian endive salad with a Dijon mustard vinaigrette, and sliced papaya sprinkled with lime juice for dessert.

FAT: 6G/14%
CALORIES: 387
SATURATED FAT: .9G
CARBOHYDRATE: 52G
PROTEIN: 30G
CHOLESTEROL: 106MG
SODIUM: 416MG

Vegetable Lasagna

SERVES: 8
WORKING TIME: 30 MINUTES
TOTAL TIME: 50 MINUTES

To ensure perfect results with this inviting lasagna, cool the cooked vegetables before adding the cottage cheese mixture to prevent curdling. Boil the noodles until just slightly underdone since they are later baked. And as with any lasagna, let it stand for five to ten minutes to firm, and then cut it into serving portions.

12 lasagna noodles (12 ounces)

½ cup sun-dried (not oil-packed) tomato halves

¾ cup boiling water

1 tablespoon olive oil

4 cloves garlic, minced

1 medium red onion, cut into ½-inch chunks

2 carrots, thinly sliced

2 zucchini, halved lengthwise and cut into thin slices

1 tomato, diced

2 tablespoons balsamic vinegar

½ teaspoon dried rosemary

¼ cup chopped fresh parsley

½ teaspoon salt

¼ teaspoon freshly ground black pepper

16-ounce container low-fat (1%) cottage cheese

¼ cup low-fat (1%) milk

8 ounces shredded part-skim mozzarella cheese (2 cups)

¼ cup grated Parmesan cheese

1. Heat a large pot of water to boiling, and cook the noodles until almost tender. Drain. Transfer to a bowl of cold water to prevent sticking. Meanwhile, in a small bowl, combine the sun-dried tomatoes and the boiling water. Let stand until softened, about 15 minutes. Drain, reserving the liquid. Coarsely chop the tomatoes.

2. In a large nonstick skillet, heat the oil until hot but not smoking over medium heat. Add the garlic and onion and cook until fragrant, about 2 minutes. Add the carrots and zucchini and cook until they begin to soften, about 4 minutes. Add the sun-dried tomatoes and their liquid, diced tomato, vinegar, and rosemary. Cover and cook until the vegetables are tender, about 5 minutes. Remove from the heat. Stir in the parsley, salt, and pepper. Cool slightly.

3. Preheat the oven to 450°. In a food processor or blender, purée the cottage cheese and milk until smooth, 1 minute. Stir half of the purée into the vegetable sauce. Stir 1½ cups of the mozzarella into the remaining cottage cheese purée. In a 13 x 9-inch baking dish, spread 2 tablespoons of the vegetable sauce. Lay 3 noodles on top and spoon one-third of the remaining sauce over. Repeat twice with the remaining noodles and sauce, ending with noodles. Top with the cottage cheese-mozzarella mixture and Parmesan. Bake for 10 minutes. Sprinkle the remaining ½ cup mozzarella on top and bake for 3 minutes longer, or until the top is golden.

Suggested accompaniment: A mixed green salad with a garlic vinaigrette.

FAT: 9G/23%
CALORIES: 354
SATURATED FAT: 4.5G
CARBOHYDRATE: 45G
PROTEIN: 23G
CHOLESTEROL: 24MG
SODIUM: 570MG

LINGUINE WITH FRESH CLAMS IN RED SAUCE

SERVES: 4
WORKING TIME: 35 MINUTES
TOTAL TIME: 35 MINUTES

10 ounces fresh linguine

1 teaspoon olive oil

3 shallots or scallions, coarsely chopped

2 cloves garlic, minced

¼ cup dry red wine

1 bay leaf

½ teaspoon dried oregano

½ teaspoon dried basil

24 cherrystone clams

28-ounce can no-salt-added tomatoes, drained and finely chopped

1 tablespoon no-salt-added tomato paste

2 tablespoons chopped fresh parsley

1. In a large pot of boiling water, cook the linguine until just tender. Drain well.

2. Meanwhile, in a large nonstick skillet, heat the oil until hot but not smoking over medium heat. Add the shallots and garlic and cook until the shallots are softened, about 2 minutes. Add the wine, bay leaf, oregano, and basil and bring to a boil. Add the clams, cover, and cook until the clams open up, about 4 minutes. With a slotted spoon, transfer the clams to a bowl.

3. Add the tomatoes to the skillet along with the tomato paste. Cook, stirring occasionally, for 4 minutes to thicken slightly. Remove the bay leaf. Add the cooked pasta, tossing to coat. Transfer the pasta to a serving bowl, surround with the clams in their shells, sprinkle with the parsley, and serve.

Helpful hints: If any of the clams remain unopened after 4 minutes of cooking, remove the others and cook the unopened clams for 1 to 2 minutes longer. If they still do not open, discard them. If you prefer, use two 7¼-ounce cans of minced clams in place of the fresh clams.

You may never open another can of clam sauce once you discover how easy it is to prepare this lavish seafood dinner. You could serve this dish as individual portions, but there's something particularly extravagant about presenting a big bowl brimming with the steaming linguine and succulent clams.

FAT: 4G/10%
CALORIES: 355
SATURATED FAT: .5G
CARBOHYDRATE: 53G
PROTEIN: 24G
CHOLESTEROL: 87MG
SODIUM: 108MG

SAUTÉED CHICKEN WITH PESTO FETTUCCINE

SERVES: 4
WORKING TIME: 20 MINUTES
TOTAL TIME: 30 MINUTES

*U*p *with carbos, down with fat: This pesto is thickened with puréed potatoes rather than copious quantities of oil and cheese.*

6 ounces all-purpose potatoes, peeled and thinly sliced

¾ teaspoon salt

3 cloves garlic, peeled

1½ cups packed fresh basil leaves

⅔ cup reduced-sodium chicken broth, defatted

4 teaspoons olive oil

2 tablespoons pine nuts

1 tablespoon balsamic or red wine vinegar

8 ounces fettuccine

½ teaspoon dried rosemary

⅛ teaspoon cayenne pepper

4 skinless, boneless chicken breast halves (about 1 pound total)

2 tablespoons flour

1. In a medium saucepan of boiling water, cook the potatoes with ¼ teaspoon of the salt until the potatoes are firm-tender, about 10 minutes. Add the garlic for the last 2 minutes of cooking time. Drain well. In a food processor, combine the basil, broth, 1 teaspoon of the oil, the pine nuts, vinegar, and ¼ teaspoon of the salt and process to a smooth purée. Add the drained potatoes and garlic and process just until smooth, about 30 seconds.

2. In a large pot of boiling water, cook the fettuccine until just tender. Drain well. In a large bowl, toss the pasta with the basil mixture.

3. Meanwhile, in a small bowl, stir together the rosemary, cayenne, and the remaining ¼ teaspoon salt. Rub the herb mixture into the chicken breasts. On a sheet of waxed paper, dredge the chicken in the flour, shaking off the excess.

4. In a large nonstick skillet, heat the remaining 1 tablespoon oil until hot but not smoking over medium heat. Add the chicken and cook until browned and cooked through, about 5 minutes per side. Divide the fettuccine among 4 plates. Slice the chicken on the diagonal and serve alongside the pasta.

Helpful hint: Save a few sprigs of basil for garnishing the finished dish.

FAT: 9G/29%
CALORIES: 271
SATURATED FAT: 1.3G
CARBOHYDRATE: 19G
PROTEIN: 31G
CHOLESTEROL: 66MG
SODIUM: 601MG

EGG NOODLES WITH HAM, CABBAGE, AND APPLES

SERVES: 4
WORKING TIME: 30 MINUTES
TOTAL TIME: 30 MINUTES

8 ounces "yolkless" egg noodles

1 tablespoon vegetable oil

1 onion, coarsely chopped

6 ounces reduced-fat ham, diced

1 teaspoon cumin seeds, or ½ teaspoon ground cumin

2 cups shredded cabbage

1 Red Delicious apple, cored and diced

1 cup reduced-sodium chicken broth, defatted

1 tablespoon cider vinegar

2 teaspoons Dijon mustard

1 tablespoon cornstarch

1. In a large pot of boiling water, cook the noodles until just tender. Drain well.

2. Meanwhile, in a large nonstick skillet, heat the oil until hot but not smoking over medium heat. Add the onion and ham and cook until the ham is lightly browned, about 4 minutes. Add the cumin seeds and cook until fragrant, about 1 minute. Add the cabbage, apple, and broth and bring to a boil. Reduce the heat to a simmer and cook until the cabbage is just tender, about 4 minutes.

3. In a small bowl, combine the vinegar, mustard, and cornstarch. Add the cornstarch mixture to the skillet and cook until the liquid is slightly thickened, about 1 minute.

4. Transfer the ham and cabbage mixture to a large bowl, add the noodles, and toss to combine. Divide the noodle mixture among 4 bowls and serve.

Helpful hint: Smoked turkey or chicken can be substituted for the ham.

FAT: 7G/18%
CALORIES: 345
SATURATED FAT: 1.4G
CARBOHYDRATE: 53G
PROTEIN: 18G
CHOLESTEROL: 20MG
SODIUM: 850MG

Here's the German way to warm a cold winter day. Mustard, vinegar, and cumin seeds flavor the sauce.

Vegetable Chow Mein

SERVES: 4
WORKING TIME: 30 MINUTES
TOTAL TIME: 30 MINUTES

Although "chow mein" is an authentic Cantonese dish, it has been in this country for so long (probably since the early 1850s) that it has nearly achieved traditional American cuisine status. Basically a noodle stir-fry, it can include all manner of ingredients; here we present a light, meatless version made with fettuccine in place of the usual fresh Chinese egg noodles.

8 ounces fettuccine

1 tablespoon dark Oriental sesame oil

6 scallions, thinly sliced

4 cloves garlic, finely chopped

2 tablespoons finely chopped fresh ginger

1 red bell pepper, cut into thin strips

1 green bell pepper, cut into thin strips

2 ribs celery, cut into ¼-inch slices

½ pound button mushrooms, halved

¼ teaspoon salt

2 teaspoons cornstarch

¾ cup reduced-sodium chicken broth, defatted

3 tablespoons reduced-sodium soy sauce

2 tablespoons dry sherry

1 tablespoon fresh lemon juice

1. In a large pot of boiling water, cook the fettuccine until just tender. Drain well.

2. Meanwhile, in a large nonstick skillet or wok, heat 2 teaspoons of the sesame oil until hot but not smoking over medium heat. Add the scallions, garlic, and ginger and stir-fry until the scallions are crisp-tender, about 1 minute. Add the bell peppers, celery, and mushrooms and stir-fry until the bell peppers and celery are crisp-tender, about 4 minutes. Add the pasta to the skillet and stir-fry until lightly crisped, about 1 minute.

3. In a small bowl, combine the salt, cornstarch, broth, soy sauce, sherry, lemon juice, and the remaining 1 teaspoon oil. Pour the mixture into the skillet and cook, stirring, until slightly thickened, about 1 minute.

Helpful hint: You can cut up the bell peppers and celery a few hours ahead of time; combine them in a sealable bag or a covered bowl and refrigerate until needed.

FAT: 6G/17%
CALORIES: 313
SATURATED FAT: 1G
CARBOHYDRATE: 52G
PROTEIN: 12G
CHOLESTEROL: 54MG
SODIUM: 744MG

If you're looking for a quick meal with flair, search no further. Sweet, delicate scallops are always a treat; dusted with cumin, sautéed with vegetables, and served over freshly cooked linguine, they make a fine dinner for family or friends. Partner the main dish with a salad of dark leafy greens and cherry tomatoes.

SPICY SCALLOPS WITH LINGUINE

SERVES: 4
WORKING TIME: 30 MINUTES
TOTAL TIME: 30 MINUTES

8 ounces linguine

1 tablespoon flour

1 teaspoon ground cumin

¼ teaspoon salt

¼ teaspoon freshly ground black pepper

1 pound bay scallops or quartered sea scallops (see tip)

1 tablespoon olive oil

1 cup sliced scallions

1 clove garlic, minced

1 zucchini, cut into ¼-inch dice

1 yellow summer squash, cut into ¼-inch dice

2 tomatoes, diced

1 small fresh or pickled jalapeño pepper, seeded and minced

½ cup reduced-sodium chicken broth, defatted

1. In a large pot of boiling water, cook the linguine until just tender. Drain well.

2. Meanwhile, in a sturdy plastic bag, combine the flour, cumin, salt, and pepper. Add the scallops to the bag, tossing to coat. In a large nonstick skillet or wok, heat 2 teaspoons of the oil until hot but not smoking over medium-high heat. Add the scallops and stir-fry until the scallops are just opaque, 2 to 3 minutes. With a slotted spoon, transfer the scallops to a plate.

3. Add the remaining 1 teaspoon oil to the skillet. Add the scallions and garlic and stir-fry until the scallions are softened, about 1 minute. Add the zucchini, summer squash, tomatoes, jalapeño, and broth and bring to a boil. Cook, stirring, until the squash is crisp-tender, about 3 minutes. Return the scallops to the pan and cook until heated through, about 1 minute.

4. Divide the pasta among 4 plates, spoon the scallops and sauce over, and serve.

Helpful hints: It's best to buy scallops no longer than one day before you plan to use them. Before dredging them in the flour mixture, use paper towels to pat the scallops dry.

TIP

If the smaller and sweeter bay scallops are not available, use the larger sea scallops. Cut each one into quarters so they are about the same size as the bay variety.

FAT: 6G/14%
CALORIES: 389
SATURATED FAT: 0.7G
CARBOHYDRATE: 55G
PROTEIN: 29G
CHOLESTEROL: 38MG
SODIUM: 415MG

PEPERONATA PASTA

SERVES: 4
WORKING TIME: 25 MINUTES
TOTAL TIME: 40 MINUTES

1 tablespoon olive oil

2 green bell peppers, diced

1 red bell pepper, diced

1 yellow or red bell pepper, diced

1 clove garlic, minced

2 large tomatoes, diced

½ cup reduced-sodium chicken broth, defatted, or reduced-sodium vegetable broth

2 tablespoons chopped fresh basil

2 tablespoons chopped fresh parsley

2 tablespoons chopped Calamata olives

½ teaspoon salt

¼ teaspoon freshly ground black pepper

8 ounces ruote (wagon wheel) pasta

1. In a large nonstick skillet, heat the oil until hot but not smoking over medium heat. Add the bell peppers and garlic and cook, stirring frequently, until the peppers are softened, about 8 minutes.

2. Stir in the tomatoes, broth, basil, parsley, olives, salt, and black pepper and bring to a boil. Reduce to a simmer and cook, stirring occasionally, until the flavors have blended and the mixture is slightly thickened, about 15 minutes.

3. Meanwhile, in a large pot of boiling water, cook the pasta until just tender. Drain well. Add the pasta to the sauce, toss to coat, and cook until the pasta is just warmed through, about 1 minute. Divide the pasta mixture among 4 shallow bowls and serve.

Helpful hints: Wagon wheel pasta is one of our favorite shapes—the nooks and crannies fill up with the sauce—but rotelle, radiatore, or medium pasta shells would also be good choices. You can replace the Calamata olives with another flavorful imported variety, such as Gaeta or Niçoise.

FAT: 6G/18%
CALORIES: 295
SATURATED FAT: 0.8G
CARBOHYDRATE: 52G
PROTEIN: 9G
CHOLESTEROL: 0MG
SODIUM: 448MG

Here we've taken an Italian specialty, peperonata—a fragrant mix of bell peppers, tomatoes, and herbs cooked in olive oil—and transformed it into a great pasta sauce. Keeping the oil to a minimum, we've added some broth to make the vegetables saucy, and tossed in a small amount of chopped black olives for tang. Serve with garlic bread sprinkled with chopped fresh basil or parsley.

FETTUCCINE WITH SPINACH AND FETA CHEESE

SERVES: 4
WORKING TIME: 20 MINUTES
TOTAL TIME: 30 MINUTES

If you've ever eaten spanakopita (Greek spinach pie), you know that spinach and tangy feta cheese taste great together. Here, the feta is "stretched" with part-skim ricotta, making this a cheese-rich—but low-fat—Mediterranean-style dish. Sun-dried tomatoes add a splash of color and bright tomato taste; to save time, they're heated in the broth rather than presoaked.

8 ounces fettuccine

1 cup reduced-sodium chicken broth, defatted

10-ounce package frozen chopped spinach, thawed and squeezed dry

⅓ cup sun-dried (not oil-packed) tomato halves

1 clove garlic, minced

1 cup part-skim ricotta cheese

¼ teaspoon freshly ground black pepper

¼ cup crumbled feta cheese

1. In a large pot of boiling water, cook the fettuccine until just tender. Drain well.

2. Meanwhile, in a medium saucepan, bring the broth, spinach, sun-dried tomatoes, and garlic to boil over high heat. Reduce the heat to a simmer, cover, and cook until the spinach is warmed through, about 5 minutes.

3. Stir the ricotta and pepper into the saucepan and cook until just warmed through, about 1 minute. Transfer the mixture to a large bowl, add the pasta and feta, and toss to combine. Divide the pasta mixture among 4 bowls and serve.

Helpful hint: To thaw the spinach in the microwave, remove all of the packaging, place the frozen spinach in a microwave-safe container, and microwave on high power for 2 to 3 minutes.

FAT: 9G/22%
CALORIES: 362
SATURATED FAT: 4.8G
CARBOHYDRATE: 51G
PROTEIN: 20G
CHOLESTEROL: 80MG
SODIUM: 402MG

SHELLS WITH LEMON CHICKEN AND VEGETABLES

Fresh mint enhances the lemony flavor of this dish. We swirl in a little light mayonnaise just before serving for a luxurious creaminess.

⅔ cup reduced-sodium chicken broth, defatted

3 cloves garlic, slivered

6 ounces skinless, boneless chicken breasts, cut into ½-inch chunks

1 carrot, cut into matchsticks

1 zucchini, cut into matchsticks

2 tablespoons chopped fresh mint

2 teaspoons grated lemon zest

¾ teaspoon dried oregano

½ teaspoon salt

½ teaspoon freshly ground black pepper

1½ teaspoons cornstarch

2 tablespoons fresh lemon juice

1 tablespoon olive oil

2 tablespoons reduced-fat mayonnaise

10 ounces medium pasta shells

1. Start heating a large pot of water to boiling for the pasta. In a large skillet, combine the broth and garlic. Bring to a boil over medium-high heat, add the chicken, carrot, zucchini, mint, lemon zest, oregano, salt, and pepper, reduce to a simmer, and cover. Cook until the chicken is almost cooked through, about 4 minutes.

2. In a cup, combine the cornstarch and 1 tablespoon of water, stir to blend, and stir into the chicken mixture. Add the lemon juice and oil, bring to a boil over medium-high heat, and cook, uncovered, stirring constantly, until the chicken is cooked through, about 1 minute longer. Remove from the heat and stir in the mayonnaise.

3. Meanwhile, cook the pasta shells in the boiling water until just tender. Drain well. Transfer the chicken mixture to a large bowl, add the pasta shells, and toss to combine. Spoon the pasta mixture into 4 shallow bowls and serve.

Suggested accompaniments: Salad of mixed lettuces sprinkled with a little balsamic vinegar and grated Parmesan. For dessert, strawberry ice milk served with a drizzle of nonfat chocolate sauce.

FAT: 7G/16%
CALORIES: 392
SATURATED FAT: 1.3G
CARBOHYDRATE: 60G
PROTEIN: 20G
CHOLESTEROL: 27MG
SODIUM: 464MG

FETTUCCINE WITH CHICKEN AND TANGY ONION SAUCE

SERVES: 4
WORKING TIME: 20 MINUTES
TOTAL TIME: 30 MINUTES

6 ounces fettuccine

1 teaspoon vegetable oil

1 pound skinless, boneless chicken thighs, cut into 2-inch chunks

1 large onion, halved and thinly sliced

3 cloves garlic, minced

2 carrots, cut into julienne strips

½ pound mushrooms, cut into quarters

½ teaspoon sugar

½ teaspoon salt

2 tablespoons red wine vinegar

1 scallion, cut into julienne strips

1. In a large pot of boiling water, cook the pasta until just tender. Drain.

2. Meanwhile, in a large nonstick skillet, heat the oil until hot but not smoking over medium heat. Add the chicken and cook, stirring frequently, until lightly browned, about 3 minutes. With a slotted spoon, transfer the chicken to a plate.

3. Add the onion and garlic to the pan and cook, stirring frequently, until the onion begins to soften, about 3 minutes. Add the carrots, mushrooms, sugar, and salt and cook until the vegetables begin to soften, about 4 minutes. Return the chicken to the pan and cook until the chicken is cooked through, about 4 minutes longer.

4. Stir in the vinegar and scallion. Place the pasta on 4 plates, spoon the chicken and vegetables on top, and serve.

Suggested accompaniments: Mixed greens with a mustard vinaigrette. For dessert, fresh fruit salad topped with raspberries puréed with a little red currant jelly.

FAT: 8G/20%
CALORIES: 360
SATURATED FAT: 1.7G
CARBOHYDRATE: 42G
PROTEIN: 31G
CHOLESTEROL: 135MG
SODIUM: 397MG

I*n*
this distinctive dish, a bit of wine vinegar complements the richness of the chicken and mushrooms.

CURRIED VEGETABLE COUSCOUS

SERVES: 4
WORKING TIME: 25 MINUTES
TOTAL TIME: 25 MINUTES

Though it looks like no other pasta, North Africa's couscous is made of the same semolina flour and water that go into spaghetti and macaroni. This innovative dish crosses borders, combining the grainlike pasta with India's curry seasonings and chutney. Unlike other pastas, couscous is cooked very quickly in a small amount of liquid, so this entire meal can be cooked in one skillet.

2 teaspoons olive oil
1 red onion, diced
2 carrots, thinly sliced
2 cloves garlic, minced
2 teaspoons curry powder
2 teaspoons ground cumin
13¾-ounce can reduced-sodium chicken broth, defatted
15-ounce can chick-peas, rinsed and drained
¼ cup dried currants or raisins
2 tablespoons mango chutney
1 tablespoon white wine vinegar
2 teaspoons grated fresh ginger
½ teaspoon salt
¾ cup couscous
3 tablespoons chopped fresh cilantro or parsley

1. In a large nonstick skillet, heat the oil until hot but not smoking over medium heat. Add the onion and carrots and cook until the onion is softened, about 5 minutes. Stir in the garlic, curry powder, and cumin and cook for 1 minute to blend the flavors.

2. Add the broth, chick-peas, currants, chutney, vinegar, ginger, and salt to the skillet and bring to a boil. Remove the skillet from the heat, stir in the couscous, cover, and let stand until the couscous is tender, about 5 minutes. Stir in the cilantro and serve.

Helpful hints: If the fresh ginger you are using has thin skin, you don't need to peel it before grating. If the skin is thick and leathery, however, it's best to remove it with a vegetable peeler. Mango chutney often contains large chunks of mango; for even flavoring, you may need to chop the chutney before using it in this dish.

FAT: 5G/14%
CALORIES: 323
SATURATED FAT: 0.4G
CARBOHYDRATE: 60G
PROTEIN: 12G
CHOLESTEROL: 0MG
SODIUM: 780MG

PASTA AND VEGETABLE SALAD WITH PESTO

SERVES: 4
WORKING TIME: 25 MINUTES
TOTAL TIME: 35 MINUTES

Pesto is one of those wonderful culinary creations that brings delectable flavor to all kinds of dishes—but it can harbor fat. Our slimmed-down pesto uses just a small amount of walnuts, and substitutes nonfat yogurt and reduced-fat mayonnaise for the usual olive oil. Served alone or with some crusty bread, this salad makes a great lunch or light supper.

3 cloves garlic, peeled
8 ounces medium pasta shells
½ pound green beans, cut into 1-inch pieces
2 carrots, cut into 1-inch-long julienne strips
1 yellow summer squash, halved lengthwise and cut into thin slices
1 cup fresh basil leaves
½ cup plain nonfat yogurt
¼ cup grated Parmesan cheese
3 tablespoons reduced-fat mayonnaise
2 tablespoons coarsely chopped walnuts
½ teaspoon salt

1. In a large pot of boiling water, cook the garlic for 3 minutes to blanch. Reserve the boiling water for the pasta and, with a slotted spoon, transfer the garlic to a food processor and set aside.

2. Cook the pasta in the reserved boiling water for 7 minutes. Add the green beans and carrots and cook until the pasta is just tender and the beans and carrots are crisp-tender, about 3 minutes longer. Drain, rinse under cold water, and drain again. Transfer to a large bowl along with the squash.

3. Add the basil, yogurt, Parmesan, mayonnaise, walnuts, and salt to the garlic in the food processor and purée until smooth. Pour the dressing over the pasta mixture and toss to combine. Divide the salad among 4 plates and serve.

Helpful hints: This salad is equally good served at room temperature or chilled. The dressing can be made up to 2 days ahead, and then mixed with the salad just before serving. Sugar snap peas or snow peas can be substituted for the green beans, and fusilli or penne for the pasta shells.

FAT: 7G/19%
CALORIES: 357
SATURATED FAT: 1.7G
CARBOHYDRATE: 60G
PROTEIN: 14G
CHOLESTEROL: 5MG
SODIUM: 501MG

ASIAN-STYLE CHICKEN AND VEGETABLE PASTA

SERVES: 4
WORKING TIME: 30 MINUTES
TOTAL TIME: 30 MINUTES

There's never a boring bite with this dish: Tender chicken contrasts with crisp vegetables, while ginger and garlic play against sesame and soy.

8 ounces angel hair pasta

2 teaspoons vegetable oil

½ pound skinless, boneless chicken breasts, cut into 1-inch chunks

1 teaspoon dark Oriental sesame oil

2 cups sliced mushrooms

1 cup frozen snow peas, thawed

1 red or yellow bell pepper, cut into strips

1 clove garlic, minced

½ cup reduced-sodium chicken broth, defatted

8-ounce can sliced water chestnuts, drained

½ cup sliced scallions

1 tablespoon ground ginger

2 tablespoons reduced-sodium soy sauce

1. In a large pot of boiling water, cook the pasta until just tender. Drain well.

2. Meanwhile, in a large nonstick skillet, heat the vegetable oil until hot but not smoking over medium-high heat. Add the chicken and cook, stirring, until browned, about 4 minutes. With a slotted spoon, transfer the chicken to a plate.

3. Add the sesame oil, mushrooms, snow peas, bell pepper, and garlic to the skillet. Cook, stirring, until the snow peas and bell pepper are crisp-tender, about 4 minutes. Add the broth, water chestnuts, scallions, ginger, and soy sauce. Return the chicken to the skillet. Cook until the vegetables are tender and the chicken is cooked through, about 3 minutes. Transfer the mixture to a large bowl, add the pasta, and toss to combine. Divide the pasta mixture among 4 plates and serve.

Helpful hint: Fans of spicy Szechuan dishes might like to add ¼ teaspoon of Chinese chili oil to this dish. Chinese chili oil is a fiery condiment made by steeping chilies in oil. It can be found in Asian grocery stores. Reduce the sesame oil by ¼ teaspoon and add the chili oil to the skillet at the same time.

FAT: 5G/12%
CALORIES: 366
SATURATED FAT: 0.8G
CARBOHYDRATE: 55G
PROTEIN: 24G
CHOLESTEROL: 33MG
SODIUM: 431MG

SPAGHETTI WITH CHILI AGLIATA

SERVES: 4
WORKING TIME: 35 MINUTES
TOTAL TIME: 45 MINUTES

6 cloves garlic, peeled

3 slices firm-textured white sandwich bread, torn into pieces

½ cup reduced-sodium chicken broth, defatted, or reduced-sodium vegetable broth

1 cup jarred roasted red peppers, rinsed and drained

⅓ cup coarsely chopped walnuts, toasted

¼ cup packed parsley leaves

2 teaspoons mild or medium-hot chili powder

¾ teaspoon salt

½ teaspoon freshly ground black pepper

2 teaspoons olive oil

1 zucchini, quartered lengthwise and cut into thin slices

1 cup chopped fresh tomatoes

8 ounces spaghetti

1. In a small saucepan of boiling water, cook the garlic for 3 minutes to blanch. Drain and let cool. Meanwhile, in a medium bowl, stir together the bread and broth until all the liquid is absorbed. Transfer the bread mixture to a food processor along with the garlic, roasted peppers, walnuts, parsley, chili powder, salt, and black pepper and purée until the mixture is smooth. Set aside.

2. In a large nonstick skillet, heat the oil until hot but not smoking over medium heat. Add the zucchini and cook, stirring frequently, until the zucchini is softened, about 5 minutes. Add the tomatoes and cook, stirring frequently, until the mixture is slightly thickened, about 5 minutes. Stir in the pepper purée.

3. Meanwhile, in a large pot of boiling water, cook the spaghetti until just tender. Drain well. Add the spaghetti to the sauce and toss well to combine. Place the spaghetti mixture in a large bowl and serve.

Helpful hints: Thinly sliced French or Italian bread can replace the sandwich bread. The pepper purée can be made up to 2 days ahead and refrigerated—bring to room temperature before proceeding. The purée is also wonderful as a topping for baked potatoes or other cooked vegetables, especially green vegetables for the color contrast.

FAT: 10G/24%
CALORIES: 393
SATURATED FAT: 1.2G
CARBOHYDRATE: 63G
PROTEIN: 12G
CHOLESTEROL: 0MG
SODIUM: 704MG

Our agliata sauce, based on an Italian classic, stars puréed roasted peppers, walnuts, garlic, and chili powder for zip.

RAVIOLI IN TOMATO-MUSHROOM SAUCE

SERVES: 4
WORKING TIME: 25 MINUTES
TOTAL TIME: 35 MINUTES

Pasta is basically a low-fat entrée—it's the heavy sauces that get us into trouble, nutritionally, that is. But not so here: We've cooked juicy tomatoes with meaty-tasting mushrooms and a few other vegetables, and that's our fat-trimmed sauce. Serve with a salad of mixed greens and sliced radishes drizzled with a lemon vinaigrette.

1 medium onion, chopped

1 clove garlic, minced

½ cup reduced-sodium chicken broth, defatted, or reduced-sodium vegetable broth

3 tomatoes, diced

2 tablespoons chopped fresh basil

½ teaspoon salt

¼ teaspoon freshly ground black pepper

½ pound mushrooms, thinly sliced

2 carrots, thinly sliced

1½ cups fresh or frozen corn kernels

8 ounces refrigerated or frozen spinach-cheese or vegetable ravioli

1. In a large skillet, combine the onion, garlic, and broth. Bring to a boil, reduce to a simmer, and cook, stirring frequently, until the onion is softened, about 5 minutes. Stir in the tomatoes, basil, salt, and pepper and bring to boil. Reduce to a simmer, cover, and cook, stirring occasionally, until the mixture is slightly thickened, about 15 minutes.

2. Stir in the mushrooms, carrots, and corn, cover again, and cook until the vegetables are tender, about 10 minutes longer.

3. Meanwhile, in a large pot of boiling water, cook the ravioli until just tender. Drain well. Add the ravioli to the sauce and toss to combine. Divide the ravioli mixture among 4 shallow bowls and serve.

Helpful hints: For a really special dish, take advantage of the variety of mushrooms available in the supermarket: oyster, portobello, cremini, and shiitake. The tomato-mushroom sauce can be made up to 1 day ahead and refrigerated, and then gently reheated while you cook the ravioli. The sauce is good over any sturdy pasta, such as penne, rigatoni, or rotini.

FAT: 10G/29%
CALORIES: 297
SATURATED FAT: 0.2G
CARBOHYDRATE: 42G
PROTEIN: 14G
CHOLESTEROL: 47MG
SODIUM: 670MG

M eatballs are sublimely flavored with dill and yogurt— classic Middle Eastern partners—and combined with pasta and vegetables to create this satisfying supper. Any short, sturdy pasta, such as ziti or penne, will do well here if spinach fusilli is not available. If you don't see lean ground lamb in your meat case, ask the butcher to trim and grind you some, or use lean ground beef.

LAMB MEATBALLS WITH SPINACH FUSILLI

SERVES: 4
WORKING TIME: 20 MINUTES
TOTAL TIME: 40 MINUTES

6 ounces spinach fusilli pasta

½ pound lean ground lamb or beef

⅓ cup minced scallions

¼ cup snipped fresh dill (see tip)

3 tablespoons plain low-fat yogurt

2 tablespoons plain dried bread crumbs

½ teaspoon salt

¼ teaspoon freshly ground black pepper

2 teaspoons olive oil

3 cups cauliflower florets

1 red bell pepper, diced

14½-ounce can no-salt-added stewed tomatoes, chopped with their juices

⅓ cup reduced-sodium chicken broth, defatted

2 tablespoons no-salt-added tomato paste

1. In a large pot of boiling water, cook the fusilli until just tender. Drain well and set aside.

2. Meanwhile, in a medium bowl, combine the lamb, scallions, 2 tablespoons of the dill, the yogurt, bread crumbs, ¼ teaspoon of the salt, and the black pepper. Mix until well combined and form into 12 meatballs. Set aside.

3. In a large skillet, heat the oil until hot but not smoking over medium heat. Add the cauliflower and bell pepper and cook until the cauliflower is lightly golden, about 2 minutes. Stir in the tomatoes with their juices, the broth, tomato paste, remaining 2 tablespoons dill, and remaining ¼ teaspoon salt and bring to a boil. Add the meatballs, reduce to a simmer, cover, and cook until the meatballs are just cooked through, about 9 minutes.

4. Stir in the fusilli and cook, uncovered, until the fusilli is just heated through, about 3 minutes longer. Divide the meatballs, fusilli, and vegetables among 4 bowls and serve.

Suggested accompaniments: Spinach and feta cheese salad with a tarragon vinaigrette, and fresh figs drizzled with honey for dessert.

FAT: 7G/18%
CALORIES: 343
SATURATED FAT: 2G
CARBOHYDRATE: 49G
PROTEIN: 21G
CHOLESTEROL: 38MG
SODIUM: 456MG

TIP

After rinsing and drying fresh dill, use kitchen shears to snip the feathery fronds directly into a measuring cup, avoiding the stems, until you have the amount the recipe calls for.

You'll fool everyone with this one—a creative dish that intertwines fettuccine pasta with vegetable "fettuccine" ribbons, and then bathes them in a seductively rich (yet guilt-free) reduced-fat cheese sauce. To create the proper illusion, it really is important to use fettuccine—don't be tempted to substitute another pasta shape.

VEGETABLE RIBBON PASTA

SERVES: 4
WORKING TIME: 35 MINUTES
TOTAL TIME: 45 MINUTES

2 small zucchini

2 small yellow summer squash

1 tablespoon olive oil

1 leek (white and light green parts only), cut into 2-inch julienne strips

1 clove garlic, minced

1 green bell pepper, cut into thin strips

1 yellow bell pepper, cut into thin strips

½ cup reduced-sodium chicken broth, defatted, or reduced-sodium vegetable broth

8 ounces fettuccine

2 ounces reduced-fat cream cheese (Neufchâtel), cut into small pieces

2 tablespoons skim milk

2 tablespoons grated Parmesan cheese

½ teaspoon salt

¼ teaspoon freshly ground black pepper

1. With a vegetable peeler, cut the zucchini and yellow squash lengthwise into "ribbons" (see tip). Set aside.

2. In a large deep nonstick skillet, heat the oil until hot but not smoking over medium heat. Add the leek and garlic and cook, stirring frequently, until the leek is softened, about 7 minutes. Stir in the bell peppers and broth and cook until the peppers are softened, about 6 minutes.

3. Meanwhile, in a large pot of boiling water, cook the pasta until just tender. Drain well.

4. Add the zucchini and yellow squash to the skillet and cook until the squash are tender, about 2 minutes. Stir in the cream cheese, milk, Parmesan, salt, and black pepper and cook until the cheese is melted, about 1 minute longer. Add the pasta and toss to coat. Place the pasta mixture on a platter and serve.

Helpful hint: Be sure to shop for smaller, younger zucchini and squash, which have fewer seeds—they'll make for more attractive ribbons.

TIP

To create the vegetable ribbons, hold the squash in one hand, and draw a swivel-bladed vegetable peeler lengthwise down the squash, cutting off wide, thin strips.

SPAGHETTINI FRITTATA

SERVES: 4
WORKING TIME: 25 MINUTES
TOTAL TIME: 40 MINUTES

*T*his tempting baked frittata calls for an ovenproof skillet—if you don't have one, simply wrap the handle of a regular nonstick skillet in foil.

¾ pound thin asparagus, trimmed and cut into 2-inch lengths

8 ounces spaghettini

4 teaspoons Oriental sesame oil

5 scallions, minced

1 yellow squash, halved lengthwise and cut into thin slices

1 tablespoon fresh lemon juice

⅔ cup low-fat (1%) cottage cheese

½ cup low-fat (1%) milk

2 eggs

4 egg whites

¼ cup grated Parmesan cheese

½ teaspoon salt

½ teaspoon dried marjoram

1. Heat a large pot of water to boiling, and cook the asparagus until crisp-tender, about 2 minutes. Reserve the boiling water for the pasta and, with a slotted spoon, transfer the asparagus to a colander. Drain, rinse under cold water, and drain again. Cook the spaghettini in the reserved boiling water until just tender. Drain.

2. Meanwhile, preheat the oven to 350°. In a 10-inch ovenproof nonstick skillet, heat 2 teaspoons of the oil until hot but not smoking over medium heat. Add the scallions and cook until tender, about 3 minutes. Add the squash and cook, stirring occasionally, until tender, about 4 minutes. Remove from the heat. Add the lemon juice.

3. In a blender or food processor, purée the cottage cheese until very smooth, about 1 minute. Transfer to a large bowl and whisk in the milk, eggs, and egg whites until well combined. Stir in the Parmesan, salt, and marjoram until blended. Fold in the scallion mixture, asparagus, and spaghettini. Wipe the skillet with paper towels.

4. In the same pan, heat the remaining 2 teaspoons oil until hot but not smoking over medium heat. Add the egg mixture and cook without stirring until the bottom is set, about 5 minutes. Place in the oven and bake for 12 to 15 minutes, or until the frittata is set. Cut the frittata into wedges, place on 4 plates, and serve.

Suggested accompaniments: Yellow pear tomatoes or cherry tomatoes. For dessert, sliced bananas drizzled with honey, and then broiled.

FAT: 10G/23%
CALORIES: 399
SATURATED FAT: 3G
CARBOHYDRATE: 52G
PROTEIN: 25G
CHOLESTEROL: 113MG
SODIUM: 631MG

Home-Style Baked Ziti

Serves: 8
Working time: 30 minutes
Total time: 55 minutes

12 ounces ziti

2 teaspoons olive oil

1 large onion, minced

3 cloves garlic, minced

2 carrots, minced

1 rib celery, minced

6 ounces extra-lean ground beef

4 ounces lean ground pork

½ cup dry white wine

2 tablespoons flour

½ cup low-fat (1%) milk

Three 8-ounce cans no-salt-added tomato sauce

¾ teaspoon dried oregano

½ teaspoon dried rosemary

½ teaspoon salt

¼ teaspoon freshly ground black pepper

4 ounces shredded part-skim mozzarella cheese (about 1 cup)

¼ cup grated Parmesan cheese

1. Heat a large pot of water to boiling, and cook the ziti until just tender. Drain well. Transfer to a large bowl. Meanwhile, in a large nonstick skillet, heat the oil until hot but not smoking over medium heat. Add the onion and garlic and cook, stirring frequently, until the onion has softened, about 7 minutes. Add the carrots and celery and cook until the vegetables have softened, about 5 minutes longer.

2. Preheat the oven to 400°. Spray a shallow 3-quart baking dish with nonstick cooking spray. Stir the beef and pork into the vegetable mixture and cook, stirring frequently, until no longer pink, about 4 minutes. Add the wine and cook until the liquid has almost evaporated, about 5 minutes longer. Stir in the flour until well combined. Gradually stir in the milk and cook until the mixture is slightly thickened, about 4 minutes. Stir in the tomato sauce, oregano, rosemary, salt, and pepper and cook until the flavors have blended, about 4 minutes longer. Add the meat mixture to the ziti and toss well to combine.

3. Spoon the ziti mixture into the prepared baking dish and bake for 10 minutes. Sprinkle the mozzarella and Parmesan on top and bake for 5 minutes longer, or until the cheese has melted and the pasta is piping hot.

Suggested accompaniments: Crusty peasant bread, and a fresh fruit cup.

Fat: 11g/27%
Calories: 365
Saturated Fat: 4.2g
Carbohydrate: 46g
Protein: 19g
Cholesterol: 34mg
Sodium: 314mg

This tasty ziti benefits from two kinds of ground meat—it would also be delicious made with all ground beef.

*T*he
Alsace region of France
borders Germany, so it
should come as no
surprise that Alsatian
food is renowned for
its heartiness as well
as its lush flavors.
Here, the combination
of noodles, cabbage,
and apple reflects this
German influence.
Even without long
cooking, these
ingredients readily take
on the smoky goodness
of Canadian bacon.

ALSATIAN CABBAGE AND NOODLE STIR-FRY

SERVES: 4
WORKING TIME: 25 MINUTES
TOTAL TIME: 35 MINUTES

8 ounces wide egg noodles

1 tablespoon olive oil

3 tablespoons slivered Canadian bacon (1 ounce)

1 large onion, coarsely chopped

¾ pound Savoy cabbage, cut into 1-inch chunks (see tip)

1 large McIntosh, Cortland, or Empire apple, cored and cut into ½-inch chunks

¾ teaspoon salt

½ teaspoon freshly ground black pepper

⅓ cup reduced-fat sour cream

3 tablespoons plain nonfat yogurt

2 teaspoons flour

½ cup snipped fresh dill

1. In a large pot of boiling water, cook the noodles until just tender. Drain well.

2. In a large nonstick skillet or wok, heat the oil until hot but not smoking over medium heat. Add the Canadian bacon and onion and stir-fry until the bacon is lightly browned and the onion is crisp-tender, about 4 minutes. Add the cabbage, apple, salt, and pepper and stir-fry until the apple is crisp-tender, about 4 minutes. Stir in the noodles and stir-fry until lightly browned, about 4 minutes.

3. In a small bowl, combine the sour cream, yogurt, and flour. Add the sour cream mixture to the skillet and cook, stirring, until slightly thickened, about 1 minute. Stir in the dill, divide among 4 plates, and serve.

Helpful hint: Savoy cabbage is a green cabbage with very crinkly leaves. Its unique texture makes this dish special, but regular green cabbage could be used instead.

FAT: 9G/22%
CALORIES: 375
SATURATED FAT: 2.5G
CARBOHYDRATE: 61G
PROTEIN: 14G
CHOLESTEROL: 64MG
SODIUM: 571MG

TIP

To prepare the cabbage for this recipe, first halve the head and cut out the dense white core. Cut the cabbage half into 1-inch-wide wedges, then cut the wedges crosswise into 1-inch pieces.

59

Scallops make for speedy meals from start to finish. Because they're sold shucked, there's nothing to shell, clean, or fillet —and they cook in a flash. Here, sautéed scallops are tossed with linguine, a citrus-kissed tomato sauce, and fresh mint. It's a meal you'd be proud to serve to dinner guests, and they needn't know how little time you spent in the kitchen.

LINGUINE WITH SCALLOPS

SERVES: 4
WORKING TIME: 20 MINUTES
TOTAL TIME: 20 MINUTES

8 ounces linguine

2 teaspoons olive oil

¾ pound bay scallops or
quartered sea scallops (see tip)

1 clove garlic, minced

14½-ounce can no-salt-added
stewed tomatoes

½ cup bottled clam juice

1 tablespoon frozen orange juice
concentrate

¼ teaspoon salt

¼ teaspoon freshly ground black
pepper

1 cup shredded carrots

2 tablespoons chopped fresh mint

1. In a large pot of boiling water, cook the linguine until just tender. Drain well.

2. Meanwhile, in a large nonstick skillet, heat the oil until hot but not smoking over medium heat. Add the scallops and garlic and cook, stirring, until the scallops are just opaque, about 4 minutes. With a slotted spoon, transfer the scallops to a plate.

3. Add the tomatoes, clam juice, orange juice concentrate, salt, and pepper to the skillet. Bring to a boil, stir in the carrots, reduce to a simmer, and cook, stirring, until the sauce is thickened and slightly reduced, about 5 minutes. Return the scallops to the skillet, along with the mint. Cook until the scallops are warmed through, about 1 minute.

4. Transfer the scallop mixture to a large bowl, add the pasta, and toss to combine. Divide the pasta mixture among 4 bowls and serve.

Helpful hint: You can shred the carrots ahead of time, in the food processor or by hand; if you do, toss them with the orange juice concentrate to keep them from turning brown, and store them in a covered container in the refrigerator for up to 8 hours. Add them in step 3 as directed.

FAT: 4G/10%
CALORIES: 353
SATURATED FAT: 0.5G
CARBOHYDRATE: 56G
PROTEIN: 23G
CHOLESTEROL: 28MG
SODIUM: 369MG

TIP

Tender, sweet bay scallops, no bigger across than a dime, may only be available seasonally. The larger sea scallops—about 1½ inches in diameter—are usually available year round. If the smaller bay scallops are unavailable, cutting a sea scallop into quarters produces a reasonable facsimile.

SUMMER SHRIMP AND TOMATO PASTA

SERVES: 4
WORKING TIME: 30 MINUTES
TOTAL TIME: 30 MINUTES

8 ounces rotelle pasta

1 tablespoon olive oil

2 yellow summer squash, thinly sliced

1 onion, coarsely chopped

1 clove garlic, minced

14-ounce can no-salt-added tomatoes

¼ cup ketchup

1 teaspoon dried tarragon

½ teaspoon salt

¼ teaspoon freshly ground black pepper

½ pound medium shrimp, shelled and deveined

1 cup frozen peas

1. In a large pot of boiling water, cook the pasta until just tender. Drain well.

2. Meanwhile, in a large nonstick skillet, heat the oil until hot but not smoking over medium heat. Add the squash, onion, and garlic, and cook, stirring, until the squash is crisp-tender, about 5 minutes.

3. Stir the tomatoes into the skillet, breaking them up with the back of a spoon. Add the ketchup, tarragon, salt, and pepper and bring to a boil. Reduce the heat to a simmer, cover, and cook for 3 minutes to blend the flavors. Add the shrimp and peas and cook until the shrimp are just opaque, about 2 minutes.

4. Transfer the mixture to a large bowl, add the pasta, and toss to combine. Divide the pasta mixture among 4 plates and serve.

Helpful hint: For a Tex-Mex twist, use salsa-style ketchup, substitute oregano for the tarragon, and sprinkle the pasta and sauce with minced fresh cilantro.

Ketchup is a familiar component of "fast food." But for this quick dish, it is more than just a condiment. Here, ketchup plays a subtler role, adding sweetness and spice—as well as concentrated tomato taste—to the sauce. The shrimp cook right in the sauce, so they're absolutely drenched in flavor. Add a greens-and-tomato salad and the meal is ready.

FAT: 6G/14%
CALORIES: 388
SATURATED FAT: 0.8G
CARBOHYDRATE: 64G
PROTEIN: 21G
CHOLESTEROL: 71MG
SODIUM: 581MG

Just a small amount of ham adds meaty flavor to the rich yet very low-fat cottage cheese-based filling, which is sparked with jarred roasted red peppers. The manicotti can be filled earlier in the day and refrigerated. Just before baking, stir together the sauce ingredients and spoon over the manicotti in the baking dish.

STUFFED MANICOTTI WITH HAM AND CHEESE

SERVES: 8
WORKING TIME: 25 MINUTES
TOTAL TIME: 50 MINUTES

16 manicotti shells

7-ounce jar roasted red peppers, rinsed and drained

⅓ cup fresh parsley leaves

2 scallions, cut into 1-inch pieces

1½ cups low-fat (1%) cottage cheese

1 cup frozen peas, thawed

¾ cup finely chopped reduced-sodium baked ham

⅓ cup diced Provolone cheese, plus ⅔ cup thin strips Provolone cheese

14½-ounce can no-salt-added stewed tomatoes, chopped with their juices

½ cup chopped fresh basil

¼ cup no-salt-added tomato paste

½ teaspoon dried oregano

⅛ teaspoon hot pepper sauce

1. Spray two 11 x 7-inch baking dishes with nonstick cooking spray. In a large pot of boiling water, cook the manicotti until almost tender. Drain, rinse under cold water, and drain again. Set aside.

2. Meanwhile, preheat the oven to 400°. In a blender or food processor, purée the roasted peppers, parsley, and scallions until smooth. Scrape the purée into a large bowl and stir in the cottage cheese, peas, ham, and diced Provolone. Spoon the mixture into a sturdy plastic bag and snip off a bottom corner (see tip; top photo). Pipe the mixture into the manicotti (bottom photo) and place the shells in the prepared baking dishes.

3. In a small bowl, stir together the tomatoes with their juices, basil, tomato paste, oregano, and hot pepper sauce and spoon the mixture over the manicotti. Cover with foil and bake for 25 minutes, or until the manicotti is piping hot. Remove the foil, sprinkle the Provolone strips on top, and bake for 3 minutes longer, or until the cheese is melted. Divide the stuffed manicotti among 8 plates and serve.

Suggested accompaniments: Arugula and cherry tomato salad with a nonfat Italian dressing. Follow with sliced fresh pears drizzled with chocolate sauce.

FAT: 6G/20%
CALORIES: 250
SATURATED FAT: 2.9G
CARBOHYDRATE: 33G
PROTEIN: 17G
CHOLESTEROL: 18MG
SODIUM: 499MG

TIP

Spoon the cheese mixture into a large plastic food-storage bag. Pack the filling into the bag, twist the top of the bag closed, and snip off a bottom corner. Squeezing the top and sides of the bag, pipe the filling into each end of the manicotti, making sure to fill the shell completely.

Fresh
asparagus, the
harbinger of spring, is
played to full
advantage against a
background of pasta
and tender chunks of
chicken, all tossed in a
creamy sauce made
with reduced-fat sour
cream. When shopping
for asparagus, select
medium-green, firm,
straight spears with
smooth, unwrinkled
stems and compact tips.

STIR-FRIED CHICKEN AND ASPARAGUS WITH LINGUINE

SERVES: 4
WORKING TIME: 20 MINUTES
TOTAL TIME: 20 MINUTES

6 ounces linguine

2 teaspoons olive oil

1 ounce smoked turkey, finely chopped

1 pound skinless, boneless chicken breasts, cut into 1-inch pieces

½ teaspoon salt

¾ pound asparagus, trimmed, peeled (see tip), and cut diagonally into 1-inch pieces

¾ cup reduced-sodium chicken broth, defatted

3 tablespoons light sour cream

2 tablespoons snipped fresh chives or finely chopped scallion

4 teaspoons coarsely chopped pecans

1. In a large pot of boiling water, cook the pasta until just tender. Drain, return the pasta to the cooking pot, and cover to keep warm.

2. Meanwhile, in a large nonstick skillet, heat the oil until hot but not smoking over medium heat. Add the turkey and cook, stirring frequently, until the turkey begins to brown, about 1 minute. Add the chicken and salt and cook, stirring frequently, until the chicken is lightly browned, about 3 minutes.

3. Stir in the asparagus and cook for 1 minute. Add the broth. Bring to a boil over medium-high heat, reduce to a simmer, and cook until the chicken is cooked through and the asparagus is tender, about 3 minutes longer. Remove from the heat. With a slotted spoon, transfer the chicken mixture to the pasta pot.

4. Stir the sour cream and chives into the sauce, pour over the chicken and pasta mixture, and toss to combine. Spoon the chicken-pasta mixture onto 4 plates, sprinkle with the pecans, and serve.

Suggested accompaniments: Shredded carrot salad with a reduced-fat poppy seed dressing, and small scoops of raspberry and orange sherbet for dessert.

FAT: 8G/20%
CALORIES: 359
SATURATED FAT: 1.7G
CARBOHYDRATE: 35G
PROTEIN: 36G
CHOLESTEROL: 73MG
SODIUM: 543MG

TIP

To prepare for cooking, rinse asparagus well, paying particular attention to the tips. Trim off the woody ends. Unless the asparagus is pencil-thin, the outer layers can be tough, so peeling is recommended. Using a swivel-bladed vegetable peeler, remove the outside layers of the stems until you reach the tender centers.

CHICKEN WITH SPAGHETTI AND SUMMER SQUASH

SERVES: 4
WORKING TIME: 20 MINUTES
TOTAL TIME: 20 MINUTES

6 ounces spaghetti

2 teaspoons olive oil

3 cloves garlic, minced

1 pound skinless, boneless chicken thighs, cut into 1-inch chunks

10 ounces yellow summer squash, halved lengthwise and cut into ½-inch-thick pieces

1 red bell pepper, cut into ½-inch chunks

¾ teaspoon dried sage

1½ cups diced plum tomatoes

1 tablespoon red wine vinegar

½ teaspoon salt

2 tablespoons grated Parmesan cheese

1. In a large pot of boiling water, cook the pasta until just tender. Drain.

2. Meanwhile, in a large nonstick skillet, heat the oil until hot but not smoking over low heat. Add the garlic and cook, stirring frequently, until fragrant, about 30 seconds. Increase the heat to medium, add the chicken, and cook, stirring occasionally, until the chicken is lightly browned, about 3 minutes.

3. Add the squash, bell pepper, and sage and cook, stirring frequently, until the vegetables begin to soften, about 3 minutes. Add the tomatoes, vinegar, and salt and cook until the chicken is cooked through and the vegetables are tender, about 4 minutes longer.

4. Place the pasta on 4 plates and spoon the chicken and vegetables on top. Sprinkle with the Parmesan and serve.

Suggested accompaniment: Belgian endive and sliced tomato salad sprinkled with lemon juice and chopped fresh parsley.

This simple chicken sauce is ready in the amount of time it takes to cook the pasta. And you may substitute freely; zucchini for the yellow squash, balsamic vinegar for the red wine vinegar, and dried oregano or rosemary for the sage. Bow-ties or wagon wheels would be fun alternate pasta shapes to use in this dish.

FAT: 8G/21%
CALORIES: 348
SATURATED FAT: 1.6G
CARBOHYDRATE: 40G
PROTEIN: 29G
CHOLESTEROL: 94MG
SODIUM: 380MG

CHICKEN & TURKEY

Left, Chicken Teriyaki (p. 123).
Above, Maple-Broiled Chicken (p. 103).

*O*ur molasses-chili sauce marinade gives these skewers a delicious kick. For a tasty and decorative touch, we've wrapped scallion "ribbons" around the kebabs. Blanching the scallions first makes them pliable and easier to thread onto the skewers. Serve with crusty biscuits or whole-wheat rolls.

SKEWERED CHICKEN AND SUMMER VEGETABLES

SERVES: 4
WORKING TIME: 25 MINUTES
TOTAL TIME: 35 MINUTES

8 thin scallions, as long as possible, trimmed

⅔ cup chili sauce

2 tablespoons molasses

2 teaspoons Dijon mustard

½ teaspoon firmly packed light brown sugar

¼ teaspoon salt

1 pound skinless, boneless chicken breasts, cut into 12 pieces

1 large yellow summer squash, halved lengthwise and cut into 12 pieces

1 large red bell pepper, cut into 12 pieces

1. In a large pot of boiling water, cook the scallions for 2 minutes to blanch. Drain and rinse under cold water. Set aside.

2. In a large bowl, stir together the chili sauce, molasses, mustard, brown sugar, and salt. Add the chicken, squash, and bell pepper and toss to coat.

3. Preheat the broiler or prepare the grill. Alternately thread the chicken, squash, and bell pepper onto 4 skewers, at the same time weaving the blanched scallions in between the other ingredients (see tip). Reserve the marinade.

4. Broil or grill the kebabs 6 inches from the heat, turning and brushing with the reserved marinade, for 8 minutes, or until the chicken and vegetables are cooked through.

Helpful hints: Assemble the kebabs earlier in the day, coat with the marinade, and refrigerate until time to cook. Let the kebabs return to room temperature before proceeding. Experiment with other vegetables, such as cherry tomatoes, zucchini, and mushrooms.

FAT: 2G/7%
CALORIES: 231
SATURATED FAT: 0.4G
CARBOHYDRATE: 25G
PROTEIN: 29G
CHOLESTEROL: 66MG
SODIUM: 891MG

TIP

To weave the scallions onto the kebabs, start by piercing one end of a blanched scallion with a skewer. Next add, for example, a piece of chicken, keeping the chicken close to the pointed end of the skewer. Pierce the scallion again so that it wraps around one side of the piece of chicken. Alternate adding kebab ingredients with threading the scallions, gradually moving the ingredients down the skewer, using 2 scallions per skewer.

Mom's Chicken Noodle Soup

SERVES: 4
WORKING TIME: 15 MINUTES
TOTAL TIME: 35 MINUTES

*S*ure to chase the chill from a winter evening, this simple soup encourages variations. Try substituting turnips or potatoes for the parsnips, and other shapes, such as rotelle, fusilli, or ditalini, for the pasta shells.

3 cups reduced-sodium chicken broth, defatted

1¼ pounds whole chicken legs, split and skinned

3 cloves garlic, peeled

¼ teaspoon salt

2 medium onions, diced

2 carrots, thinly sliced

2 parsnips, thinly sliced (about 1½ cups)

2 ribs celery, thinly sliced

4 ounces small pasta shells

2 tablespoons chopped fresh dill

1. In a large saucepan, combine the broth, 2 cups of water, chicken, garlic, and salt. Bring to a boil over high heat, reduce to a simmer, cover, and cook until the chicken is cooked through, about 15 minutes. With a slotted spoon, transfer the chicken and garlic to a cutting board. Strip the chicken meat from the bones and dice the chicken. Discard the garlic. Skim the fat from the broth.

2. Add the onions, carrots, parsnips, and celery to the broth. Return to a boil, reduce to a simmer, cover, and cook until the vegetables are almost tender, about 5 minutes. Stir in the pasta and cook, uncovered, for 7 minutes. Add the diced chicken and cook until the pasta is tender, about 3 minutes longer. Stir in the dill, ladle the soup into 4 bowls, and serve.

Suggested accompaniments: Crusty rolls, and a tossed green salad with an herbed buttermilk dressing.

FAT: 5G/15%
CALORIES: 307
SATURATED FAT: .9G
CARBOHYDRATE: 42G
PROTEIN: 24G
CHOLESTEROL: 64MG
SODIUM: 737MG

The stuffing for these chicken breasts tastes decadently rich, but the fat content is surprisingly low. The trick is using a blend of reduced-fat cheeses—ricotta and cream cheese—to achieve a silky texture. Thyme-sprinkled potatoes are a wonderfully fragrant accompaniment.

SPINACH-AND-CHEESE-STUFFED CHICKEN

SERVES: 4
WORKING TIME: 15 MINUTES
TOTAL TIME: 45 MINUTES

1 pound all-purpose potatoes, peeled and thinly sliced

¼ teaspoon dried thyme

½ teaspoon salt

⅓ cup reduced-sodium chicken broth, defatted

Half 10-ounce package frozen chopped spinach, thawed and squeezed dry

½ cup part-skim ricotta cheese

2 tablespoons reduced-fat cream cheese

2 tablespoons minced shallot or scallion

1 egg white

1 teaspoon grated lemon zest

⅛ teaspoon freshly ground black pepper

Pinch ground nutmeg

4 bone-in chicken breast halves (about 1½ pounds), with skin

1. Preheat the oven to 400°. In a large saucepan, combine the potatoes with water to cover. Bring to a boil over high heat, reduce to a simmer, cover, and cook for 5 minutes. Drain and pat dry. Spray a medium baking pan with nonstick cooking spray. Add the potatoes, thyme, and ¼ teaspoon of the salt and toss to combine. Pour the broth on top and set aside.

2. In a medium bowl, combine the spinach, ricotta, cream cheese, shallot, egg white, zest, pepper, nutmeg, and the remaining ¼ teaspoon salt and stir to blend. With your fingers, carefully loosen the skin from the chicken, leaving the skin intact (see tip). Spread the spinach mixture under the skin. Place the chicken on a rack in a separate medium baking pan.

3. Place the chicken and potatoes in the oven and bake for 25 minutes, or until the chicken is cooked through and the potatoes are tender. Place the chicken and potatoes on 4 serving plates. Skim the fat from the pan juices, spoon some of the juices on top of the potatoes, and serve. Remove the skin from the chicken before eating.

Suggested accompaniments: Julienned red bell peppers and carrots, and applesauce flavored with ground ginger for dessert.

FAT: 7G/21%
CALORIES: 294
SATURATED FAT: 2.9G
CARBOHYDRATE: 24G
PROTEIN: 34G
CHOLESTEROL: 79MG
SODIUM: 497MG

TIP

Tucking the stuffing beneath the skin is a clever way to have stuffing without roasting a whole bird. Carefully loosen the chicken skin from the flesh from an open side, leaving the skin attached along the other side. Spoon the stuffing under the skin and then press gently down on the skin, spreading the stuffing evenly.

Turkey Orloff Casserole

Serves: 4
Working time: 20 minutes
Total time: 50 minutes

2 medium onions, finely chopped

10 ounces mushrooms, finely chopped

¾ cup long-grain rice

1 tablespoon julienned lemon zest

½ teaspoon dried tarragon

½ cup low-fat (1.5%) buttermilk

⅓ cup reduced-fat sour cream

½ pound thinly sliced smoked turkey

¼ teaspoon freshly ground black pepper

Two 10-ounce packages frozen chopped broccoli, thawed and squeezed dry

3 tablespoons grated Parmesan cheese

1. In a large saucepan, combine the onions, mushrooms, 1½ cups of water, the rice, lemon zest, and tarragon. Bring to a boil over high heat, reduce to a simmer, cover, and cook for 10 minutes. Remove from the heat and let stand, covered, until the rice is almost tender, about 5 minutes.

2. Meanwhile, preheat the oven to 375°. In a small bowl, stir together the buttermilk and sour cream until smooth. Set aside.

3. Spray a 2½-quart baking dish with nonstick cooking spray. Sprinkle the turkey with the pepper. Place half of the broccoli in the prepared baking dish, lay half of the turkey slices on top, and spoon half of the rice mixture over. Repeat with the remaining broccoli, turkey, and rice mixture. Spoon the buttermilk mixture over, sprinkle the Parmesan on top, and cover with foil. Bake for 25 minutes, or until the casserole is piping hot.

4. Preheat the broiler. Remove the foil and broil the casserole 4 inches from the heat for 3 minutes, or until the top is golden brown.

Suggested accompaniments: Mixed green and red leaf lettuce salad with a reduced-fat poppy seed dressing. Follow with apple slices and currants sautéed with a splash of bourbon.

Fat: 7g/19%
Calories: 346
Saturated Fat: 3.2g
Carbohydrate: 49g
Protein: 24g
Cholesterol: 41mg
Sodium: 701mg

Here we've lightened the classic French veal Orloff by using lean turkey instead of veal, and buttermilk and reduced-fat sour cream instead of heavy cream in the sauce. For a taste twist, substitute a nutty basmati or Texmati rice for the long-grain white. To get a jump on dinner, assemble the casserole early in the day, refrigerate it, and then just add a few minutes to the baking time.

Watercress and water chestnuts add crunch and pepperiness to this Mediterranean-inspired salad, while the broiled, herb-coated chicken breasts and bell pepper lend a smoky flavor. If weather permits, grill the chicken and the pepper outdoors.

BROILED CHICKEN AND ORANGE SALAD

SERVES: 4
WORKING TIME: 25 MINUTES
TOTAL TIME: 30 MINUTES

¾ teaspoon dried oregano

½ teaspoon ground cumin

½ teaspoon dried rosemary

½ teaspoon salt

1 pound skinless, boneless chicken breasts

1 yellow or red bell pepper, halved

2 tablespoons cider vinegar

1 tablespoon low-sodium ketchup

1 teaspoon vegetable oil

⅛ teaspoon cayenne pepper

8-ounce can sliced water chestnuts, rinsed and drained

3 navel oranges, peeled and sectioned

1 bunch watercress (about 6 ounces), thick stems trimmed

1 tablespoon coarsely chopped pecans

1. Preheat the broiler. In a cup, combine ½ teaspoon of the oregano, ¼ teaspoon of the cumin, the rosemary, and salt. Rub the chicken with the herb mixture.

2. Place the chicken and the bell pepper halves, cut-sides down, on the broiler rack. Broil the chicken 4 inches from the heat for about 4 minutes per side, or until just cooked through. Transfer the chicken to a cutting board. Continue to broil the pepper halves for 4 minutes longer, or until the skin is blackened (see tip). Transfer the pepper halves to a small bowl, cover with plastic wrap, and let stand for 5 minutes.

3. Meanwhile, cut the chicken into diagonal slices. Transfer the pepper halves to the cutting board. Remove the peel from the peppers, remove any seeds, and cut the peppers into thin strips.

4. In a medium bowl, combine the vinegar, ketchup, oil, cayenne, remaining ¼ teaspoon oregano, and remaining ¼ teaspoon cumin. Add the pepper strips, water chestnuts, orange sections, and watercress and toss to coat. Place the watercress-orange salad on 4 plates and arrange the chicken slices on top. Sprinkle with the pecans and serve.

Suggested accompaniments: Whole-grain rolls and, for dessert, peach nonfat yogurt sprinkled with fresh blueberries.

FAT: 4G/15%
CALORIES: 238
SATURATED FAT: .6G
CARBOHYDRATE: 23G
PROTEIN: 29G
CHOLESTEROL: 66MG
SODIUM: 259MG

TIP

The skin of broiled or roasted bell peppers can be removed easily by grasping the blackened skin and pulling it away from the flesh.

OVEN-BRAISED ROSEMARY CHICKEN WITH VEGETABLES

SERVES: 4
WORKING TIME: 20 MINUTES
TOTAL TIME: 50 MINUTES

Sun-dried tomatoes elegantly update this country dish. And all the cooking is done in one roasting pan in the oven.

1 tablespoon olive oil

3 cloves garlic, unpeeled

2 parsnips, thinly sliced (about 1½ cups)

2 medium onions, cut into 1-inch chunks

¾ pound sweet potatoes, peeled and thinly sliced

2 cups cut butternut squash (1-inch cubes)

6 sprigs fresh rosemary, or 4 teaspoons dried

½ teaspoon mild paprika

½ teaspoon salt

½ cup sun-dried (not oil-packed) tomato halves, coarsely chopped

⅔ cup boiling water

4 bone-in chicken breast halves (about 1½ pounds total), skinned

¼ teaspoon freshly ground black pepper

1. Preheat the oven to 400°. In a large roasting pan, combine the oil, garlic, parsnips, onions, sweet potatoes, squash, 2 sprigs of the rosemary or 1 teaspoon of the dried, the paprika, and ¼ teaspoon of the salt. Cover with foil and bake for 20 minutes, or until the vegetables begin to soften.

2. Meanwhile, in a small bowl, combine the sun-dried tomatoes and the boiling water. Let stand until the tomatoes have softened, about 10 minutes.

3. Sprinkle the chicken with the remaining ¼ teaspoon salt and the pepper and place on top of the vegetables. Add the sun-dried tomatoes and their soaking liquid and the remaining rosemary. Bake for 20 minutes longer, or until the vegetables are tender and the chicken is cooked through. Spoon the chicken and vegetables onto 4 plates and serve.

Suggested accompaniments: Caraway rye bread, and a light dessert of stewed dried apricots, pears, and cherries.

FAT: 6G/16%
CALORIES: 347
SATURATED FAT: 1G
CARBOHYDRATE: 45G
PROTEIN: 31G
CHOLESTEROL: 65MG
SODIUM: 378MG

CHICKEN IN GREEN SAUCE

Serves: 4
Working time: 15 minutes
Total time: 30 minutes

1 tablespoon flour

½ teaspoon salt

¼ teaspoon freshly ground black pepper

4 skinless, boneless chicken breast halves (about 1 pound total)

2 teaspoons olive oil

1 cup reduced-sodium chicken broth, defatted

2 cloves garlic, minced

3 tablespoons fresh lemon juice

3 tablespoons chopped fresh parsley

2 tablespoons minced chives or scallion

½ teaspoon dried tarragon

⅛ teaspoon red pepper flakes

1 cup frozen peas

1. On a plate, combine the flour, ¼ teaspoon of the salt, and the black pepper. Dredge the chicken in the flour mixture, shaking off the excess. In a large nonstick skillet, heat the oil until hot but not smoking over medium heat. Add the chicken and cook until golden brown, turning once, about 5 minutes.

2. Add the broth, garlic, lemon juice, parsley, chives, tarragon, red pepper flakes, and remaining ¼ teaspoon salt. Bring to a boil, reduce to a simmer, and cook, partially covered, until the chicken is cooked through, about 10 minutes longer.

3. With a slotted spoon, transfer the chicken to 4 serving plates. Bring the sauce to a boil over medium-high heat, add the peas, and cook, uncovered, until the sauce is reduced to ½ cup, about 3 minutes. Spoon the peas and sauce over the chicken and serve.

Suggested accompaniments: Roasted red potatoes, and a fresh fruit salad made with watermelon, cantaloupe, and seedless grapes.

Fat: 4g/19%
Calories: 193
Saturated Fat: .7g
Carbohydrate: 9g
Protein: 29g
Cholesterol: 66mg
Sodium: 550mg

This juicy chicken is bathed in a translucent sauce flecked with herbs and peas, all seasoned with hot red pepper flakes.

*T*o mellow the flavor of the garlic in this easy-to-prepare favorite, we first blanch the cloves. And for extra moistness, we've left the chicken skin on during the cooking, removing it just before eating, since it is quite fatty. Serve with steamed carrots, yellow squash, and radishes sprinkled with chopped parsley.

LEMON-GARLIC STUFFED CHICKEN BREASTS

SERVES: 4
WORKING TIME: 15 MINUTES
TOTAL TIME: 35 MINUTES

10 cloves garlic, peeled

2 slices (1 ounce each) white sandwich bread, torn into small pieces

¼ cup fresh lemon juice

⅓ cup chopped fresh parsley

½ teaspoon grated lemon zest

½ teaspoon salt

4 bone-in chicken breast halves, (about 1½ pounds total), with skin

1. Preheat the broiler. In a small pot of boiling water, cook the garlic for 3 minutes to blanch. Drain well. When cool enough to handle, mash the garlic with the flat of a knife.

2. In a small bowl, stir together the bread and lemon juice. Add the mashed garlic, parsley, lemon zest, and salt.

3. With a knife, make a pocket in the chicken flesh (see tip; top photo). Spoon the lemon-garlic stuffing into the pocket (bottom photo) and place the chicken on a broiler rack, skin-side down. Broil 6 inches from the heat for 7 minutes. Turn the chicken over and broil, skin-side up, for 10 minutes, or until the chicken is cooked through. Divide the chicken among 4 plates and serve. Remove the skin from the chicken before eating.

Helpful hint: Although we call for white sandwich bread for the stuffing, you can use whole-wheat, sourdough, or rye instead.

FAT: 2G/10%
CALORIES: 177
SATURATED FAT: 0.5G
CARBOHYDRATE: 11G
PROTEIN: 27G
CHOLESTEROL: 65MG
SODIUM: 425MG

TIP

With a paring knife, cut a 2½-inch-long pocket about 1½-inches deep along the breast-bone side of the breast, without cutting all the way through the chicken. Spoon the stuffing evenly into the pocket, then gently press the breast back into place.

CLASSIC AMERICAN CHICKEN-POTATO SALAD

SERVES: 4
WORKING TIME: 20 MINUTES
TOTAL TIME: 35 MINUTES

1½ cups reduced-sodium chicken
broth, defatted

3 cloves garlic, peeled and
smashed

2 scallions, thinly sliced

1 bay leaf

¼ teaspoon dried rosemary

¾ pound skinless, boneless
chicken breasts

¾ pound small red potatoes, cut
into ½-inch cubes

1 red bell pepper, cut into
½-inch squares

1 green bell pepper, cut into
½-inch squares

1 rib celery, halved lengthwise
and thinly sliced

3 tablespoons reduced-fat
mayonnaise

2 teaspoons Dijon mustard

2 teaspoons fresh lemon juice

¼ teaspoon salt

4 cups torn lettuce leaves, such as
Boston, Bibb, or buttercrunch

1. In a large skillet, combine the broth, garlic, scallions, bay leaf, and rosemary and bring to a boil over medium heat. Reduce the heat to a simmer, add the chicken, cover, and cook, turning once, until the chicken is just cooked through, about 10 minutes. Set the chicken aside to cool in the poaching liquid.

2. Meanwhile, in a large pot of boiling water, cook the potatoes until tender, about 10 minutes. Drain well, transfer to a large bowl, and add the bell pepper and celery.

3. With a slotted spoon, transfer the chicken to a cutting board and cut into 1-inch cubes. Strain the poaching liquid and discard the solids. Pour ½ cup of the strained liquid into a small saucepan and bring to a boil over high heat, skimming any foam that rises to the surface. Boil the liquid until it is reduced to ⅓ cup, about 3 minutes. Set aside to cool slightly.

4. In a small bowl, whisk together the mayonnaise, mustard, lemon juice, salt, and reduced poaching liquid. Pour the dressing over the vegetables, add the chicken, and toss to coat well. Place the lettuce on 4 plates and spoon the chicken mixture on top. Serve the salad warm, at room temperature, or chilled.

Helpful hint: Instead of poaching, you can microwave the chicken with the liquid mixture in step 1, tightly covered, on high power for 3 to 5 minutes.

FAT: 4G/15%
CALORIES: 225
SATURATED FAT: 0.7G
CARBOHYDRATE: 24G
PROTEIN: 23G
CHOLESTEROL: 49MG
SODIUM: 483MG

This salad—perfect for picnics and backyard barbecues—is a delicious hybrid of chicken and potato salad. For really succulent chicken, we begin by poaching it to insure moistness. Then, so we don't lose any flavor, we reduce the poaching liquid to intensify its character, and use it as the base of the dressing.

LOUISIANA SMOTHERED CHICKEN

SERVES: 4
WORKING TIME: 35 MINUTES
TOTAL TIME: 50 MINUTES

In this Southern-style dish, golden brown chicken breasts are "smothered" by onions that are slowly sautéed with a touch of sugar to bring out their natural sweetness—a process known as "caramelizing." A bouquet of spices with a hint of heat flavor the sauce.

⅔ cup long-grain rice

2 tablespoons flour

½ teaspoon salt

4 bone-in chicken breast halves (about 1½ pounds total), skinned

2 teaspoons olive oil

3 large onions, halved and thinly sliced

½ teaspoon sugar

1 cup chopped tomatoes

1 cup reduced-sodium chicken broth, defatted

1 bay leaf

½ teaspoon dried thyme

¼ teaspoon dried oregano

⅛ teaspoon cayenne pepper

1 tablespoon chopped fresh parsley

1. In a medium saucepan, combine the rice and 1½ cups of water. Bring to a boil over high heat, reduce to a simmer, cover, and cook until the rice is tender, about 17 minutes. Meanwhile, on a sheet of waxed paper, combine the flour and ¼ teaspoon of the salt. Dredge the chicken in the flour mixture, shaking off the excess.

2. In a large nonstick skillet, heat the oil until hot but not smoking over medium heat. Add the chicken and cook until golden brown, about 2 minutes per side. With a slotted spoon, transfer the chicken to a plate.

3. Reduce the heat to low. Add the onions to the skillet and sprinkle the sugar over. Cook, stirring frequently, until the onions are softened and golden brown, about 10 minutes. Stir in the tomatoes, broth, bay leaf, thyme, oregano, cayenne, and remaining ¼ teaspoon salt. Bring to a boil, return the chicken to the pan, and reduce to a simmer. Cover and cook, stirring occasionally, until the chicken is cooked through, about 15 minutes. Discard the bay leaf. Spoon the rice onto 4 plates, top with the chicken mixture, sprinkle the parsley over, and serve.

Helpful hints: Well-drained canned whole tomatoes would work equally well in this dish. You can make the chicken up to 8 hours in advance. Gently reheat it, covered, over low heat, before serving with warm rice.

FAT: 4G/11%
CALORIES: 352
SATURATED FAT: 0.8G
CARBOHYDRATE: 46G
PROTEIN: 32G
CHOLESTEROL: 65MG
SODIUM: 518MG

TEX-MEX BARBECUED CHICKEN WITH SALSA

SERVES: 4
WORKING TIME: 10 MINUTES
TOTAL TIME: 40 MINUTES

For this simple down-home dish, we begin with a bottled salsa and then enhance it with spices and honey to give it a barbecue flavor. The barbecue sauce is used both as a marinade for the chicken and to flavor a delicious corn relish. Serve this with a basket of jalapeño corn bread and a shredded lettuce, tomato, and red onion salad garnished with an avocado slice.

1½ cups mild prepared salsa
2 teaspoons chili powder
1 teaspoon honey
1 teaspoon ground coriander
¾ teaspoon ground cumin
4 skinless, boneless chicken breast halves (about 1 pound total)
½ cup frozen corn kernels
1 tablespoon fresh lime juice

1. In a medium bowl, stir together the salsa, chili powder, honey, coriander, and cumin. Remove 1 cup of the salsa mixture and combine it with the chicken in a shallow pan. Turn the chicken to coat well with the salsa and set aside to marinate for 20 minutes.

2. Meanwhile, in a small pot of boiling water, cook the corn for 30 seconds to blanch. Drain the corn well and add to the salsa mixture remaining in the bowl, along with the lime juice. Set aside.

3. Preheat the broiler or prepare the grill. Broil or grill the chicken 6 inches from the heat for about 8 minutes, or until cooked through. Place the chicken on 4 plates, spoon the salsa-corn mixture over, and serve.

Helpful hints: This dish is especially good when grilled outdoors—consider tossing mesquite or wood chips into the fire for a flavor twist. Make a double batch of the chicken, and you'll have wonderful leftovers for chicken sandwiches.

FAT: 2G/9%
CALORIES: 180
SATURATED FAT: 0.4G
CARBOHYDRATE: 12G
PROTEIN: 27G
CHOLESTEROL: 66MG
SODIUM: 888MG

CREOLE TURKEY AND RICE STEW

SERVES: 8
WORKING TIME: 25 MINUTES
TOTAL TIME: 55 MINUTES

In our simple version of this Southern favorite, we use okra to thicken the stew. Green peppers add a smokier flavor than the sweeter red (or yellow) peppers, so be sure not to replace them with the other colors. Surprisingly, just a tiny amount of baked ham lends a deeply rich taste. Leftovers are easily reheated on the stovetop or in the microwave.

1 tablespoon olive oil

4 ribs celery, chopped

2 green bell peppers, chopped

1 red bell pepper, chopped

1 large red onion, chopped

1½ teaspoons dried thyme

1 teaspoon dried oregano

Two 14½-ounce cans reduced-sodium chicken broth, defatted

16-ounce can no-salt-added whole tomatoes, coarsely chopped with their juices

3 ounces baked ham, cut into ¼-inch cubes

1¼ cups long-grain rice

10-ounce package frozen cut okra

Two 10-ounce packages frozen corn kernels

10-ounce package frozen lima beans

1½ pounds turkey breast, cut into ¾-inch cubes

2 teaspoons Worcestershire sauce

½ to 1 teaspoon hot pepper sauce

1. In a large Dutch oven, heat the oil until hot but not smoking over medium-high heat. Add the celery, bell peppers, and onion and cook, stirring frequently, until the vegetables are softened, about 8 minutes. Add the thyme and oregano and cook, stirring constantly, until well coated, about 2 minutes.

2. Stir in the broth, 2 cups of water, the tomatoes with their juices, ham, and rice. Bring to a boil, reduce to a simmer, and cook, stirring occasionally, until the flavors have blended, about 10 minutes.

3. Stir in the okra, increase the heat to medium, and cook for 5 minutes. Stir in the corn, lima beans, and turkey and cook until the rice is tender and the turkey is cooked through, 5 to 10 minutes longer. Stir in the Worcestershire sauce and hot pepper sauce. Ladle the stew into 8 shallow bowls and serve.

Suggested accompaniments: Chicory and watercress salad drizzled with a buttermilk dressing. For dessert, bananas sautéed with brown sugar and almond liqueur.

FAT: 4G/10%
CALORIES: 388
SATURATED FAT: .9G
CARBOHYDRATE: 56G
PROTEIN: 33G
CHOLESTEROL: 59MG
SODIUM: 563MG

OVEN-BARBECUED CHICKEN BREASTS

SERVES: 4
WORKING TIME: 10 MINUTES
TOTAL TIME: 40 MINUTES

F*inishing these tempting chicken breasts with a quick pass under the broiler richly caramelizes the honey- and pineapple-sweetened sauce.*

1 teaspoon olive oil
2 cloves garlic, minced
1 cup no-salt-added canned tomatoes
½ cup pineapple juice
3 tablespoons honey
1 tablespoon cider vinegar
1 tablespoon molasses
¾ teaspoon ground ginger
½ teaspoon salt
4 bone-in chicken breast halves (about 1½ pounds total), skinned

1. Preheat the oven to 425°. In a medium saucepan, heat the oil until hot but not smoking over medium heat. Add the garlic and cook, stirring frequently, until softened, about 30 seconds. Stir in the tomatoes, breaking them up with the back of a spoon. Add the pineapple juice, honey, vinegar, molasses, ginger, and salt, bring to a boil, and cook until the sauce has thickened, about 5 minutes.

2. Spray a shallow medium roasting pan with nonstick cooking spray. Place the chicken in the prepared pan, spoon the sauce on top, and bake for 20 minutes, or until the chicken is cooked through.

3. Preheat the broiler. Broil the chicken 4 inches from the heat for 2 minutes, or until the sauce has caramelized. Place the chicken on 4 plates and serve.

Suggested accompaniments: Dilled corn on the cob and crusty rolls. Follow with lemon frozen yogurt.

FAT: 3G/12%
CALORIES: 226
SATURATED FAT: .5G
CARBOHYDRATE: 24G
PROTEIN: 27G
CHOLESTEROL: 65MG
SODIUM: 357MG

CHICKEN, VEGETABLE, AND CORN BREAD CASSEROLE

SERVES: 4
WORKING TIME: 15 MINUTES
TOTAL TIME: 40 MINUTES

Two 8-ounce cans no-salt-added tomato sauce

1 green bell pepper, diced

1 large onion, diced

2 teaspoons sugar

½ teaspoon dried oregano

1 cup frozen corn kernels

¾ teaspoon salt

1 pound skinless, boneless chicken thighs, cut into 2-inch pieces

⅓ cup yellow cornmeal

⅓ cup flour

½ teaspoon baking powder

¼ teaspoon baking soda

½ cup low-fat buttermilk

1 teaspoon vegetable oil

1 egg white

1. Preheat the oven to 400°. In a medium saucepan, combine the tomato sauce, bell pepper, onion, 1 teaspoon of the sugar, and oregano. Bring to a boil over medium-high heat, reduce to a simmer, and cook, stirring occasionally, until the vegetables begin to soften, about 5 minutes. Stir in the corn and ½ teaspoon of the salt. Return to a boil, add the chicken, and cook for 1 minute. Spoon the chicken mixture into a 9-inch pie pan.

2. In a medium bowl, combine the cornmeal, flour, baking powder, baking soda, the remaining 1 teaspoon sugar, and the remaining ¼ teaspoon salt. Stir in the buttermilk, oil, and egg white until just combined. Spoon the cornmeal mixture onto the center of the chicken mixture. Place the pie pan on a baking sheet and bake the casserole for 20 to 25 minutes, or until the chicken is cooked through and the corn bread is golden brown.

Suggested accompaniment: Stewed rhubarb and strawberry compote for dessert.

FAT: 7G/18%
CALORIES: 347
SATURATED FAT: 1.5G
CARBOHYDRATE: 42G
PROTEIN: 30G
CHOLESTEROL: 95MG
SODIUM: 721MG

The golden corn bread "crust" gives this easy chicken and vegetable combination extra appeal.

O_{ne} of our favorite ways to cook vegetables is to roast them, which brings out their flavor without adding fat. This salad was inspired by the classic version from the south of France, but we've nutritionally fine-tuned it by omitting the eggs and keeping the oil in the dressing to a minimum. Serve with a basket of bread sticks.

CHICKEN NIÇOISE

SERVES: 4
WORKING TIME: 30 MINUTES
TOTAL TIME: 1 HOUR

1 pound skinless, boneless
chicken breasts

1 teaspoon Italian herb seasoning

1 yellow bell pepper, cut into
large squares

1 green bell pepper, cut into large
squares

1½ pounds small red potatoes,
quartered

¾ pound green beans

6 cloves garlic, unpeeled

2 tablespoons red wine vinegar

2 tablespoons balsamic vinegar

1 tablespoon olive oil

½ teaspoon salt

¼ teaspoon freshly ground black
pepper

20 Boston lettuce leaves

2 tomatoes, cut into wedges

¼ cup slivered Calamata or
other brine-cured black olives

1. Preheat the oven to 425°. Rub the chicken with the Italian seasoning and set aside. Spray a roasting pan with nonstick cooking
spray. Place the bell peppers, potatoes, green beans, and garlic on
the roasting pan, keeping each ingredient separate from the others,
and bake for 15 minutes. Add the chicken to the pan and bake for
15 minutes, or until the chicken and vegetables are cooked
through. Transfer the chicken to a cutting board and when just
cool enough to handle, cut into 1-inch cubes.

2. Meanwhile, in a medium bowl, whisk together 2 tablespoons of
water, the red wine vinegar, balsamic vinegar, oil, salt, and black
pepper. Squeeze the roasted garlic (see tip; top photo) into a small
bowl, mash with a fork (bottom photo), and add to the dressing.
Add the still-hot chicken cubes to the dressing and toss to coat.

3. Line 4 plates with lettuce. Arrange the bell peppers, potatoes, green
beans, and tomato wedges in separate piles on top of the lettuce.
With a slotted spoon, transfer the chicken to the plates. Sprinkle
the olives on top of the chicken and drizzle the remaining dressing
over the entire salad, or serve on the side. Serve the salad warm or
at room temperature.

*Helpful hint: If you don't have any balsamic vinegar, you can simply
double the amount of red wine vinegar called for and add ¼ teaspoon
of honey to soften the acid.*

FAT: 8G/19%
CALORIES: 388
SATURATED FAT: 1.2G
CARBOHYDRATE: 47G
PROTEIN: 33G
CHOLESTEROL: 66MG
SODIUM: 533MG

TIP

*After the garlic cloves have
been roasted until soft,
and they are cool enough
to handle, squeeze the pulp
from the skins. Mash the
cloves with a fork to make
a smooth paste to add to
the other ingredients to
create the dressing.*

Fruity and savory flavors give this dish a sunny disposition that will brighten any table. We enliven the chicken with fresh peaches as well as peach jam, and then accent that with a touch of ginger. Serve with your favorite low-fat biscuits and a simple green salad.

GEORGIA PEACH-BRAISED CHICKEN

SERVES: 4
WORKING TIME: 20 MINUTES
TOTAL TIME: 35 MINUTES

2 tablespoons flour

½ teaspoon salt

½ teaspoon freshly ground black pepper

4 skinless, boneless chicken breast halves (about 1 pound total), cut crosswise in half

2 teaspoons olive oil

4 scallions, cut into 1-inch pieces

1 red bell pepper, cut into 1-inch squares

1 yellow summer squash, quartered lengthwise and cut into ½-inch-thick slices

1 teaspoon grated orange zest

¾ teaspoon ground ginger

½ teaspoon dried rosemary

⅓ cup dry white wine

⅔ cup reduced-sodium chicken broth, defatted

¼ cup orange juice

2 tablespoons peach jam

2 peaches, peeled (see tip) and cut into thick wedges

1. On a sheet of waxed paper, combine the flour, ¼ teaspoon of the salt, and ¼ teaspoon of the black pepper. Dredge the chicken in the flour mixture, shaking off the excess. In a large nonstick skillet, heat the oil until hot but not smoking over medium heat. Add the chicken and cook until lightly browned, about 2 minutes per side. With a slotted spoon, transfer the chicken to a plate.

2. Add the scallions, bell pepper, and squash to the skillet, stirring to coat. Stir in the orange zest, ginger, rosemary, remaining ¼ teaspoon salt, and remaining ¼ teaspoon black pepper. Add the wine, increase the heat to high, and cook until the liquid is almost evaporated, about 2 minutes.

3. Stir in the broth, orange juice, and jam and bring to a boil. Return the chicken to the pan, reduce to a simmer, cover, and cook until the chicken is cooked through, about 7 minutes. Add the peaches and cook, uncovered, until the peaches are warmed through and barely tender, about 4 minutes. Divide the chicken mixture among 4 bowls and serve.

Helpful hint: If fresh peaches are out of season, replace with 1½ cups frozen peach slices, thawed.

FAT: 4G/14%
CALORIES: 255
SATURATED FAT: 3.7G
CARBOHYDRATE: 23G
PROTEIN: 29G
CHOLESTEROL: 66MG
SODIUM: 464MG

TIP

Place the peaches in a medium saucepan of boiling water and cook for 30 seconds to blanch. This will help loosen the skins without cooking the fruit. With a sharp paring knife, carefully pull away the skin and discard.

Easy Chicken, Red Beans, and Rice

SERVES: 4
WORKING TIME: 15 MINUTES
TOTAL TIME: 50 MINUTES

This quickly assembled meal-in-one, based on a Southern classic, is jazzed up with a crisp Parmesan-and-bread crumb topping.

2 teaspoons olive oil

3 cloves garlic, minced

1 large onion, diced

1 green bell pepper, diced

⅔ cup long-grain rice

1 tablespoon no-salt-added tomato paste

1⅔ cups reduced-sodium chicken broth, defatted

16-ounce can red kidney beans, rinsed and drained

½ teaspoon dried marjoram

¾ pound skinless, boneless chicken thighs, cut into 2-inch pieces

1 ounce Canadian bacon, diced

2 tablespoons chopped fresh parsley

2 tablespoons grated Parmesan cheese

2 tablespoons dried bread crumbs

1. Preheat the oven to 350°. In a shallow medium casserole, heat the oil until hot but not smoking over medium-high heat. Add the garlic, onion, and bell pepper and cook, stirring frequently, until the vegetables are tender, about 5 minutes.

2. Add the rice, stirring to coat, and cook for 1 minute. Stir in the tomato paste. Add the broth, kidney beans, and marjoram and cook for 5 minutes longer. Stir in the chicken, bacon, and parsley. Cover, place the casserole in the oven, and bake for 30 minutes, or until the chicken is cooked through and the rice is tender.

3. Preheat the broiler. Sprinkle the Parmesan and bread crumbs over the chicken mixture. Broil the casserole 4 inches from the heat for 2 minutes, or until the topping is crisp and well browned. Spoon the chicken mixture onto 4 plates and serve.

Suggested accompaniments: Tossed salad with an oregano vinaigrette, and dark roast coffee flavored with cinnamon.

FAT: 8G/19%
CALORIES: 388
SATURATED FAT: 1.9G
CARBOHYDRATE: 47G
PROTEIN: 30G
CHOLESTEROL: 76MG
SODIUM: 664MG

CHICKEN PARMESAN WITH HERBED TOMATOES

SERVES: 4
WORKING TIME: 10 MINUTES
TOTAL TIME: 30 MINUTES

2 egg whites

⅓ cup dried bread crumbs

¼ cup grated Parmesan cheese

¼ teaspoon salt

4 skinless, boneless chicken breast halves (about 1 pound total)

2 teaspoons olive oil

2 tomatoes, cut into 12 slices

¾ teaspoon sugar

¾ teaspoon dried oregano

¼ teaspoon dried marjoram

1. Preheat the oven to 400°. Spray a baking sheet with nonstick cooking spray.

2. In a shallow dish, using a fork, beat the egg whites and 1 tablespoon water until foamy. On a plate, combine the bread crumbs, Parmesan, and salt. Set aside 2 tablespoons of the crumb mixture. Dip the chicken into the egg whites, then into the crumb mixture, gently pressing crumbs into the chicken. Place the chicken on the prepared baking sheet, drizzle with the oil, and bake for 12 minutes, or until the chicken is crisp, golden, and cooked through.

3. Meanwhile, arrange the tomatoes in a single layer on another baking sheet and sprinkle with the sugar, oregano, and marjoram. Spoon the reserved 2 tablespoons crumb mixture on top, gently pressing crumbs into the tomatoes. Place the tomatoes in the oven with the chicken and bake for 6 to 8 minutes, or until the tomatoes are heated through and the topping is crisp. Place the chicken and tomatoes on 4 plates and serve.

Suggested accompaniments: Roasted zucchini chunks, followed by toasted slices of reduced-fat pound cake topped with fresh blueberries.

FAT: 6G/23%
CALORIES: 230
SATURATED FAT: 1.8G
CARBOHYDRATE: 11G
PROTEIN: 32G
CHOLESTEROL: 70MG
SODIUM: 412MG

C heese is not off limits in this Italian-inspired entrée—aromatic Parmesan adds just the right flavor.

*T*his sophisticated entrée features sharp, peppery watercress as the perfect foil for the sweet and spicy chicken breasts. The maple syrup glaze is also a delectable partner for lean pork chops. If watercress is unavailable, substitute shredded Belgian endive, curly endive, or romaine lettuce.

Maple-Broiled Chicken

Serves: 4
Working time: 15 minutes
Total time: 30 minutes

2 cloves garlic, minced

½ cup maple syrup

½ cup orange juice

1 teaspoon grated orange zest

½ teaspoon dried thyme

½ teaspoon salt

⅛ teaspoon red pepper flakes

1 teaspoon olive oil

1 red bell pepper, cut into thin strips

2 bunches watercress (about 12 ounces), thick stems trimmed

4 bone-in chicken thighs (about 1¼ pounds total), skinned

2 navel oranges, peeled, pith removed, and thinly sliced (see tip)

1. In a medium saucepan, combine the garlic, maple syrup, orange juice, orange zest, thyme, salt, and pepper flakes. Bring to a boil over medium heat and cook until the maple mixture is reduced by one-half, about 5 minutes. Set aside to cool slightly.

2. Meanwhile, preheat the broiler or prepare the grill. If using a broiler, line the broiler pan with foil. In a medium skillet, heat the oil until hot but not smoking over medium heat. Add the bell pepper and cook, stirring occasionally, until the bell pepper begins to soften, about 5 minutes. Add the watercress, cover, and cook until the watercress is wilted, about 5 minutes longer. Set aside.

3. Brush the chicken with half of the maple mixture and broil or grill 6 inches from the heat for 7 minutes. Turn the chicken, brush with the remaining maple mixture, and broil or grill for about 8 minutes longer, or until the chicken is just cooked through.

4. Spoon the watercress mixture onto 4 plates and place the chicken on top. Place the orange slices on the side and serve.

Suggested accompaniments: Orzo or other small pasta. For dessert, toasted slices of fat-free pound cake drizzled with strawberry purée.

TIP

The bitter white pith of an orange, lemon, or lime lies between the flesh of the fruit and the zest. Use a small, sharp paring knife to cut away the white pith from the flesh of the peeled fruit; discard the pith.

Fat: 6g/18%
Calories: 300
Saturated Fat: 1.2g
Carbohydrate: 41g
Protein: 23g
Cholesterol: 86mg
Sodium: 402mg

MEXICAN CHICKEN AND RICE CASSEROLE

SERVES: 4
WORKING TIME: 30 MINUTES
TOTAL TIME: 1 HOUR 10 MINUTES

This Mexican-inspired casserole has been enlivened in several ways: First we sauté the rice with the vegetables, which imparts a toasty hint. Then, we spice up the sauce with cumin, chili powder, and a dose of lime. Finally, we keep the chicken tender and juicy by browning it before baking—allowing the casserole to be cooked, covered, in moist heat.

2 teaspoons olive oil
1¼ cups long-grain rice
1 red bell pepper, cut into thin strips
6 scallions, coarsely chopped
3 cloves garlic, minced
1 teaspoon ground cumin
1 teaspoon chili powder
½ teaspoon dried oregano
13¾-ounce can reduced-sodium chicken broth, defatted
½ teaspoon salt
½ cup chopped fresh cilantro or parsley
1 teaspoon grated lime zest
2 tablespoons fresh lime juice
2 zucchini, halved lengthwise and thinly sliced
4 skinless, boneless chicken breast halves (about 1 pound total)

1. Preheat the oven to 350°. Spray a 13 x 9-inch baking dish with nonstick cooking spray. Meanwhile, in a large skillet, heat 1 teaspoon of the oil until hot but not smoking over medium heat. Add the rice, bell pepper, scallions, and garlic. Cook until the vegetables are softened, about 5 minutes. Stir in the cumin, chili powder, and oregano and cook for 1 minute to blend the flavors. Add the broth and salt and bring to a boil over medium heat. Remove from the heat and stir in the cilantro, lime zest, and lime juice. Transfer the mixture to the prepared baking dish. Spread the zucchini evenly on top, cover tightly with foil, and bake for 25 minutes.

2. Meanwhile, wipe out the skillet and heat the remaining 1 teaspoon oil until hot but not smoking over medium heat. Add the chicken and cook on one side until golden brown, about 2 minutes. Remove from the heat.

3. Carefully remove the foil from the baking dish and drizzle ½ cup of water over the rice. Top with the chicken, browned-side up, and any juices that have collected in the skillet. Re-cover and bake for 15 to 20 minutes, or until the rice is tender and the chicken is cooked through.

Helpful hint: Leftovers can be gently reheated, covered, in the oven or in a microwave—you may want to stir in a little chicken broth since the rice continues to absorb moisture upon standing.

FAT: 5G/11%
CALORIES: 396
SATURATED FAT: 0.8G
CARBOHYDRATE: 53G
PROTEIN: 33G
CHOLESTEROL: 66MG
SODIUM: 641MG

The
sunny, assertive flavors
of the Mediterranean
are unmistakably at
work in this salad:
The sweetness of orange
and honey is
deliciously contrasted
with the sharp and
savory combination of
red wine vinegar,
mustard, and mint.

MEDITERRANEAN CHICKEN SALAD

SERVES: 4
WORKING TIME: 25 MINUTES
TOTAL TIME: 30 MINUTES

3 slices (2 ounces each) crusty bread

1 clove garlic, peeled and halved

½ pound green beans, cut into 2-inch pieces

1 pound skinless, boneless chicken breasts

¾ teaspoon grated orange zest

1 cup orange juice

2 tablespoons honey

2 tablespoons red wine vinegar

1 tablespoon Dijon mustard

1 tablespoon olive oil

½ teaspoon salt

¾ pound plum tomatoes (about 3), cut into wedges

2 tablespoons chopped fresh mint

3 cups torn green-leaf lettuce leaves

1. Preheat the oven to 400°. Place the bread on a baking sheet and bake for 5 minutes, or until crisp and golden. Immediately rub the warm bread with the cut sides of the garlic (see tip). Cut the bread into small cubes for croutons. Set aside.

2. In a large pot of boiling water, cook the green beans until crisp-tender, about 2 minutes. Drain, rinse with cold water, and drain again.

3. In a large skillet, combine the chicken, orange zest, and orange juice. Bring to a boil over high heat, reduce to a simmer, cover, and cook until the chicken is cooked through, about 8 minutes. With a slotted spoon, transfer the chicken to a cutting board. Add the honey to the sauce, bring to a boil, and cook, uncovered, until reduced to ½ cup, about 5 minutes. Remove from the heat and cool slightly. Cut the chicken into thin diagonal slices.

4. In a large bowl, combine the cooled sauce, vinegar, mustard, oil, and salt. Add the green beans, tomatoes, mint, and chicken slices and toss to combine. Place the lettuce on 4 plates and spoon the chicken salad on top. Sprinkle with the croutons and serve.

Suggested accompaniments: Homemade limeade. Follow with assorted melon balls sprinkled with crushed macaroons and drizzled with honey.

TIP

The garlic toast used for croutons in this salad contains none of the oil or butter of traditional garlic bread, but tastes just as good. Use this easy method whenever garlic bread is called for.

FAT: 8G/22%
CALORIES: 322
SATURATED FAT: 1.3G
CARBOHYDRATE: 33G
PROTEIN: 30G
CHOLESTEROL: 66MG
SODIUM: 495MG

HUNTER'S-STYLE CHICKEN

SERVES: 4
WORKING TIME: 40 MINUTES
TOTAL TIME: 1 HOUR

A dish prepared in this manner, hunter's style, almost always has tomatoes and mushrooms, and occasionally bacon. Here there's no bacon, but we've added crunchy croutons instead. The white wine sauce, thickened with flavorful tomato paste, makes this a stick-to-your-ribs favorite. Garnish with sprigs of fresh rosemary and serve with mashed sweet potatoes.

4 ounces peasant bread, cut into ½-inch cubes

2 tablespoons flour

½ teaspoon salt

½ teaspoon freshly ground black pepper

4 bone-in chicken breast halves (about 1½ pounds total), skinned

2 teaspoons olive oil

8 shallots, peeled

½ pound mushrooms, quartered

4 cloves garlic, minced

½ cup dry red wine

1 cup chopped fresh tomato

½ cup reduced-sodium chicken broth, defatted

2 tablespoons no-salt-added tomato paste

½ teaspoon dried rosemary

¼ cup chopped fresh parsley

1. Preheat the oven to 375°. Spread the bread cubes on a baking sheet and bake for 5 minutes, or until golden brown. Meanwhile, on a sheet of waxed paper, combine the flour, ¼ teaspoon of the salt, and ¼ teaspoon of the pepper. Dredge the chicken in the flour mixture, shaking off the excess.

2. In a large nonstick skillet, heat the oil until hot but not smoking over medium heat. Add the chicken and cook until golden brown, about 2 minutes per side. With a slotted spoon, transfer the chicken to a plate.

3. Add the shallots, mushrooms, and garlic to the pan and cook, stirring frequently, until the vegetables are lightly browned, about 5 minutes. Add the wine, increase the heat to high, and cook until the wine is reduced by half, about 4 minutes. Add the fresh tomato, broth, tomato paste, rosemary, remaining ¼ teaspoon salt, and remaining ¼ teaspoon pepper. Bring to a boil, return the chicken to the pan, reduce to a simmer, cover, and cook, stirring occasionally, until the chicken is cooked through, about 20 minutes. Spoon the chicken mixture onto 4 plates, sprinkle with the parsley, top with the toasted bread cubes, and serve.

Helpful hint: Shallots are small, mild-flavored onions. Since they remain whole in this recipe, you can substitute thawed frozen pearl onions.

FAT: 5G/16%
CALORIES: 288
SATURATED FAT: 1G
CARBOHYDRATE: 28G
PROTEIN: 32G
CHOLESTEROL: 65MG
SODIUM: 609MG

MADRAS CHICKEN KEBABS

Serves: 4
Working time: 15 minutes
Total time: 35 minutes

¾ cup plain nonfat yogurt

¼ cup chopped fresh cilantro or parsley

½ teaspoon grated lime zest

¼ cup fresh lime juice

1 teaspoon ground coriander

½ teaspoon ground cumin

½ teaspoon ground ginger

¼ teaspoon salt

¼ teaspoon freshly ground black pepper

1 pound skinless, boneless chicken breasts, cut into 1½-inch chunks

¼ cup reduced-sodium chicken broth, defatted

1 teaspoon olive oil

8 large mushroom caps

2 zucchini, cut into 16 pieces total

16 cherry tomatoes

1. In a large bowl, stir together ½ cup of the yogurt, 3 tablespoons of the cilantro, the lime zest, 1 tablespoon of the lime juice, ¾ teaspoon of the ground coriander, the cumin, ginger, salt, and pepper. Add the chicken, tossing well to coat.

2. Preheat the broiler or prepare the grill. In a small bowl, whisk together 2 tablespoons of the lime juice, the broth, and oil. Add the mushroom caps, zucchini, and cherry tomatoes, tossing to coat. Thread the chicken, mushrooms, zucchini, and cherry tomatoes onto 8 skewers. Broil or grill 6 inches from the heat, turning the skewers, for 8 minutes, or until the chicken is cooked through.

3. Meanwhile, in a small bowl, combine the remaining ¼ cup yogurt, remaining 1 tablespoon cilantro, remaining 1 tablespoon lime juice, and remaining ¼ teaspoon coriander. Remove the chicken and vegetables from the skewers onto 4 plates. Spoon the yogurt sauce over and serve.

Helpful hints: You can marinate the chicken and vegetables separately for up to 2 hours in advance. If you have Madras curry powder in your cupboard, you can use 2 teaspoons of that instead of the coriander, cumin, and ginger.

Fat: 3g/14%
Calories: 198
Saturated Fat: 0.6g
Carbohydrate: 11g
Protein: 31g
Cholesterol: 67mg
Sodium: 290mg

The quick and easy marinade for this dish is a combination of spices typical of Indian cuisine—cumin, ginger, and coriander—mixed into nonfat yogurt. For a low-fat side sauce, we've taken a little yogurt and flavored it with cilantro. Rice with sautéed onion, colored with turmeric, would be a great accompaniment.

Chicken Salad with Spicy Sesame Sauce

SERVES: 4
WORKING TIME: 30 MINUTES
TOTAL TIME: 40 MINUTES

We miss no opportunity to infuse this salad with exciting Asian flavors. First, we marinate the chicken in soy sauce and garlic. Then, the salad is tossed with a tangy orange dressing, tempered with dark, nutty Oriental sesame oil, and finished with a scattering of sesame seeds. For best results, serve at room temperature—chilling will mute the flavors.

1 pound skinless, boneless chicken breasts

2 tablespoons reduced-sodium soy sauce

2 cloves garlic, minced

½ pound asparagus, tough ends trimmed

¼ cup orange juice

2 tablespoons chopped fresh cilantro or parsley

2 teaspoons red wine vinegar

2 teaspoons Dijon mustard

1 teaspoon firmly packed brown sugar

¼ teaspoon hot pepper sauce

1 tablespoon dark Oriental sesame oil

3 carrots, shredded

1 red bell pepper, cut into 2-inch julienne strips

6 cups shredded romaine lettuce

1 tablespoon sesame seeds

1. Preheat the broiler or prepare the grill. Combine the chicken, soy sauce, and garlic in a sturdy plastic bag. Push out all the air, seal, and marinate in the refrigerator for 20 minutes. Remove the chicken from the bag and broil or grill 6 inches from the heat, turning once, for 8 to 10 minutes, or until the chicken is just cooked through. Set the chicken aside to cool slightly.

2. Meanwhile, bring a medium skillet of water to a boil and reduce to a simmer. Add the asparagus and cook until crisp-tender, about 6 minutes. Drain and set aside to cool slightly.

3. In a small bowl, whisk together the orange juice, cilantro, vinegar, mustard, sugar, pepper sauce, and sesame oil.

4. Cut the chicken into strips and place in a large bowl. Cut the asparagus into 2-inch lengths and add them to the chicken. Add the carrots, bell pepper, and orange juice mixture, tossing to coat. Place the lettuce in 4 bowls and spoon the salad on top. Sprinkle with the sesame seeds and serve warm or at room temperature.

Helpful hint: The asparagus can be cooked in the microwave: put the spears on a plate, cover with plastic wrap, and cook on high for 2 to 3 minutes, or until tender.

FAT: 6G/23%
CALORIES: 243
SATURATED FAT: 1.1G
CARBOHYDRATE: 15G
PROTEIN: 31G
CHOLESTEROL: 66MG
SODIUM: 470MG

Sautéed Chicken and Sweet Potato "Chips"

Serves: 4
Working time: 25 minutes
Total time: 50 minutes

½ cup low-fat (1.5%) buttermilk

1 tablespoon honey

2 tablespoons fresh lime juice

1 teaspoon chili powder

¾ teaspoon salt

¼ teaspoon cayenne pepper

4 skinless, boneless chicken breast halves (about 1 pound total), each cut lengthwise into 3 strips

¾ pound sweet potatoes, peeled and cut into ¼-inch-thick slices

2 tablespoons olive oil

2 teaspoons sugar

¼ cup flour

1. In a medium bowl, combine the buttermilk, honey, lime juice, chili powder, ½ teaspoon of the salt, and the cayenne. Remove ¼ cup of the mixture and set aside. Add the chicken to the mixture remaining in the bowl, stirring to coat. Cover and refrigerate for at least 30 minutes or up to 12 hours.

2. Meanwhile, in a medium pot of boiling water, cook the sweet potatoes for 5 minutes to partially cook. Drain well and pat dry with paper towels. In a large nonstick skillet, heat 1 tablespoon of the oil until hot but not smoking over medium heat. Add the sweet potato slices and sprinkle them with the sugar and the remaining ¼ teaspoon salt. Cook, tossing frequently, until many of the "chips" are browned around the edges, about 5 minutes. Transfer the chips to a plate.

3. Add the remaining 1 tablespoon oil to the pan and heat until hot but not smoking over medium heat. Place the flour on a sheet of waxed paper. Lift the chicken from its marinade and dredge in the flour, shaking off the excess; discard the marinade. Add the chicken to the skillet and cook until golden brown and cooked through, about 4 minutes per side. Divide the chicken and chips among 4 plates and serve with the reserved buttermilk mixture.

Helpful hint: To keep the sweet potato chips warm, place them in a 200° oven while you prepare the rest of the meal.

Fat: 9g/25%
Calories: 321
Saturated Fat: 1.6g
Carbohydrate: 30g
Protein: 29g
Cholesterol: 68mg
Sodium: 516mg

Sweet potato slices, quickly skillet-browned with a little sugar to glaze them, make nutritious "chips" to accompany sautéed chicken breast strips. The marinade for the chicken is a blend of buttermilk and lime juice, which contributes more than just a sprightly tang: Because it's acidic, it tenderizes the chicken. Serve with a crisp salad and steamed broccoli florets.

Broiled Orange Chicken with Basil

SERVES: 4
WORKING TIME: 25 MINUTES
TOTAL TIME: 35 MINUTES

B alsamic vinegar and orange marmalade are the flavor partners that create a tart sweetness here. For a more pungent flavor, substitute one-half teaspoon minced fresh ginger for the ground. In our silky orange sauce, we've used a little cornstarch as a thickener—no extra fat here.

⅔ cup orange juice

⅓ cup orange marmalade

3 tablespoons finely chopped fresh basil

2 tablespoons balsamic vinegar

1 teaspoon olive oil

½ teaspoon salt

¼ teaspoon ground ginger

4 skinless, boneless chicken breast halves (about 1 pound total)

1¼ teaspoons cornstarch mixed with 1 tablespoon water

2 navel oranges, peeled and sectioned

1. In a shallow nonaluminum pan, whisk together ⅓ cup of the orange juice, the marmalade, basil, vinegar, oil, salt, and ginger. Transfer ⅓ cup of the mixture to a small saucepan and set aside.

2. Add the chicken to the orange-basil mixture in the pan, turning to coat well. Set aside to marinate for 30 minutes.

3. Preheat the broiler. Place the chicken, bone-side up, on the broiler rack, spoon some of the marinade on top, and broil 6 inches from the heat for 4 minutes. Turn the chicken over, spoon on the remaining marinade, and broil for 4 minutes, or until the chicken is golden brown and just cooked through.

4. Meanwhile, add the remaining ⅓ cup orange juice to the saucepan of reserved orange-basil mixture. Bring to a boil over medium heat, stir in the cornstarch mixture, and cook until slightly thickened, about 1 minute. Fold in the orange sections. Divide the chicken among 4 plates, spoon the sauce over, and serve.

Helpful hint: Although fresh basil is worth searching for, 1 tablespoon of dried will do the trick.

FAT: 3G/10%
CALORIES: 241
SATURATED FAT: 0.5G
CARBOHYDRATE: 27G
PROTEIN: 27G
CHOLESTEROL: 66MG
SODIUM: 364MG

CHICKEN WITH MASHED POTATOES AND PAN GRAVY

SERVES: 4
WORKING TIME: 45 MINUTES
TOTAL TIME: 45 MINUTES

With so much old-fashioned goodness here, you'll think you're indulging in a real cream gravy. Serve with flaky buttermilk biscuits.

1½ pounds baking potatoes, peeled and thinly sliced

3 cloves garlic, minced

¾ teaspoon salt

¼ cup low-fat (1.5%) buttermilk

¼ cup flour

½ teaspoon freshly ground black pepper

1 pound skinless, boneless chicken breasts, cut into 2-inch chunks

2 teaspoons olive oil

1 green bell pepper, cut into 1-inch squares

1 carrot, cut into 2-inch-long julienne strips

4 scallions, cut into 1-inch pieces

⅓ cup reduced-sodium chicken broth, defatted

½ teaspoon dried thyme

1⅔ cups low-fat (1%) milk

1. In a large saucepan, combine the potatoes, garlic, ¼ teaspoon of the salt, and 3 cups of water. Bring to a boil over high heat, reduce to a simmer, and cook until the potatoes are tender, about 20 minutes. Drain well and transfer to a large bowl. Add the buttermilk and mash until the potatoes are light and fluffy.

2. Meanwhile, on a sheet of waxed paper, combine 2 tablespoons of the flour, ¼ teaspoon of the salt, and ¼ teaspoon of the black pepper. Dredge the chicken in the flour mixture, shaking off the excess. In a large nonstick skillet, heat the oil until hot but not smoking over medium heat. Add the chicken and cook until golden brown, about 3 minutes per side. With a slotted spoon, transfer the chicken to a plate.

3. Add the bell pepper, carrot, scallions, and broth to the pan and cook until the bell pepper and carrot are softened, about 5 minutes. Stir in the remaining 2 tablespoons flour, remaining ¼ teaspoon salt, remaining ¼ teaspoon black pepper, and the thyme. Gradually add the milk and cook, stirring frequently, until the mixture is slightly thickened, about 3 minutes. Return the chicken to the skillet, reduce to a simmer, and cook until the chicken is just cooked through, about 3 minutes. Divide the mashed potatoes among 4 plates, spoon the chicken mixture on top, and serve.

Helpful hint: Serve the mashed potatoes as a side dish to any meal.

FAT: 5G/14%
CALORIES: 348
SATURATED FAT: 1.5G
CARBOHYDRATE: 40G
PROTEIN: 35G
CHOLESTEROL: 71MG
SODIUM: 615MG

Pan-Fried Chicken with Pepper-Garlic Sauce

SERVES: 4
WORKING TIME: 20 MINUTES
TOTAL TIME: 30 MINUTES

6 ounces all-purpose potatoes, peeled and thinly sliced

12 cloves garlic, peeled

¾ teaspoon salt

¾ cup jarred roasted red peppers, rinsed and drained

1 teaspoon chili powder

2 tablespoons flour

¼ teaspoon freshly ground black pepper

4 skinless, boneless chicken breast halves (about 1 pound total)

1 tablespoon olive oil

½ cup reduced-sodium chicken broth, defatted

½ cup evaporated low-fat milk

1 tablespoon no-salt-added tomato paste

½ teaspoon dried rosemary

1. In a medium saucepan of boiling water, cook the potatoes and garlic with ¼ teaspoon of the salt until tender, about 10 minutes. Reserving ¼ cup of the cooking liquid, drain the potatoes and garlic and transfer to a medium bowl. Mash with the reserved cooking liquid until smooth. In a food processor, process the peppers to a smooth purée. Stir the pepper purée and the chili powder into the mashed potatoes; set aside.

2. Meanwhile, on a sheet of waxed paper, combine the flour, ¼ teaspoon of the salt, and the black pepper. Dredge the chicken in the flour mixture, shaking off the excess.

3. In a large nonstick skillet, heat the oil until hot but not smoking over medium heat. Add the chicken and cook until golden brown and cooked through, about 5 minutes per side. With a slotted spoon, transfer the chicken to a plate.

4. Add the broth, evaporated milk, tomato paste, rosemary, and the remaining ¼ teaspoon salt to the skillet and bring to a boil. Add the roasted pepper mixture and cook, stirring occasionally, until slightly thickened, about 3 minutes. Return the chicken to the pan and cook until just heated through, about 1 minute. Divide the chicken among 4 plates, top with the sauce, and serve.

FAT: 6G/21%
CALORIES: 256
SATURATED FAT: 0.8G
CARBOHYDRATE: 19G
PROTEIN: 31G
CHOLESTEROL: 71MG
SODIUM: 666MG

Serve this chicken sauté and its lush (but light) pepper-garlic sauce with steamed Italian green beans.

A *definite for lemon-lovers, our easy take on the classic veal dish is complete down to the caper and parsley finish. Once you've prepared the ingredients, the cooking is done in a flash. Steamed sliced carrots and zucchini and a colorful salad of greens and radicchio are deliciously light accompaniments.*

CHICKEN PICCATA

SERVES: 4
WORKING TIME: 25 MINUTES
TOTAL TIME: 30 MINUTES

1 cup orzo

2 tablespoons flour

½ teaspoon salt

¼ teaspoon freshly ground black pepper

4 skinless, boneless chicken breast halves (about 1 pound total)

Half a lemon, plus ¼ cup fresh lemon juice (see tip)

⅓ cup dry white wine

¼ cup reduced-sodium chicken broth, defatted

1 tablespoon olive oil

2 cloves garlic, minced

½ pound mushrooms, halved

4 teaspoons capers, rinsed and drained

2 tablespoons chopped fresh parsley

1. In a large pot of boiling water, cook the orzo until just tender. Drain well.

2. Meanwhile, on a sheet of waxed paper, combine the flour, salt, and pepper. Dredge the chicken in the flour mixture, shaking off and reserving the excess. Thinly slice the lemon half and set the slices aside. In a jar with a tight-fitting lid, combine the lemon juice, wine, broth, and reserved flour mixture and shake until smooth.

3. In a large nonstick skillet, heat the oil until hot but not smoking over medium heat. Add the chicken and cook until lightly browned, about 2 minutes per side. Add the garlic and mushrooms and cook, stirring frequently, until the mushrooms are slightly softened, about 2 minutes.

4. Shake the lemon juice mixture and add it to the pan, stirring to combine. Bring to a boil, reduce to a simmer, and cook until the chicken is cooked through, about 5 minutes. Add the lemon slices and cook for 1 minute. Divide the orzo among 4 plates and spoon the chicken mixture on top. Sprinkle with the capers and parsley and serve.

Helpful hint: Even though the orzo, a smooth, rice-shaped pasta, is a pleasant change, you can serve this with white rice or noodles, if desired.

FAT: 6G/13%
CALORIES: 393
SATURATED FAT: 1G
CARBOHYDRATE: 47G
PROTEIN: 35G
CHOLESTEROL: 66MG
SODIUM: 469MG

TIP

To juice a lemon: first let it sit at room temperature for about 30 minutes, then roll it on a flat surface such as a countertop while pressing on it, to loosen the pulp and release more juice. It may be helpful to use a juicer attached to a small cup or bowl that catches the juices and strains out any seeds. Generally, you will get 2 to 3 tablespoons of juice from 1 medium lemon.

CHICKEN TERIYAKI

SERVES: 4
WORKING TIME: 20 MINUTES
TOTAL TIME: 35 MINUTES

The honey glaze caramelizes as these kabobs cook, imparting a golden color to the chicken and a deeply rich flavor. If using wooden skewers, be sure to soak them in cold water for ten minutes first to prevent burning. Cherry tomatoes, sold year-round, are especially sweet. Try the yellow variety that are often found at the end of the summer at farmstands.

1½ tablespoons reduced-sodium soy sauce
1 tablespoon honey
1 teaspoon ground ginger
½ teaspoon Oriental sesame oil
1 clove garlic, peeled and crushed
1 pound skinless, boneless chicken breasts, cut into 2-inch pieces
⅔ cup long-grain rice
¼ teaspoon salt
1 green bell pepper, cut into 1-inch squares
1 pint cherry tomatoes
2 scallions, finely chopped

1. In a shallow bowl, combine the soy sauce, honey, ginger, sesame oil, and garlic and stir to blend. Add the chicken, toss to coat thoroughly, and let stand while you start the rice.

2. In a medium saucepan, combine the rice, 1⅓ cups of water, and the salt. Bring to a boil over high heat, reduce to a simmer, cover, and cook until the rice is tender, about 17 minutes.

3. Meanwhile, preheat the broiler or prepare the grill. Alternately thread the chicken, bell pepper, and tomatoes on 8 skewers. Broil or grill the kabobs 5 inches from the heat, turning once halfway through cooking time, for about 8 minutes, or until the chicken is just cooked through.

4. Stir the scallions into the rice. Spoon the rice mixture onto 4 plates, place the kabobs on top, and serve.

Suggested accompaniments: Green leaf lettuce and red onion salad with an orange vinaigrette. Follow with poached plums topped with bits of candied ginger.

FAT: 2G/6%
CALORIES: 283
SATURATED FAT: .5G
CARBOHYDRATE: 34G
PROTEIN: 30G
CHOLESTEROL: 66MG
SODIUM: 444MG

TAMALE PIE

SERVES: 4
WORKING TIME: 20 MINUTES
TOTAL TIME: 55 MINUTES

This festive pie features a lean ground turkey-salsa filling in a cornmeal crust, which gets an added kick from zippy spices.

¼ teaspoon salt

1 cup reduced-sodium chicken broth, defatted

¾ cup yellow cornmeal

2 teaspoons mild chili powder

1 teaspoon ground cumin

1 teaspoon dried oregano

¾ pound lean ground turkey

1½ cups mild or medium-hot chunky prepared low-sodium salsa

1 cup frozen corn kernels, thawed

2 tablespoons tomato paste

2 tablespoons chopped fresh parsley

1. Preheat the oven to 400°. Spray a 9-inch pie plate with nonstick cooking spray. In a large pot, bring 1 cup of water and the salt to a boil.

2. Meanwhile, in a medium bowl, combine the broth and cornmeal and stir well to blend. Add the cornmeal mixture to the boiling water, stirring constantly. Stir in 1 teaspoon of the chili powder, ½ teaspoon of the cumin, and ½ teaspoon of the oregano. Cook, stirring constantly, until the mixture is thickened and leaves the sides of the pot, about 5 minutes.

3. Spoon the cornmeal mixture into the prepared pie plate, smoothing evenly over the bottom and up the sides. Bake for 10 minutes, or until the crust is set. Transfer to a wire rack and cool slightly.

4. Meanwhile, in a large bowl, combine the turkey, salsa, corn, tomato paste, remaining 1 teaspoon chili powder, remaining ½ teaspoon cumin, and remaining ½ teaspoon oregano. Mix well. Spoon the turkey mixture into the crust and bake for 25 minutes, or until the crust is lightly golden and the turkey is cooked through. Sprinkle the parsley over the top and serve.

Suggested accompaniments: Boston or Bibb lettuce salad sprinkled with a little Parmesan cheese, and grapefruit slices broiled with brown sugar and cinnamon afterward.

FAT: 8G/24%
CALORIES: 288
SATURATED FAT: 1.8G
CARBOHYDRATE: 36G
PROTEIN: 20G
CHOLESTEROL: 62MG
SODIUM: 462MG

ITALIAN-STYLE CHICKEN WITH GREEN BEANS

SERVES: 4
WORKING TIME: 30 MINUTES
TOTAL TIME: 45 MINUTES

2 tablespoons flour

½ teaspoon salt

¼ teaspoon freshly ground black pepper

4 skinless, boneless chicken breast halves (about 1 pound total)

2 teaspoons olive oil

1 large onion, thinly sliced

3 cloves garlic, slivered

1 cup reduced-sodium chicken broth, defatted

2 tablespoons no-salt-added tomato paste

½ teaspoon dried sage

¼ teaspoon dried oregano

1 cup canned chick-peas, rinsed and drained

½ pound Italian or regular green beans, halved lengthwise

1. On a sheet of waxed paper, combine the flour, ¼ teaspoon of the salt, and the pepper. Dredge the chicken in the flour mixture, shaking off the excess.

2. In a large nonstick skillet, heat the oil until hot but not smoking over medium heat. Add the chicken and cook until lightly browned, about 2 minutes per side. With a slotted spoon, transfer the chicken to a plate.

3. Add the onion and garlic to the skillet and cook, stirring frequently, until the onion is softened, about 7 minutes. Stir in the broth, tomato paste, sage, oregano, and remaining ¼ teaspoon salt and bring to a boil. Return the chicken to the pan, reduce to a simmer, cover, and cook for 5 minutes.

4. Stir in the chick-peas and green beans and simmer, uncovered, until the chicken is cooked through and the beans are tender, about 7 minutes. Divide the chicken mixture among 4 plates and serve.

Helpful hint: Instead of the chick-peas, you could toss in cannellini or other white beans.

FAT: 5G/17%
CALORIES: 261
SATURATED FAT: 0.8G
CARBOHYDRATE: 21G
PROTEIN: 32G
CHOLESTEROL: 66MG
SODIUM: 600MG

Sage and oregano robustly flavor this elegant dish—it's a satisfying meal in itself.

CHICKEN À LA KING

SERVES: 4
WORKING TIME: 35 MINUTES
TOTAL TIME: 45 MINUTES

4 slices (1 ounce each) peasant bread

1 clove garlic, halved

1 tablespoon olive oil

3 tablespoons flour

½ teaspoon salt

¼ teaspoon freshly ground black pepper

1 pound skinless, boneless chicken breasts, cut into 1½-inch chunks

1 green bell pepper, diced

1 red bell pepper, diced

½ pound mushrooms, thickly sliced

¼ cup dry sherry

1 cup evaporated low-fat milk

¾ cup reduced-sodium chicken broth, defatted

½ teaspoon dried tarragon

⅛ teaspoon nutmeg

1. Preheat the oven to 400°. Rub the bread with the cut side of the garlic, then brush the bread with 1 teaspoon of the oil. Discard the garlic. Place the bread on a baking sheet and toast for 2 minutes per side, or until golden brown. Set aside.

2. Meanwhile, on a sheet of waxed paper, combine 2 tablespoons of the flour, ¼ teaspoon of the salt, and the black pepper. Dredge the chicken in the flour mixture, shaking off the excess. In a large non-stick skillet, heat the remaining 2 teaspoons oil until hot but not smoking over medium heat. Add the chicken and cook until lightly browned, about 2 minutes per side. With a slotted spoon, transfer the chicken to a plate.

3. Add the bell peppers and mushrooms to the skillet and cook, stirring frequently, until the peppers are almost tender, about 5 minutes. Remove the pan from the heat, add the sherry, and return to the heat. Increase the heat to high and cook until the liquid is evaporated, about 2 minutes. Stir in the remaining 1 tablespoon flour until blended, about 1 minute. Add the milk, broth, tarragon, nutmeg, and the remaining ¼ teaspoon salt and bring to a boil. Return the chicken to the pan, reduce to a simmer, cover, and cook until the chicken is cooked through and the sauce is slightly thickened, about 8 minutes. Place the toast on 4 plates, spoon the chicken mixture over, and serve.

FAT: 7G/19%
CALORIES: 355
SATURATED FAT: 1.1G
CARBOHYDRATE: 31G
PROTEIN: 36G
CHOLESTEROL: 76MG
SODIUM: 704MG

This is one of our favorite comfort foods—deliciously satisfying for a supper, a weekend lunch, or any time you want a homey treat. There is no heavy cream either, instead, low-fat evaporated milk provides the richness and sherry adds a flavorful undertone (don't worry about the alcohol—it cooks off). The peasant bread adds a nice rustic touch.

Hearty Turkey Chowder

Serves: 8
Working time: 35 minutes
Total time: 45 minutes

1 tablespoon olive oil

6 tablespoons chopped Canadian bacon (2 ounces)

1 large onion, diced

2 leeks, halved lengthwise and thinly sliced

2 green bell peppers, cut into ½-inch squares

3 cups reduced-sodium chicken broth, defatted

½ teaspoon dried rosemary

½ teaspoon dried thyme

½ teaspoon freshly ground black pepper

½ teaspoon salt

1½ pounds all-purpose potatoes, peeled and cut into ½-inch cubes

2 pounds skinless, boneless turkey breast, cut into ½-inch chunks

1 cup frozen peas

¾ cup canned sliced water chestnuts, drained (optional)

1½ cups evaporated skimmed milk

2 tablespoons cornstarch mixed with 3 tablespoons water

1. In a large Dutch oven or flameproof casserole, heat the oil until hot but not smoking over medium heat. Add the Canadian bacon, onion, and leeks and cook, stirring frequently, until the onion is softened, about 7 minutes.

2. Add the bell peppers and cook, stirring frequently, until softened, about 5 minutes. Stir in the broth, 3 cups of water, the rosemary, thyme, black pepper, and salt and bring to a boil. Add the potatoes and turkey, reduce the heat to a simmer, and cook until the soup is richly flavored and the vegetables are tender, about 7 minutes.

3. Stir in the peas, water chestnuts, and evaporated milk and return to a boil. Add the cornstarch mixture and cook, stirring constantly, until the soup is creamy, about 1 minute.

Helpful hint: If making the chowder in advance, complete steps 1 and 2; cool, cover, and refrigerate. At serving time, reheat the chowder to a simmer and then continue with step 3.

Fat: 3g/9%
Calories: 310
Saturated Fat: 0.7g
Carbohydrate: 32g
Protein: 38g
Cholesterol: 76mg
Sodium: 622mg

The holiday season brings many opportunities for entertaining: An informal gathering of close friends would offer a welcome respite from the seasonal bustle, and a steaming pot of turkey chowder is the perfect dish for the occasion. Along with turkey and leeks, this chowder has a smoky undertone of Canadian bacon and the surprising crunch of water chestnuts.

CRISPY CHICKEN WITH CORN CHOWCHOW

SERVES: 4
WORKING TIME: 20 MINUTES
TOTAL TIME: 45 MINUTES

4 whole chicken legs (about
2 pounds total), skinned

⅔ cup low-fat buttermilk

¼ cup red wine vinegar

3 tablespoons sugar

1 cup frozen corn kernels

1 red bell pepper, diced

1 green bell pepper, diced

6 scallions, finely chopped

2 tablespoons chopped fresh
parsley

¾ teaspoon salt

⅓ cup yellow cornmeal

⅓ cup flour

¼ cup dried bread crumbs

1. Preheat the oven to 400°. Spray a baking sheet with nonstick cooking spray. In a shallow bowl, combine the chicken and buttermilk and let stand for 10 minutes.

2. In a medium saucepan, combine the vinegar and sugar. Bring to a boil over medium-high heat and cook, stirring constantly, until the sugar has dissolved. Stir in the corn and bell peppers. Return to a boil, reduce to a simmer, cover, and cook until the mixture is slightly syrupy, about 4 minutes. Stir in the scallions, parsley, and ¼ teaspoon of the salt. Remove from the heat and cool slightly.

3. On a plate, combine the cornmeal, flour, bread crumbs, and remaining ½ teaspoon salt. Dredge the chicken in the cornmeal mixture, shaking off the excess. Place the chicken on the prepared baking sheet and bake, turning once, for 25 minutes, or until the chicken is crisp, golden, and cooked through. Place the chicken and corn chowchow on 4 plates and serve.

Suggested accompaniments: Slices of seven-grain bread, and baked apricot halves sprinkled with crumbled gingersnaps to finish.

The sweet-and-sour chowchow, a type of mixed vegetable pickle popular in the South, is a colorful and tangy partner for this satisfying oven-fried chicken. The chowchow can be made up to four days ahead. Simply cover and refrigerate until ready to use, and serve at room temperature for the best flavor.

FAT: 7G/17%
CALORIES: 371
SATURATED FAT: 1.6G
CARBOHYDRATE: 46G
PROTEIN: 32G
CHOLESTEROL: 105MG
SODIUM: 631MG

There's no reason to roast a whole chicken just to have stuffing. Here we spoon an aromatically seasoned bulghur mixture under the skin of chicken breast halves, and then wrap the extra in foil to bake alongside the chicken. Fill in the dinner plate with steamed asparagus or any other green vegetable, and garnish with a sprig of parsley.

ROAST CHICKEN BREASTS WITH PARSLEY STUFFING

SERVES: 4
WORKING TIME: 20 MINUTES
TOTAL TIME: 1 HOUR 10 MINUTES

½ cup plus 1 tablespoon bulghur (cracked wheat)

1 cup chopped fresh parsley

3 tablespoons chopped fresh mint

3 cloves garlic, minced

3 tablespoons fresh lemon juice

1½ teaspoons dried oregano

¾ teaspoon cinnamon

¾ teaspoon salt

¾ teaspoon freshly ground black pepper

4 bone-in chicken breast halves (about 1½ pounds total), with skin

1. Preheat the oven to 375°. In a medium bowl, combine the bulghur and ¾ cup of hot water. Let stand for 15 minutes. Add the parsley, mint, garlic, lemon juice, oregano, cinnamon, salt, and pepper, stirring to combine.

2. Spread ¼ of the bulghur mixture under the skin of each chicken breast half (see tip). Place the chicken in a 13 x 9-inch baking pan and tent loosely with foil.

3. Bake the chicken for 45 minutes. Uncover and bake for 10 minutes, or until the chicken is cooked through. Place the chicken on 4 plates and serve. Remove the chicken skin before eating.

Helpful hint: When fresh parsley is called for, we like to use flat-leaf, which is more assertively flavored than the curly variety.

TIP

To form a pocket for the stuffing, loosen and separate the skin, without tearing, from the flesh. Spoon the stuffing under the skin, spreading evenly, and pull the skin back to its original position.

FAT: 8G/26%
CALORIES: 264
SATURATED FAT: 2.1G
CARBOHYDRATE: 19G
PROTEIN: 30G
CHOLESTEROL: 77MG
SODIUM: 488MG

CHICKEN BREASTS WITH HEARTY MUSHROOM SAUCE

SERVES: 4
WORKING TIME: 30 MINUTES
TOTAL TIME: 35 MINUTES

2 tablespoons flour

½ teaspoon salt

¼ teaspoon freshly ground black pepper

¾ pound skinless, boneless chicken breasts, cut into 1-inch chunks

2 teaspoons olive oil

3 cloves garlic, minced

½ pound mushrooms, quartered

1 yellow or red bell pepper, cut into ½-inch squares

½ teaspoon dried rosemary

1 cup reduced-sodium chicken broth, defatted

¼ cup balsamic vinegar

1 tablespoon no-salt-added tomato paste

1 teaspoon anchovy paste

½ cup chopped fresh basil

1. On a sheet of waxed paper, combine the flour, ¼ teaspoon of the salt, and the black pepper. Dredge the chicken in the flour mixture, shaking off the excess.

2. In a large nonstick skillet, heat the oil until hot but not smoking over medium heat. Add the chicken and cook, stirring frequently, until golden brown, about 6 minutes. With a slotted spoon, transfer the chicken to a plate.

3. Add the garlic, mushrooms, bell pepper, rosemary, and ⅓ cup of the broth to the pan and cook until the mushrooms and bell pepper are softened, about 7 minutes. Add the vinegar and cook for 1 minute, scraping up any browned bits that cling to the bottom of the pan.

4. Stir in the tomato paste, anchovy paste, the remaining ⅔ cup broth, and remaining ¼ teaspoon salt, and bring to a simmer. Return the chicken to the pan and cook until just cooked through, about 4 minutes. Stir in the basil. Divide the chicken mixture among 4 plates and serve.

Helpful hints: Here's a great opportunity to experiment with some of the wild mushrooms, such as chanterelles, shiitakes, and portobellos, that are newly available in the market. You can leave out the anchovy paste if you like.

We've laced the sauce in this boldly flavored dish with Mediterranean accents: basil, rosemary, and tomato paste, adding anchovy paste and balsamic vinegar for depth. To soak up every last delicious drop of the sauce, serve with parslied white rice, and whole-grain rolls.

FAT: 4G/20%
CALORIES: 166
SATURATED FAT: 0.6G
CARBOHYDRATE: 11G
PROTEIN: 23G
CHOLESTEROL: 49MG
SODIUM: 497MG

CLASSIC CHICKEN CURRY

SERVES: 4
WORKING TIME: 30 MINUTES
TOTAL TIME: 50 MINUTES

⅔ cup long-grain rice

2 tablespoons flour

½ teaspoon salt

4 bone-in chicken breast halves
(about 1½ pounds total),
skinned

1 tablespoon olive oil

1 large onion, finely chopped

1 green bell pepper, diced

3 cloves garlic, minced

2 teaspoons curry powder

½ pound all-purpose potatoes,
peeled and cut into ½-inch dice

1½ cups reduced-sodium chicken
broth, defatted

2 tablespoons chopped mango
chutney

¼ cup chopped fresh cilantro

1. In a medium saucepan, combine the rice and 1½ cups of water. Bring to a boil over high heat, reduce to a simmer, cover, and cook until the rice is tender, about 17 minutes.

2. Meanwhile, on a sheet of waxed paper, combine the flour and ¼ teaspoon of the salt. Dredge the chicken in the flour mixture, shaking off the excess. In a large nonstick skillet, heat the oil until hot but not smoking over medium heat. Add the chicken and cook until lightly browned, about 2 minutes per side. With a slotted spoon, transfer the chicken to a plate.

3. Add the onion, bell pepper, and garlic to the skillet and cook, stirring frequently, until the onion and pepper are softened, about 5 minutes. Add the curry powder, stirring to coat. Add the potatoes, broth, chutney, and remaining ¼ teaspoon salt and bring to a boil. Return the chicken to the pan, reduce to a simmer, cover, and cook until the chicken is cooked through and the potatoes are tender, about 20 minutes.

4. Divide the chicken mixture among 4 plates and sprinkle the cilantro on top. Spoon the rice on the side and serve.

Helpful hint: Although the cilantro adds a sweet pungency to this dish, you can omit it, or substitute fresh parsley.

FAT: 5G/13%
CALORIES: 374
SATURATED FAT: 0.9G
CARBOHYDRATE: 49G
PROTEIN: 32G
CHOLESTEROL: 65MG
SODIUM: 612MG

Leaving the chicken on the bone adds extra flavor to our simplified rendition of this traditional dish. For bolder flavor, use Madras curry powder, packaged in a tin—it contains a more complex blend of spices and is somewhat hotter than the usual commercially prepared curry powders. Serve with steamed green beans.

ROSEMARY CHICKEN WITH BROCCOLI AND POTATOES

SERVES: 4
WORKING TIME: 30 MINUTES
TOTAL TIME: 50 MINUTES

*T*he strong flavors of garlic and rosemary work well together in this delectable one-dish meal.

¾ pound small red potatoes, thinly sliced

2 tablespoons flour

½ teaspoon salt

½ teaspoon freshly ground black pepper

4 bone-in chicken breast halves (about 1½ pounds total), skinned

1 tablespoon olive oil

8 cloves garlic, peeled

½ teaspoon dried rosemary

⅛ teaspoon red pepper flakes

¼ cup dry vermouth or dry white wine

1½ cups reduced-sodium chicken broth, defatted

3 cups broccoli florets

1. In a medium pot of boiling water, cook the potatoes for 5 minutes to blanch. Drain well and set aside. Meanwhile, on a sheet of waxed paper, combine the flour, ¼ teaspoon of the salt, and ¼ teaspoon of the black pepper. Dredge the chicken in the flour mixture, shaking off the excess. Set aside.

2. In a large nonstick skillet, heat the oil until hot but not smoking over low heat. Add the garlic, rosemary, and red pepper flakes, reduce the heat to low, and cook, turning the garlic frequently, until the garlic is golden, about 4 minutes. Increase the heat to medium, add the chicken, and cook until golden brown, about 2 minutes per side.

3. Add the vermouth to the pan and cook until the liquid is reduced by half, about 1 minute. Add the broth, potatoes, remaining ¼ teaspoon salt, and remaining ¼ teaspoon black pepper and bring to a boil. Reduce to a simmer, cover, and cook until the chicken is almost cooked through, about 17 minutes. Add the broccoli and cook, uncovered, until the broccoli is crisp-tender and the chicken is cooked through, about 3 minutes longer. Spoon the chicken mixture onto 4 plates and serve.

Helpful hint: Asparagus or green beans would work just as well as the broccoli; increase or decrease the cooking time, depending upon the thickness of the vegetables, to make sure they are crisp-tender.

FAT: 5G/16%
CALORIES: 300
SATURATED FAT: 0.8G
CARBOHYDRATE: 27G
PROTEIN: 33G
CHOLESTEROL: 65MG
SODIUM: 620MG

HONEY-MUSTARD CHICKEN WITH VEGETABLES

SERVES: 4
WORKING TIME: 30 MINUTES
TOTAL TIME: 40 MINUTES

4 bone-in chicken breast halves (about 1½ pounds total), skinned

2 tablespoons flour

½ teaspoon salt

½ teaspoon freshly ground black pepper

2 teaspoons olive oil

1 green bell pepper, cut into 1-inch squares

1 large red onion, cut into 1-inch chunks

2 cloves garlic, minced

½ teaspoon grated lemon zest

½ teaspoon dried sage

1 cup reduced-sodium chicken broth, defatted

2 tablespoons Dijon mustard

1 tablespoon honey

2 tablespoons fresh lemon juice

2 teaspoons cornstarch mixed with 1 tablespoon water

1. With poultry shears or a knife, cut the chicken through the bone into 2-inch pieces. On a sheet of waxed paper, combine the flour, ¼ teaspoon of the salt, and ¼ teaspoon of the black pepper. Dredge the chicken in the flour mixture, shaking off the excess.

2. In a large nonstick skillet, heat the oil until hot but not smoking over medium heat. Add the chicken and cook until golden brown, about 2 minutes per side. With a slotted spoon, transfer the chicken to a plate.

3. Add the bell pepper, onion, garlic, lemon zest, sage, remaining ¼ teaspoon salt, and remaining ¼ teaspoon black pepper to the skillet, stirring to coat. Add the broth, mustard, and honey and bring to a boil. Return the chicken to the pan, reduce to a simmer, cover, and cook until the chicken is cooked through, about 10 minutes. Return to a boil, stir in the lemon juice and the cornstarch mixture, and cook, stirring frequently, until the sauce is slightly thickened, about 1 minute.

Helpful hint: You could use boneless chicken breast halves in place of the bone-in here. Use only 1 pound total and check for doneness a few minutes early.

FAT: 4G/15%
CALORIES: 223
SATURATED FAT: 0.7G
CARBOHYDRATE: 17G
PROTEIN: 28G
CHOLESTEROL: 65MG
SODIUM: 694MG

The time-honored and tasty combination of honey and mustard are accented here with lemon; serve with rice.

CHICKEN VÉRONIQUE

SERVES: 4
WORKING TIME: 35 MINUTES
TOTAL TIME: 35 MINUTES

A recipe described as *Véronique* means seedless grapes are in attendance. Here we add them at the very end, and a scattering of fresh rosemary and a dash of Worcestershire complement their sweetness. To thicken the sauce without adding too much fat, evaporated skimmed milk, shaken with a little flour, is stirred into the skillet. Serve with potato wedges.

2 tablespoons flour

½ teaspoon salt

¼ teaspoon freshly ground black pepper

4 skinless, boneless chicken breast halves (about 1 pound total)

2 teaspoons vegetable oil

4 shallots or scallions, finely chopped

⅓ cup dry white wine

½ cup reduced-sodium chicken broth, defatted

½ cup evaporated skimmed milk

1 tablespoon chopped fresh rosemary

½ teaspoon Worcestershire sauce

½ pound seedless green grapes, halved

1. On a sheet of waxed paper, combine the flour, salt, and pepper. Dredge the chicken in the flour mixture, shaking off and reserving the excess.

2. In a large nonstick skillet, heat the oil until hot but not smoking over medium heat. Add the chicken and and cook until golden brown on one side, about 3 minutes. Turn the chicken, add the shallots, and cook until the chicken is golden brown on the other side, about 3 minutes. With a slotted spoon, transfer the chicken to a plate.

3. Add the wine and broth to the skillet and bring to a boil, scraping up any browned bits that cling to the bottom of the pan. In a jar with a tight-fitting lid, combine the evaporated milk and the reserved flour mixture and shake until smooth. Stir the flour mixture into the skillet along with the rosemary and Worcestershire sauce. Return the chicken to the pan, reduce to a simmer, and cook until the mixture is slightly thickened, and the chicken is cooked through, about 6 minutes. Stir in the grapes and cook until the grapes are heated through, about 1 minute. Divide the chicken among 4 plates, spoon the sauce on top, and serve.

Helpful hint: You can substitute 1 teaspoon dried rosemary for the fresh if you wish.

FAT: 4G/15%
CALORIES: 248
SATURATED FAT: 0.7G
CARBOHYDRATE: 19G
PROTEIN: 30G
CHOLESTEROL: 67MG
SODIUM: 475MG

ASIAN-STYLE SKEWERED CHICKEN

SERVES: 4
WORKING TIME: 20 MINUTES
TOTAL TIME: 40 MINUTES

1 sweet potato, peeled and cut into 1-inch chunks

¼ cup sherry

1 tablespoon honey

1 tablespoon grated fresh ginger

2 cloves garlic, minced

1 pound skinless, boneless chicken breasts, cut into 2-inch chunks

1 red bell pepper, cut into 16 pieces

1 green bell pepper, cut into 16 pieces

1 large onion, cut into 1-inch chunks

1. In a small pot of boiling water, cook the sweet potato until almost tender, about 10 minutes. Drain well.

2. In a large bowl, stir together the sherry, honey, ginger, and garlic. Add the chicken, bell peppers, and onion, tossing to coat.

3. Preheat the broiler or prepare the grill. Thread the chicken, bell peppers, onion, and sweet potato onto 8 skewers. Broil or grill 6 inches from the heat, turning the skewers and brushing them with the sauce, for 10 minutes, or until the chicken is cooked through. Divide the skewers among 4 plates and serve.

Helpful hints: If you'd like, assemble the kebabs earlier in the day and marinate in the refrigerator. Regular white potatoes or even acorn squash could replace the sweet potato.

For this simple yet delectable dish, we first marinate all the ingredients in an Asian-style honey and sherry marinade. We then load the skewers with chicken, onion, sweet potato, and bell pepper. The chicken tastes great served over white or brown rice, garnished with a wedge of lime and a sprig of parsley.

FAT: 2G/6%
CALORIES: 252
SATURATED FAT: 0.4G
CARBOHYDRATE: 26G
PROTEIN: 28G
CHOLESTEROL: 66MG
SODIUM: 85MG

HERB-ROASTED CHICKEN BREASTS

SERVES: 4
WORKING TIME: 20 MINUTES
TOTAL TIME: 1 HOUR 5 MINUTES

This dish would be perfect for a holiday meal, yet it's simple enough for everyday. For a touch of color, serve with broccoli.

2½ cups herb-seasoned stuffing mix

⅔ cup reduced-sodium chicken broth, defatted

½ cup finely chopped red bell pepper

1 teaspoon dried rosemary

2 tablespoons chopped fresh parsley

1 clove garlic, minced

1 tablespoon reduced-fat sour cream

½ teaspoon dried thyme

¼ teaspoon salt

¼ teaspoon freshly ground black pepper

4 bone-in chicken breast halves (about 1½ pounds total), skinned

1. Preheat the oven to 375°. In an 11 x 7-inch baking dish, combine the stuffing mix, broth, ⅔ cup of water, 5 tablespoons of the bell pepper, and ½ teaspoon of the rosemary, stirring to thoroughly moisten the stuffing. Spread the stuffing evenly over the bottom of the dish.

2. In a small bowl, combine the parsley, garlic, remaining 3 tablespoons bell pepper, the sour cream, thyme, salt, black pepper, and the remaining ½ teaspoon rosemary. Rub the sour cream mixture into the chicken breasts and place them on top of the stuffing. Spray a piece of foil with nonstick cooking spray and place it loosely over the baking dish, sprayed-side down.

3. Bake for 45 minutes, or until the chicken is cooked through. Place the chicken on 4 plates, spoon the stuffing alongside, and serve.

Helpful hint: Instead of chicken, try turkey cutlets—you may need to reduce the baking time for the turkey, removing it from the oven when cooked through.

FAT: 3G/10%
CALORIES: 308
SATURATED FAT: 0.6G
CARBOHYDRATE: 36G
PROTEIN: 31G
CHOLESTEROL: 66MG
SODIUM: 951MG

BROILED CHICKEN À LA DIABLE

SERVES: 4
WORKING TIME: 20 MINUTES
TOTAL TIME: 35 MINUTES

2 tablespoons fresh lemon juice

1 teaspoon dried rosemary

½ teaspoon salt

½ teaspoon freshly ground
black pepper

¼ teaspoon cayenne pepper

4 bone-in chicken breast halves
(about 1½ pounds total),
skinned

3 shallots, peeled and finely
chopped, or 3 scallions, finely
chopped

3 tablespoons red wine vinegar

4 plum tomatoes, coarsely
chopped (1 cup)

¼ cup reduced-sodium chicken
broth, defatted

½ teaspoon cornstarch mixed
with 1 tablespoon water

2 tablespoons chopped fresh
parsley

4 teaspoons Dijon mustard

½ cup plain dried bread
crumbs

1. In a small bowl, stir together the lemon juice, rosemary, salt, black pepper, and cayenne. Rub the mixture onto the skinned side only of the chicken and set aside while the broiler preheats.

2. Preheat the broiler. Broil the chicken 6 inches from the heat, turning once, for 8 minutes, or until cooked through.

3. Meanwhile, in a small saucepan, combine the shallots and vinegar. Bring to a boil over medium heat and cook until the liquid is almost evaporated, about 1 minute. Add the tomatoes and broth, return to a boil, and cook just until slightly reduced, about 3 minutes. Stir in the cornstarch mixture, return to a boil, and cook, stirring frequently, until slightly thickened, about 1 minute. Stir in the parsley and set aside.

4. Brush the skinned side only of the chicken with the mustard and pat on the bread crumbs. Broil for 2 minutes, or until the topping is crisp and golden brown. Divide the chicken among 4 plates, spoon the tomato-shallot sauce over, and serve.

Helpful hints: For flavorful variations, experiment with different mustards such as horseradish, wine vinegar, or tarragon. The sauce can be prepared up to 1 day ahead, but don't stir in the parsley until just before serving.

FAT: 2G/10%
CALORIES: 203
SATURATED FAT: 0.6G
CARBOHYDRATE: 15G
PROTEIN: 28G
CHOLESTEROL: 65MG
SODIUM: 629MG

This deviled chicken features a lemon-pepper marinade, a crisp mustardy coating, and a tangy tomato sauce.

CHICKEN IN PIQUANT TOMATO SAUCE

SERVES: 4
WORKING TIME: 30 MINUTES
TOTAL TIME: 40 MINUTES

This is certainly not a dish with timid flavors— red wine vinegar and horseradish marry deliciously with chopped fresh tomatoes. And for an extra flair, a splash of vodka is added off the heat—to avoid any flare-ups. Although the alcohol cooks off, the vodka imparts a subtle richness to the sauce. Serve with steamed small red potatoes and a green salad.

2 tablespoons flour
½ teaspoon salt
½ teaspoon freshly ground black pepper
4 skinless, boneless chicken breast halves (about 1 pound total)
2 teaspoons olive oil
6 scallions, thinly sliced
¼ cup vodka, brandy, or dry white wine
2 cups chopped tomatoes
⅓ cup reduced-sodium chicken broth, defatted
1 tablespoon red wine vinegar
½ teaspoon dried rosemary
2 tablespoons drained white prepared horseradish
1 teaspoon cornstarch mixed with 1 tablespoon water
1 tablespoon reduced-fat sour cream

1. On a sheet of waxed paper, combine the flour, ¼ teaspoon of the salt, and ¼ teaspoon of the pepper. Dredge the chicken in the flour mixture, shaking off the excess. In a large nonstick skillet, heat the oil until hot but not smoking over medium heat. Add the chicken and cook until golden brown, about 2 minutes per side. Reduce the heat to low and cook until the chicken is cooked through, about 6 minutes. With a slotted spoon, transfer the chicken to a plate.

2. Add the scallions and cook, stirring frequently, until the scallions are tender, about 4 minutes. Remove the pan from the heat, add the vodka, then return the pan to the heat. Cook for 1 minute, scraping up any browned bits that cling to the bottom of the pan. Add the tomatoes, broth, vinegar, and rosemary and bring to a boil. Reduce to a simmer and cook for 5 minutes to blend.

3. Stir the horseradish, remaining ¼ teaspoon salt, and remaining ¼ teaspoon pepper into the skillet and return to a boil. Return the chicken to the pan and cook until the chicken is warmed through, about 2 minutes. Return to a boil, stir in the cornstarch mixture, and cook, stirring frequently, until the sauce is slightly thickened, about 1 minute. Remove from the heat and stir in the sour cream. Divide the chicken mixture among 4 plates, spoon the sauce on top, and serve.

FAT: 5G/18%
CALORIES: 232
SATURATED FAT: 1G
CARBOHYDRATE: 11G
PROTEIN: 28G
CHOLESTEROL: 67MG
SODIUM: 422MG

LEMON CHICKEN WITH ROAST POTATOES AND GARLIC

SERVES: 4
WORKING TIME: 20 MINUTES
TOTAL TIME: 1 HOUR 20 MINUTES

This scrumptious recipe could easily become a favorite for Sunday dinner. The whole chicken is scented with lemon and herbs tucked inside the cavity and under the skin. Roasting the chicken on a rack in a pan lets the fat drain away. To prevent the potatoes from absorbing fat from the chicken, they're roasted in a separate pan.

1 pound small red potatoes, cut into quarters

6 cloves garlic, 2 unpeeled and 4 peeled

4 sprigs fresh thyme, or 1 teaspoon dried

2 sprigs fresh rosemary, or ¾ teaspoon dried

¾ teaspoon salt

½ teaspoon freshly ground black pepper

1 teaspoon olive oil

3½-pound whole chicken

1 bay leaf

2 lemons, 1 pierced several times with a fork, the other thinly sliced

1. Preheat the oven to 375°. In a medium baking pan, combine the potatoes, the 2 unpeeled garlic cloves, 2 sprigs of the thyme or ½ teaspoon of the dried, 1 sprig of the rosemary or ½ teaspoon of the dried, ¼ teaspoon of the salt, and ¼ teaspoon of the pepper. Drizzle the potatoes with the oil and toss to combine. Set aside.

2. Sprinkle the chicken cavity with the remaining ½ teaspoon salt and remaining ¼ teaspoon pepper. Place the bay leaf, the 4 peeled cloves garlic, and the pierced lemon in the cavity. With your fingers, carefully loosen the skin from the breast, leaving the skin intact. Tuck the remaining 2 sprigs thyme or ½ teaspoon dried, remaining 1 sprig rosemary or ¼ teaspoon dried, and the lemon slices under the skin. Truss the chicken by tying together the legs with string. Place the chicken, breast-side down, on a rack in a small roasting pan.

3. Place the chicken and potatoes in the oven and roast for 30 minutes. Turn the chicken breast-side up, and continue to roast for 30 minutes longer, basting the chicken with pan juices and stirring the potatoes occasionally, or until the chicken is cooked through and the potatoes are tender. Place the chicken and potatoes on a platter. Remove the skin from the chicken before eating.

Suggested accompaniments: Steamed broccoli with diced red onion, and a fresh fruit bowl of apples, pears, and red and green seedless grapes.

FAT: 12G/28%
CALORIES: 392
SATURATED FAT: 3.1G
CARBOHYDRATE: 28G
PROTEIN: 44G
CHOLESTEROL: 127MG
SODIUM: 546MG

Slices of grilled chicken are added to Caesar salad to create a delicious variation of this all-time favorite. To keep the fat to a minimum, we replace the traditionally egg-based dressing with a rich blend of reduced-fat mayonnaise and reduced-fat sour cream, thinned with chicken broth. And for a crunchy treat we've included homemade garlicky croutons.

CAESAR SALAD WITH GRILLED CHICKEN BREASTS

SERVES: 4
WORKING TIME: 20 MINUTES
TOTAL TIME: 35 MINUTES

4 ounces Italian or French bread, cut into ½-inch slices

2 cloves garlic, peeled and halved

½ teaspoon salt

½ teaspoon dried oregano

¼ teaspoon freshly ground black pepper

3 tablespoons fresh lemon juice

1 pound skinless, boneless chicken breasts

½ cup reduced-sodium chicken broth, defatted

3 tablespoons reduced-fat mayonnaise

1 tablespoon reduced-fat sour cream

1 teaspoon anchovy paste

5 cups torn romaine lettuce

8 cherry tomatoes, halved

1 tablespoon capers, rinsed and drained

1. Preheat the oven to 400°. Place the bread on a baking sheet and bake for 5 minutes, or until crisp and golden. Immediately rub the warm bread with the cut sides of the garlic (see tip). Cut the bread into cubes for croutons. Set aside.

2. Preheat the broiler or prepare the grill. In a small bowl, combine the salt, oregano, pepper, and 1 tablespoon of the lemon juice. Rub the spice mixture evenly onto the chicken. Broil or grill the chicken 6 inches from the heat for about 5 minutes per side, or until cooked through. When cool enough to handle, cut the chicken into strips.

3. In a large bowl, whisk together the broth, mayonnaise, sour cream, anchovy paste, and the remaining 2 tablespoons lemon juice. Add the lettuce, cherry tomatoes, capers, and croutons, tossing to coat. Place the salad in 4 bowls, top with the sliced chicken, and serve warm or at room temperature.

Helpful hint: You can rub the spice mixture onto the chicken up to 2 hours in advance, and keep the chicken refrigerated until ready to cook. Bring to room temperature before broiling or grilling.

FAT: 5G/19%
CALORIES: 260
SATURATED FAT: 1.3G
CARBOHYDRATE: 20G
PROTEIN: 31G
CHOLESTEROL: 68MG
SODIUM: 792MG

MEAT

Left, Glazed Beef with Chunky Mashed Potatoes (p. 186).
Above, Classic Fajitas (p. 155).

It's
fun to have fajitas as a
"serve yourself" meal:
Prepare the lettuce,
salsa, and the pepper-
and-onion and yogurt
mixtures in separate
bowls, then bring out
the sizzling steak strips
and warm tortillas at
the last moment.
Fajitas can be finger
food for the dexterous,
but some people prefer
to eat them with a
knife and fork. Either
way, supply plenty of
napkins.

Classic Fajitas

SERVES: 4
WORKING TIME: 30 MINUTES
TOTAL TIME: 30 MINUTES

¼ cup fresh lime juice

1 tablespoon chili powder

3 bell peppers, mixed colors, cut into thin strips

1 red onion, thinly sliced

¾ pound well-trimmed flank steak

Eight 6-inch flour tortillas

¼ cup plain nonfat yogurt

2 tablespoons reduced-fat sour cream

1 cup mild or medium-hot prepared salsa

2 cups shredded romaine lettuce

1. Preheat the broiler. In a medium bowl, combine the lime juice, chili powder, bell peppers, and onion. With a slotted spoon, transfer the bell peppers and onion to a broiler pan. Broil 4 to 5 inches from the heat, turning occasionally, for 10 minutes.

2. Meanwhile, brush the steak with the remaining lime juice mixture. Push the vegetables to the outer edges of the broiler pan and place the steak in the center. Broil, turning once, for 10 minutes, or until medium-rare. Transfer the steak to a cutting board and with a sharp knife, cut the steak into two pieces. Then slice it into strips (see tip).

3. Place the tortillas under the broiler for 30 seconds to warm through. In a small bowl, combine the yogurt and sour cream. Place 2 tortillas on each of 4 plates. Dividing evenly, top the tortillas with the steak strips, pepper and onion mixture, salsa, lettuce, and yogurt mixture.

Helpful hint: If you have a grill topper, you can cook both the vegetables and the steak on the barbecue rather than under the broiler.

FAT: 11G/28%
CALORIES: 349
SATURATED FAT: 3.7G
CARBOHYDRATE: 38G
PROTEIN: 24G
CHOLESTEROL: 45MG
SODIUM: 926MG

TIP

Flank steak tends to be tough; for tender fajitas, cook the steak just until it is medium-rare, then carve it this way: Cut the steak in half, with the grain. Then carve it across the grain at an acute angle into ¼-inch-thick slices.

DELUXE CHEESEBURGERS

SERVES: 4
WORKING TIME: 20 MINUTES
TOTAL TIME: 30 MINUTES

½ cup reduced-sodium chicken broth, defatted

1 small onion, finely chopped

1 clove garlic, minced

½ pound well-trimmed top round, cut into large chunks

¼ pound lean ground turkey

¼ cup plain dried bread crumbs

¼ cup chili sauce

¼ teaspoon freshly ground black pepper

¼ cup shredded Swiss cheese (1 ounce)

4 hamburger rolls, split

1 cup shredded romaine lettuce

4 thick slices of tomato

1. In a small saucepan, combine the broth, onion, and garlic. Bring to a simmer over medium heat and cook until the onion is very soft and all the liquid is absorbed, about 5 minutes. Set aside to cool slightly.

2. Meanwhile, preheat the broiler. In a food processor, process the beef until coarsely ground. In a medium bowl, combine the ground beef, turkey, bread crumbs, 2 tablespoons of the chili sauce, the pepper, and the cooled onion. Blend thoroughly and form into 4 patties. Broil the burgers 3 to 4 inches from the heat, turning once, for 8 minutes, or until cooked through. Sprinkle the Swiss cheese on top and broil for 30 seconds to melt the cheese.

3. Broil the hamburger buns for 30 seconds to lightly toast. Place the buns on 4 plates and top with the lettuce, tomato, and a burger. Top the burgers with the remaining 2 tablespoons chili sauce and serve.

Helpful hint: You can customize these burgers with your favorite cheese. Cheddar, Monterey jack, Gouda, and blue cheese can all be substituted for the Swiss.

FAT: 9G/25%
CALORIES: 325
SATURATED FAT: 3.1G
CARBOHYDRATE: 35G
PROTEIN: 26G
CHOLESTEROL: 60MG
SODIUM: 686MG

Can a thick, juicy burger on a bun, crowned with melted cheese be a healthy meal? Definitely. The patty is made from lean top round plus ground turkey; bread crumbs bulk up the burgers, while braised onions and chili sauce keep them juicy. And there's just one-quarter ounce of cheese on each burger. Add a slice of raw onion, if you like, and a side order of potato salad.

STEAK WITH BALSAMIC SAUCE AND MUSHROOMS

SERVES: 4
WORKING TIME: 15 MINUTES
TOTAL TIME: 30 MINUTES PLUS MARINATING TIME

A citrus-and-vinegar marinade suffuses this steak with flavor. Serve the steak with sautéed broccoli rabe.

⅓ cup balsamic vinegar

⅓ cup dry red wine

1 teaspoon grated orange zest

⅓ cup orange juice

2 cloves garlic, slivered

½ teaspoon dried oregano

¼ teaspoon dried sage

½ teaspoon salt

½ teaspoon freshly ground black pepper

1 pound well-trimmed flank steak

1 teaspoon olive oil

1¼ pounds large mushrooms, quartered

1 teaspoon cornstarch mixed with 1 tablespoon water

¼ cup chopped fresh basil

4 slices Italian bread (6 ounces total), toasted

1. In a shallow nonaluminum pan or bowl, combine the vinegar, wine, orange zest, orange juice, garlic, oregano, sage, salt, and pepper. Add the steak, turning to coat. Set aside to marinate for at least 30 minutes at room temperature or for up to 8 hours in the refrigerator.

2. Preheat the broiler or prepare the grill. Reserving the marinade, place the steak on the rack and broil or grill 6 inches from the heat, turning once, for 8 minutes, or until medium-rare. Let stand for 5 minutes before cutting into thin diagonal slices.

3. Meanwhile, in a large nonstick skillet, heat the oil until hot but not smoking over medium heat. Add the mushrooms and cook, stirring frequently, until softened, about 4 minutes. Pour in the reserved marinade and bring to a boil. Boil until reduced by one-fourth, about 5 minutes. Stir in the cornstarch mixture and cook, stirring, until slightly thickened, about 1 minute. Stir the basil into the pan. Place the steak, mushrooms, and toasted bread on 4 plates and serve.

Helpful hint: Try handsome light-brown cremini mushrooms in this dish if you can find them; they have a little more flavor than domestic white mushrooms. Many supermarkets now carry these Italian mushrooms.

FAT: 12G/29%
CALORIES: 372
SATURATED FAT: 4.3G
CARBOHYDRATE: 33G
PROTEIN: 30G
CHOLESTEROL: 57MG
SODIUM: 601MG

SPICY BEER-BRAISED BEEF STEW

SERVES: 4
WORKING TIME: 30 MINUTES
TOTAL TIME: 50 MINUTES

3 tablespoons flour

½ teaspoon salt

¼ teaspoon freshly ground
black pepper

1 pound well-trimmed top
round of beef, cut into ¾-inch
cubes

2 teaspoons olive oil

2 Spanish onions (1 pound),
halved and thinly sliced

4 cloves garlic, minced

2 carrots, thinly sliced

1½ cups dark beer

1 cup reduced-sodium chicken
broth, defatted

2 tablespoons no-salt-added
tomato paste

¾ teaspoon dried thyme

½ teaspoon red pepper flakes

¼ teaspoon ground allspice

¼ cup chopped fresh parsley

1. On a sheet of waxed paper, combine the flour, ¼ teaspoon of the salt, and the pepper. Dredge the beef in the flour mixture, shaking off and reserving the excess. In a nonstick Dutch oven, heat the oil until hot but not smoking over medium heat. Add the beef and cook until lightly browned, about 4 minutes. With a slotted spoon, transfer the beef to a plate. Set aside.

2. Add the onions and garlic to the pan and cook, stirring, until golden brown, about 10 minutes. Add the carrots and cook, stirring frequently, until almost tender, about 5 minutes. Stir in the beer, increase the heat to high, and cook until the beer is reduced by half, about 5 minutes. Stir in the broth, tomato paste, thyme, red pepper flakes, allspice, and the remaining ¼ teaspoon salt. Bring to a boil, reduce to a simmer, cover, and cook until the vegetables are tender, about 10 minutes.

3. In a small bowl, combine the reserved dredging mixture and ¼ cup of water. Stir the flour mixture into the pan and bring to a boil. Cook, stirring, until the sauce is slightly thickened, about 2 minutes. Return the beef to the pan and cook until just cooked through, about 2 minutes. Divide among 4 bowls, sprinkle the parsley over, and serve.

Helpful hint: Sweet Vidalia, Maui, or Granex onions may be substituted for the mild Spanish onions.

FAT: 6G/18%
CALORIES: 302
SATURATED FAT: 1.6G
CARBOHYDRATE: 25G
PROTEIN: 30G
CHOLESTEROL: 65MG
SODIUM: 530MG

Here's our light take on Flemish "carbonnade." Dark beer gives it rich color and a slightly fruity bouquet.

PORK "UN-FRIED" RICE

SERVES: 4
WORKING TIME: 30 MINUTES
TOTAL TIME: 45 MINUTES

This vivid potpourri retains all the textures and colors of the usual fried rice, but without the extra fat and calories. We've used a mere two teaspoons of oil for "frying" before gently simmering the ingredients, thus fusing the flavors. Strips of beef top round or chicken breast would be equally delicious in place of the pork.

2 teaspoons vegetable oil

4 scallions (white and tender green parts only), thinly sliced

3 cloves garlic, minced

1 tablespoon minced fresh ginger

1 cup long-grain rice

1⅓ cups reduced-sodium chicken broth, defatted

½ pound lean boneless pork loin, cut into 1½-by-¼-inch strips

⅔ cup ¼-inch-wide shredded Napa cabbage

1 red bell pepper, diced

½ pound snow peas, trimmed and cut diagonally in half

1 cup frozen peas, thawed

1 tablespoon reduced-sodium soy sauce

1 tablespoon cider vinegar

1. In a large skillet, heat the oil until hot but not smoking over medium heat. Add the scallions, garlic, and ginger and cook, stirring frequently, until the mixture is softened, about 3 minutes. Add the rice, stirring to coat. Add the broth and 1 cup of water, bring to a boil, reduce to a simmer, cover, and cook until the rice is tender, about 15 minutes.

2. Stir in the pork, cabbage, bell pepper, and snow peas. Cover again and cook, stirring frequently, until the cabbage and pepper are just crisp-tender and the pork is almost cooked through, about 5 minutes.

3. Stir in the peas, soy sauce, and vinegar and cook, uncovered, stirring constantly, until the pork is cooked through and the rice is lightly golden, about 5 minutes longer.

Suggested accompaniments: Almond or oolong tea, fortune cookies, and fresh cherries steeped in red wine.

FAT: 6G/16%
CALORIES: 346
SATURATED FAT: 1.5G
CARBOHYDRATE: 51G
PROTEIN: 21G
CHOLESTEROL: 33MG
SODIUM: 443MG

Italian Beef Stir-Fry with Artichokes

SERVES: 4
WORKING TIME: 35 MINUTES
TOTAL TIME: 35 MINUTES

Artichoke hearts, mushrooms, tomatoes, and bell peppers signal the Italian inspiration here, as do the garlic and balsamic vinegar that season the sauce. Fresh artichokes take some time to prepare, so we've used frozen artichoke hearts; they have a lighter, fresher flavor than the canned ones because they're not packed in brine. A salad with cucumbers and radishes would be nice with this dish.

8 ounces ruote (wagon wheel) pasta
1 tablespoon oil
½ pound well-trimmed sirloin, cut into 2-by-⅛-inch strips
1 onion, chopped
1 clove garlic, minced
2 red bell peppers, cut into thin strips
9-ounce package frozen artichoke hearts, thawed and quartered
1 cup sliced mushrooms
13¾-ounce can reduced-sodium chicken broth, defatted
½ teaspoon dried thyme
½ teaspoon dried rosemary
½ teaspoon salt
⅛ teaspoon red pepper flakes
1 teaspoon cornstarch
1 tablespoon balsamic vinegar
3 plum tomatoes, diced
¼ cup chopped fresh parsley

1. In a large pot of boiling water, cook the pasta until just tender. Drain well.

2. Meanwhile, in a large nonstick skillet or wok, heat 2 teaspoons of the oil until hot but not smoking over medium-high heat. Add the beef and stir-fry until browned, 3 to 4 minutes. With a slotted spoon, transfer the beef to a plate.

3. Add the remaining 1 teaspoon oil to the skillet. Add the onion and garlic and stir-fry until the onion begins to soften and brown, about 2 minutes. Add the bell peppers, artichoke hearts, mushrooms, broth, thyme, rosemary, salt, and red pepper flakes. Bring to a boil, reduce to a simmer, and cook until the artichokes and bell peppers are tender, 3 to 4 minutes.

4. In a small bowl, combine the cornstarch with the balsamic vinegar and 1 tablespoon of water. Stir the mixture into the skillet along with the tomatoes and cook, stirring, until slightly thickened, about 1 minute. Return the beef to the pan along with the parsley and cook until heated through, about 1 minute. Toss with the pasta, divide among 4 bowls, and serve.

Helpful hint: An egg slicer—the kind with evenly spaced wires like guitar strings—can be used to slice mushrooms quickly and neatly.

FAT: 7G/16%
CALORIES: 389
SATURATED FAT: 1.5G
CARBOHYDRATE: 57G
PROTEIN: 24G
CHOLESTEROL: 35MG
SODIUM: 615MG

PEASANT-STYLE BEEF STEW

SERVES: 8
WORKING TIME: 40 MINUTES
TOTAL TIME: 1 HOUR 30 MINUTES

Strongly flavored with sage, thyme, and a generous splash of red wine, this homey stew satisfies even the most ravenous appetites with just three ounces of meat per serving, thanks to lots of vegetables and beans. Enjoy your own party by preparing this a day or two ahead—then place the stew, reheated in an attractive kettle, on a buffet table with a stack of serving bowls.

¼ cup plus 3 tablespoons flour

½ teaspoon salt

¼ teaspoon freshly ground black pepper

1½ pounds top round of beef, cut into ½-inch cubes

1 tablespoon olive oil

3 cloves garlic, minced

1 pound carrots, thickly sliced

Two 14½-ounce cans reduced-sodium beef broth, defatted

1 cup dry red wine

2 tablespoons tomato paste

2 teaspoons dried sage

1 teaspoon dried thyme

1 teaspoon dry mustard

1½ pounds small red potatoes, quartered

10 ounces mushrooms, quartered

10-ounce package frozen pearl onions, thawed

16-ounce can red kidney beans or chick-peas, rinsed and drained

¼ cup chopped fresh parsley

1. In a shallow bowl, combine ¼ cup of the flour, the salt, and pepper. Add half of the beef and dredge in the flour mixture, shaking off the excess. In a large Dutch oven, heat half of the oil until hot but not smoking over medium heat. Add the floured beef and cook, stirring frequently, until browned, about 8 minutes. Transfer to a plate. Repeat with the remaining beef, flour mixture, and oil.

2. Return all the beef to the pan. Stir in the garlic, carrots, broth, wine, tomato paste, sage, thyme, and mustard and bring to a boil. Reduce to a simmer, cover, and cook, stirring occasionally, until the flavors have blended, about 15 minutes.

3. Stir in the potatoes, mushrooms, and onions. Cover again and cook until the potatoes and beef are tender, about 20 minutes. Stir in the beans and parsley and cook, uncovered, until the beans are heated through, about 3 minutes.

4. In a jar with a tight-fitting lid, combine the remaining 3 tablespoons flour and ¼ cup of water, shake until smooth, and stir into the simmering stew. Cook, stirring constantly, until the stew is slightly thickened, about 2 minutes longer.

Suggested accompaniments: Crusty rolls, followed by chunky applesauce with dried currants and a dusting of cinnamon.

FAT: 11G/28%
CALORIES: 360
SATURATED FAT: 3.4G
CARBOHYDRATE: 39G
PROTEIN: 26G
CHOLESTEROL: 52MG
SODIUM: 585MG

PEPPER STEAK WITH BRANDY CREAM SAUCE

SERVES: 4
WORKING TIME: 30 MINUTES
TOTAL TIME: 30 MINUTES

There's a distinctly French accent to this sophisticated take on steak. The sauce is redolent of shallots, with their delicate garlic-onion bouquet; a splash of brandy is another fragrant addition. The steak and pepper strips are served over slabs of sourdough bread—the French "pain levain"—which soaks up the delectable sauce. Add a bistro-style salad and you're all set.

1 tablespoon olive oil

1 red bell pepper, cut into thin strips

1 green bell pepper, cut into thin strips

2 tablespoons flour

¾ teaspoon salt

¼ teaspoon freshly ground black pepper

½ pound well-trimmed top round steak, cut into thin slices

2 large shallots, minced

½ cup reduced-sodium beef broth

2 tablespoons brandy

2 tablespoons reduced-fat sour cream

4 ounces sourdough bread, cut into 4 slices, toasted, and cut in half

1. In a medium nonstick skillet, heat the oil until hot but not smoking over medium heat. Add the bell peppers and cook, stirring occasionally, until crisp-tender, about 5 minutes.

2. Meanwhile, in a sturdy plastic bag, combine the flour, salt, and black pepper. Add the steak, shaking to coat.

3. Add the shallots to the pan, increase the heat to medium-high, and cook until softened, about 1 minute. Add the beef and cook, stirring frequently, until medium-rare, about 4 minutes. Stir in the broth and then the brandy and simmer for 2 minutes. Remove from the heat and stir in the sour cream. Place 2 toast halves on each of 4 plates, spoon the steak and sauce over, and serve.

Helpful hint: Shallots look like large garlic cloves, but their skin is more like that of an onion. You can substitute 2 coarsely chopped scallions for the shallots in this recipe, if you like.

FAT: 7G/26%
CALORIES: 242
SATURATED FAT: 1.8G
CARBOHYDRATE: 22G
PROTEIN: 17G
CHOLESTEROL: 35MG
SODIUM: 628MG

HEARTY BEEF AND VEGETABLE STEW

SERVES: 4
WORKING TIME: 30 MINUTES
TOTAL TIME: 55 MINUTES

This outstanding stew brims with hefty cubes of beef, carrots, red potatoes, and rutabaga. Puréed vegetables thicken the broth.

2 tablespoons flour
½ teaspoon salt
¼ teaspoon freshly ground black pepper
¾ pound well-trimmed top round of beef, cut into ¾-inch cubes
2 teaspoons olive oil
1 large onion, cut into 1-inch cubes
½ pound rutabaga, peeled and cut into 1-inch cubes
2 large carrots, cut into 1-inch pieces
½ teaspoon sugar
¾ pound small red potatoes, quartered
⅓ cup reduced-sodium chicken broth, defatted
¾ teaspoon ground ginger
2 tablepoons chopped fresh parsley

1. On a sheet of waxed paper, combine the flour, ¼ teaspoon of the salt, and the pepper. Dredge the beef in the flour mixture, shaking off the excess.

2. In a Dutch oven or flameproof casserole, heat the oil until hot but not smoking over medium heat. Add the beef and cook until lightly browned, about 4 minutes. With a slotted spoon, transfer the beef to a plate. Add the onion, rutabaga, and carrots to the pan, sprinkle the sugar on top, and cook, stirring frequently, until the vegetables are lightly browned, about 4 minutes.

3. Add the potatoes, broth, 1 cup of water, the ginger, and remaining ¼ teaspoon salt and bring to a boil. Reduce to a simmer, cover, and cook until the vegetables are firm-tender, about 20 minutes. With a slotted spoon, transfer ½ cup of the vegetables to a food processor. Add ¼ cup of the cooking liquid and process to a coarse purée. Stir the purée into the stew, return the beef to the pan, and simmer, uncovered, until the beef is just cooked through, about 2 minutes. Divide the stew among 4 bowls, sprinkle with the parsley, and serve.

Helpful hint: Instead of transferring the vegetables to a food processor, you can use a hand blender right in the pot. Run the blender in 1 or 2 on-and-off pulses to purée about a ½ cup of the vegetables, while leaving the stew chunky.

FAT: 6G/20%
CALORIES: 277
SATURATED FAT: 1.3G
CARBOHYDRATE: 33G
PROTEIN: 24G
CHOLESTEROL: 49MG
SODIUM: 407MG

LAMB AND WHITE BEAN STEW

SERVES: 4
WORKING TIME: 30 MINUTES
TOTAL TIME: 30 MINUTES

1 tablespoon olive oil

1 pound boneless leg of lamb, cut into ¾-inch cubes

½ pound red potatoes, cut into ¾-inch cubes

1 cup reduced-sodium chicken broth, defatted

2 teaspoons paprika

1 teaspoon ground cumin

1 teaspoon chili powder

1 teaspoon minced garlic

¾ teaspoon salt

½ teaspoon dried oregano

2 tablespoons flour

5 scallions, thinly sliced

19-ounce can white kidney beans (cannellini), rinsed and drained

1. In a large nonstick skillet, heat the oil until hot but not smoking over medium heat. Add the lamb and cook until medium, 4 to 5 minutes. With a slotted spoon, transfer the lamb to a plate. Set aside.

2. Add the potatoes, ¾ cup of the broth, the paprika, cumin, chili powder, garlic, salt, and oregano to the skillet. Bring to a boil, reduce to a simmer, cover, and cook until the potatoes are tender, about 8 minutes.

3. In a small bowl, combine the remaining ¼ cup broth and the flour, whisking to blend. Add the broth mixture and the scallions to the pan and cook, stirring, until the sauce is slightly thickened, about 3 minutes. Return the lamb to the skillet, add the beans, and cook until warmed through, about 1 minute. Divide the lamb mixture among 4 bowls and serve.

Helpful hint: Red kidney beans or pinto beans would work perfectly well in this dish in place of the white kidney beans.

FAT: 10G/26%
CALORIES: 350
SATURATED FAT: 2.3G
CARBOHYDRATE: 32G
PROTEIN: 33G
CHOLESTEROL: 73MG
SODIUM: 826MG

Perhaps the most flavorful of meats, lamb is irresistibly savory when smothered in chilied white beans.

169

Americans have become great fans of Szechuan food, thanks to the explosion of Szechuan restaurants around the country. Stir-frying—one of the quickest cooking techniques—plays a major role in this cuisine. Do as the Chinese do, and have all the ingredients lined up and ready to go into the skillet before you start.

SZECHUAN PORK STIR-FRY

SERVES: 4
WORKING TIME: 25 MINUTES
TOTAL TIME: 30 MINUTES

1 cup long-grain rice

¼ teaspoon salt

2 teaspoons vegetable oil

½ pound well-trimmed pork tenderloin, cut into ½-inch-wide strips

2 red bell peppers, cut into thin strips

2 teaspoons grated fresh ginger

1 clove garlic, minced

16-ounce bag frozen broccoli florets (see tip)

1½ cups reduced-sodium chicken broth, defatted

¼ teaspoon red pepper flakes

1 teaspoon cornstarch

2 tablespoons reduced-sodium soy sauce

1 tablespoon rice vinegar

1 cup sliced scallions

1. In a medium saucepan, bring 2¼ cups of water to a boil. Add the rice and salt, reduce to a simmer, cover, and cook until the rice is tender, about 17 minutes.

2. In a large nonstick skillet or wok, heat 1 teaspoon of the oil until hot but not smoking over medium-high heat. Add the pork and cook, stirring, until browned, about 5 minutes. With a slotted spoon, transfer the pork to a plate.

3. Add the remaining 1 teaspoon oil to the skillet along with the bell peppers, ginger, and garlic. Cook, stirring, until the peppers are crisp-tender, about 2 minutes. Add the broccoli, broth, and red pepper flakes. Bring to a boil, reduce to a simmer, and cook until the peppers and broccoli are tender, about 5 minutes.

4. Meanwhile, in a small bowl, combine the cornstarch, soy sauce, and vinegar. Return the pork to the pan. Add the cornstarch mixture and scallions and bring to a boil. Cook, stirring, until the sauce is slightly thickened and the pork is cooked through, about 2 minutes. Serve the pork mixture with the rice.

Helpful hint: You can easily cook a stir-fry in a skillet, but if you do a lot of Asian-style cooking, a nonstick wok may be a worthwhile investment (and not a very great investment, at that). The wok's curved sides suit it particularly well to the rapid tossing and mixing of stir-frying.

FAT: 5G/14%
CALORIES: 323
SATURATED FAT: 1G
CARBOHYDRATE: 49G
PROTEIN: 21G
CHOLESTEROL: 37MG
SODIUM: 737MG

TIP

There's no need to thaw the broccoli florets if they separate easily. But if the florets have clumped together in an icy mass, you can quick-thaw them: Put the broccoli in a strainer or colander and run cold water over it, separating the florets with your fingers. Drain the broccoli well before using.

BARBECUED BEEF STEW

SERVES: 8
WORKING TIME: 30 MINUTES
TOTAL TIME: 45 MINUTES

The down-home flavor of barbecue is most welcome in a hunger-chasing stew. Spicy but not hot (unless you care to toss in some extra cayenne), this dish has vegetables built right in; and instead of the usual chopped or shredded meat, this stew is filled with good-sized cubes of beef. Bake up some cornsticks, corn muffins, or corn bread to serve alongside.

¼ cup flour

¾ teaspoon salt

2 pounds well-trimmed top round of beef, cut into ½-inch cubes

4 teaspoons olive oil

5 cloves garlic, minced

14½-ounce can no-salt-added stewed tomatoes, chopped with their juice

Two 8-ounce cans no-salt-added tomato sauce

2 tablespoons molasses

1 teaspoon ground ginger

1 teaspoon dried oregano

1 teaspoon Worcestershire sauce

¼ teaspoon cayenne pepper

1¼ pounds green beans, cut into 1-inch lengths

10-ounce package frozen corn kernels

1. On a sheet of waxed paper, combine the flour and ¼ teaspoon of the salt. Dredge the beef in the flour mixture, shaking off the excess.

2. In a large nonstick Dutch oven or flameproof casserole, heat 2 teaspoons of the oil until hot but not smoking over medium heat. Add half the beef and cook until lightly browned, about 4 minutes. With a slotted spoon, transfer the beef to a plate. Repeat with the remaining 2 teaspoons oil and remaining beef.

3. Add the garlic and cook, stirring frequently, until fragrant, about 2 minutes. Stir in the stewed tomatoes, tomato sauce, molasses, ginger, oregano, Worcestershire, cayenne, and the remaining ½ teaspoon salt and bring to a boil. Reduce to a simmer, cover, and cook for 5 minutes to blend the flavors.

4. Stir in the green beans and simmer, uncovered, until the beans are tender, about 6 minutes. Return the beef to the pan, add the corn, and simmer just until the beef is cooked through and the corn is hot, about 3 minutes. Divide the stew among 8 bowls and serve.

Helpful hint: You can use a 10-ounce package of frozen green beans instead of the fresh green beans if you like; add the frozen beans along with the corn, and allow an extra minute or two for the vegetables to heat through.

FAT: 7G/22%
CALORIES: 283
SATURATED FAT: 1.7G
CARBOHYDRATE: 28G
PROTEIN: 30G
CHOLESTEROL: 65MG
SODIUM: 301MG

STIR-FRIED PORK WITH SESAME GREEN BEANS

SERVES: 4
WORKING TIME: 35 MINUTES
TOTAL TIME: 35 MINUTES

The dark, deeply fragrant oil made from roasted sesame seeds is a staple in Asian kitchens. Fortunately, you'll also find it in most supermarkets. Here, sesame oil flavors green beans, summer squash, and scallions as well as stir-fried slices of pork tenderloin. A sprinkling of toasted sesame seeds reinforces the impact of the aromatic oil.

1 cup long-grain rice
¾ teaspoon salt
1 tablespoon flour
¼ teaspoon freshly ground black pepper
½ pound well-trimmed pork tenderloin, cut into very thin slices
2 teaspoons vegetable oil
1 teaspoon dark Oriental sesame oil
½ pound green beans, cut into 2-inch lengths
1 yellow summer squash, halved lengthwise and thinly sliced
1 cup sliced scallions
¾ cup reduced-sodium chicken broth, defatted
1 teaspoon cornstarch
2 tablespoons reduced-sodium soy sauce
1 tablespoon rice vinegar
½ teaspoon sugar
⅛ teaspoon red pepper flakes
2 tablespoons sesame seeds, toasted

1. In a medium saucepan, bring 2¼ cups of water to a boil. Add the rice and ¼ teaspoon of the salt, reduce to a simmer, cover, and cook until the rice is tender, about 17 minutes.

2. Meanwhile, in a sturdy plastic bag, combine the flour, pepper, and the remaining ½ teaspoon salt. Add the pork to the bag, shaking to coat with the flour mixture. In a large nonstick skillet, heat the vegetable oil until hot but not smoking over medium heat. Add the pork and cook until no longer pink in the center, 3 to 4 minutes. Transfer the pork to a plate.

3. Add the sesame oil and green beans to the skillet and cook until the green beans are browned, about 1 minute. Add the squash, scallions, and ½ cup of the broth. Bring to a boil, reduce to a simmer, and cook until the squash is crisp-tender, about 2 minutes.

4. In a small bowl, combine the cornstarch, the remaining ¼ cup broth, the soy sauce, vinegar, sugar, and red pepper flakes. Add the cornstarch mixture to the skillet and cook, stirring, until slightly thickened, about 1 minute. Return the pork to the skillet along with the sesame seeds and cook until heated through, about 1 minute. Divide the rice among 4 plates, spoon the pork alongside, and serve.

Helpful hint: Toast the sesame seeds in a dry skillet over medium heat: Cook, stirring, for 2 to 3 minutes, until the seeds are golden brown.

FAT: 8G/21%
CALORIES: 347
SATURATED FAT: 1.5G
CARBOHYDRATE: 49G
PROTEIN: 19G
CHOLESTEROL: 37MG
SODIUM: 872MG

BEEF GUMBO

SERVES: 4
WORKING TIME: 15 MINUTES
TOTAL TIME: 35 MINUTES

The word gumbo comes from an African word, "quingumbo," which means okra. Gumbos are thickened either with okra (which releases a thickening substance as it cooks) or with filé powder, which is made from sassafras leaves. We've boosted the texture of this Louisiana classic with tapioca, a starch derived from cassava roots.

1 teaspoon olive oil

3 tablespoons coarsely chopped Canadian bacon (1 ounce)

4 scallions, thinly sliced

1 green bell pepper, cut into 1-inch squares

2 cloves garlic, minced

14½-ounce can no-salt-added stewed tomatoes, chopped with their juices

2 cups reduced-sodium beef broth

2 teaspoons chili powder

¾ teaspoon dried thyme

¾ teaspoon dried oregano

½ teaspoon salt

10-ounce package frozen cut okra

1 tablespoon minute tapioca

10 ounces well-trimmed top round of beef, cut into bite-size pieces

1½ cups frozen corn kernels

1. In a nonstick Dutch oven or flameproof casserole, heat the oil until hot but not smoking over medium heat. Add the Canadian bacon, scallions, bell pepper, and garlic and cook, stirring frequently, until the vegetables are softened, about 5 minutes.

2. Stir in the tomatoes and their juices, the broth, 3 cups of water, the chili powder, thyme, oregano, and salt. Bring to a boil, reduce to a simmer, cover, and cook for 5 minutes to blend the flavors. Add the okra, cover, and cook until the okra is tender, about 10 minutes.

3. Meanwhile, place the tapioca in a small bowl and stir in ½ cup of the simmering broth; let stand for 5 minutes to soften. Stir the tapioca mixture, beef, and corn into the soup and cook, uncovered, until the soup is slightly thickened and the beef is just cooked through, about 5 minutes. Ladle the soup into 4 bowls and serve.

Helpful hint: A very effective thickener for soups and sauces, tapioca comes in powder, flake, bead, and granule form. Minute tapioca is the quick-cooking granular form of this useful ingredient.

FAT: 5G/18%
CALORIES: 251
SATURATED FAT: 1.2G
CARBOHYDRATE: 31G
PROTEIN: 24G
CHOLESTEROL: 44MG
SODIUM: 769MG

CHILI CON CARNE

SERVES: 4
WORKING TIME: 25 MINUTES
TOTAL TIME: 35 MINUTES

½ pound well-trimmed top round of beef, cut into large chunks

2 teaspoons olive oil

5 cloves garlic, minced

6 scallions, thinly sliced

1 large green bell pepper, coarsely chopped

1 jalapeño pepper, minced

1 tablespoon chili powder

½ teaspoon dried thyme

½ teaspoon dried oregano

½ teaspoon ground cumin

½ teaspoon salt

1 tablespoon flour

8-ounce can no-salt-added tomato sauce

½ cup reduced-sodium beef broth

19-ounce can red kidney beans, rinsed and drained

1 cup frozen corn kernels

¼ cup reduced-fat sour cream

1. In a food processor, process the meat until coarsely ground, about 30 seconds.

2. In a large skillet, heat the oil until hot but not smoking over medium heat. Add the garlic and all but 1 tablespoon of the scallions and cook, stirring frequently, until the scallions are softened, about 2 minutes. Add the bell pepper and jalapeño pepper and cook, stirring frequently, until the bell pepper is crisp-tender, about 3 minutes. Stir the meat into the skillet, breaking it up with a spoon. Sprinkle the meat with the chili powder, thyme, oregano, cumin, and salt and cook until the meat is no longer pink, about 2 minutes.

3. Sprinkle the meat evenly with the flour, stirring to combine. Add the tomato sauce, broth, beans, and corn and bring to a boil. Reduce to a simmer, cover, and cook until the flavors are blended and the sauce is slightly thickened, about 7 minutes. Serve with the sour cream sprinkled with the remaining 1 tablespoon scallions.

Helpful hint: You can adjust the heat of the chili by removing the seeds and membranes from the jalapeño. Most of the "burn" resides in this part of chilies, so scraping out and discarding the seeds and ribs makes for a milder dish.

FAT: 8G/24%
CALORIES: 307
SATURATED FAT: 2G
CARBOHYDRATE: 37G
PROTEIN: 25G
CHOLESTEROL: 37MG
SODIUM: 594MG

These days, chili comes in many guises—with beef or pork, chopped or ground, hot or mild, with or without beans—so there are many decisions to be made when cooking up a pot. Here's an easy way out—a recipe for a hearty chili that should please just about everybody. Warm jalapeño corn bread would be a wonderful accompaniment.

Keeping the meatballs small stretches less than a pound of meat to feed a crowd. And we avoid adding extra fat by baking the meatballs, rather than sautéing them in oil. Fresh dill is essential, both in the meatballs and as the final garnish. Store dill in the refrigerator with the stems in a glass of water and the tops covered with a plastic bag.

Swedish Meatballs

SERVES: 8
WORKING TIME: 30 MINUTES
TOTAL TIME: 50 MINUTES

2 cups fresh bread crumbs
(see tip)

⅓ cup skim milk

¾ pound lean ground beef

3 scallions, finely chopped

2 egg whites

3 teaspoons snipped fresh dill

¾ teaspoon dry mustard

12 ounces yolk-free egg noodles

14½-ounce can reduced-sodium
beef broth, defatted

1 tablespoon tomato paste

1 teaspoon paprika

½ teaspoon salt

1 red or yellow bell pepper, cut
into thin slivers

Half medium red onion, cut into
thin slivers

1 zucchini, cut into 2-inch
julienne

3 tablespoons flour

½ cup reduced-fat sour cream

1½ tablespoons fresh lemon juice

1. Preheat the oven to 400°. Line a baking sheet with foil. In a large bowl, combine the bread crumbs and milk. Add the beef, scallions, egg whites, 1 teaspoon of the dill, and the mustard and mix until well combined. Using a rounded teaspoon for each, form the mixture into 32 small meatballs. Place on the prepared baking sheet and bake for 10 minutes, or until the meatballs are cooked through.

2. Meanwhile, in a large pot of boiling water, cook the noodles until just tender. Drain well.

3. In a medium saucepan, stir together the broth, tomato paste, paprika, and salt. Bring to a simmer over medium heat, add the bell pepper and onion, and cook for 4 minutes. Add the zucchini and cook until the pepper and onion are crisp-tender, about 4 minutes.

4. In a jar with a tight-fitting lid, shake together the flour and ¼ cup of water until smooth. Whisk the flour mixture into the broth mixture and cook, whisking constantly, until the sauce comes to a simmer. Add the meatballs and cook until heated through, about 3 minutes longer. Remove from the heat and stir in the sour cream and lemon juice. Divide the noodles and meatballs among 8 shallow bowls, sprinkle the remaining 2 teaspoons dill on top, and serve.

Suggested accompaniments: Sliced cucumber salad with a horseradish and parsley vinaigrette. For dessert, assorted reduced-fat cookies.

FAT: 8G/22%
CALORIES: 315
SATURATED FAT: 3G
CARBOHYDRATE: 43G
PROTEIN: 20G
CHOLESTEROL: 32MG
SODIUM: 409MG

TIP

To make fresh bread crumbs, tear the bread into pieces and place in a food processor. Process the bread with on-off pulses until finely ground and fluffy. If not using right away, place the bread crumbs in a freezer bag, press out the air, seal, and freeze for several months.

TEX-MEX STIR-FRY

SERVES: 4
WORKING TIME: 30 MINUTES
TOTAL TIME: 30 MINUTES

A skillet dinner made with strips of sirloin is a cut above the usual ground-beef one-dish meal. And this unique stir-fry, replete with golden corn, bell peppers, chili seasonings, and fresh cilantro, is ready in half an hour, so you could hardly ask for more in the way of convenience. While you're cooking, warm some flour or corn tortillas to serve on the side.

1 tablespoon vegetable oil

½ pound well-trimmed sirloin, cut into 2-by-⅛-inch strips

1 tablespoon chili powder

1 teaspoon ground cumin

⅛ teaspoon cayenne pepper

1 red bell pepper, cut into thin strips

1 green bell pepper, cut into thin strips

1 red onion, sliced

2 ribs celery, sliced

¾ cup reduced-sodium chicken broth, defatted

2 tablespoons ketchup

10-ounce package frozen corn kernels, thawed

1 cup canned red kidney beans, rinsed and drained

1 cup halved cherry tomatoes

¼ cup chopped fresh cilantro or parsley

1. In a large nonstick skillet or wok, heat 2 teaspoons of the oil until hot but not smoking over medium heat. Add the beef and stir-fry until browned, about 3 minutes. Reduce the heat to medium and add the chili powder, cumin, and cayenne. Stir-fry until fragrant, about 1 minute. With a slotted spoon, transfer the beef to a plate.

2. Add the remaining 1 teaspoon oil to the skillet. Add the bell peppers, onion, and celery and stir-fry until the onions are slightly softened, 2 to 3 minutes. Add the broth, ketchup, corn, and beans. Bring to a boil, reduce to a simmer, and cook until the vegetables are tender, 2 to 3 minutes.

3. Increase the heat to high, return the beef to the skillet along with the tomatoes and cilantro, and cook until heated through, about 1 minute.

Helpful hint: To save time later, you can cut up and combine the bell peppers, onion, and celery up to 12 hours in advance and keep them covered in the refrigerator until ready to use.

FAT: 8G/27%
CALORIES: 270
SATURATED FAT: 1.4G
CARBOHYDRATE: 34G
PROTEIN: 20G
CHOLESTEROL: 35MG
SODIUM: 377MG

STEAK WITH CHUNKY TOMATO SAUCE AND POTATOES

SERVES: 4
WORKING TIME: 40 MINUTES
TOTAL TIME: 45 MINUTES

Hold the ketchup! No need to sully steaks with something from a bottle when you can savor this fresh, summery tomato sauce, enlivened with bits of carrot, onion, and garlic. The steaks and sauce cook while you boil the accompanying potatoes. Serve a simple salad, too, and put a pinch of oregano in the dressing to complement the sauce.

1 pound all-purpose potatoes, peeled and cut into 1-inch cubes
¼ cup chopped fresh parsley
1 tablespoon extra-virgin olive oil
½ teaspoon salt
1 large onion, finely chopped
2 cloves garlic, minced
¾ cup reduced-sodium chicken broth, defatted
1 carrot, finely chopped
2 tomatoes, coarsely chopped
½ teaspoon dried oregano
½ teaspoon dried rosemary
1 pound well-trimmed top round of beef, cut into 4 thin steaks

1. In a large pot of boiling water, cook the potatoes until tender, about 15 minutes. Drain well and toss with the parsley, ½ teaspoon of the oil, and ¼ teaspoon of the salt. Set aside.

2. In a large nonstick skillet, heat 1 teaspoon of the remaining oil until hot but not smoking over medium heat. Add the onion and garlic and stir to coat. Add ¼ cup of the broth and cook, stirring frequently, until the onion is softened, about 5 minutes. Add the carrot and cook, stirring frequently, until the carrot is softened, about 4 minutes. Stir in the remaining ½ cup broth and cook until slightly reduced, about 4 minutes. Stir in the tomatoes, oregano, and rosemary and cook until the sauce is slightly reduced, about 5 minutes.

3. Meanwhile, in another large nonstick skillet, heat the remaining 1½ teaspoons oil until hot but not smoking over medium-high heat. Sprinkle the steaks with the remaining ¼ teaspoon salt and cook until lightly browned and just cooked through, about 2 minutes per side. Place the steaks and potatoes on 4 plates, spoon the sauce over the steaks, and serve.

Helpful hint: Tan-skinned "long white" all-purpose potatoes are good for boiling; don't confuse them with "long russets"—baking potatoes—which are starchier and will fall apart if peeled and boiled.

FAT: 10G/29%
CALORIES: 304
SATURATED FAT: 2.4G
CARBOHYDRATE: 26G
PROTEIN: 29G
CHOLESTEROL: 66MG
SODIUM: 479MG

GLAZED BEEF WITH CHUNKY MASHED POTATOES

SERVES: 4
WORKING TIME: 30 MINUTES
TOTAL TIME: 30 MINUTES

5 tablespoons frozen orange juice concentrate, thawed

¼ cup firmly packed light brown sugar

1 tablespoon spicy brown mustard

2½ teaspoons chili powder

¾ pound well-trimmed flank steak

1½ pounds red potatoes, cut into 2-inch chunks

½ cup plain low-fat yogurt

3 scallions, coarsely chopped

¼ teaspoon salt

¼ teaspoon ground white pepper

1. Start heating a medium pot of water to boiling for the potatoes. In a shallow bowl, combine 3 tablespoons of the orange juice concentrate, the brown sugar, mustard, and 2 teaspoons of the chili powder. Add the steak, turning to coat.

2. Preheat the broiler. Cook the potatoes in the pot of boiling water until tender, about 12 minutes. Drain well and transfer to a large bowl. Add the yogurt, scallions, salt, white pepper, the remaining ½ teaspoon chili powder, and remaining 2 tablespoons orange juice concentrate and coarsely mash.

3. Meanwhile, broil the steak 5 inches from the heat, turning once, for 10 minutes, or until medium-rare. Let stand for 5 minutes before slicing. Divide the steak among 4 plates, spoon the potatoes alongside, and serve.

Helpful hints: Don't be tempted to mash the potatoes in the food processor: They'll be smooth, but gummy and gluey. To save precious minutes at dinnertime (and get even deeper flavor), marinate the steak: Prepare the recipe through step 1, cover the steak and marinade with plastic wrap, and refrigerate for up to 8 hours.

FAT: 8G/19%
CALORIES: 387
SATURATED FAT: 3.1G
CARBOHYDRATE: 56G
PROTEIN: 23G
CHOLESTEROL: 44MG
SODIUM: 289MG

You can't oven-roast (or even pot-roast) a family-size chunk of beef in half an hour, but you can broil a deliciously glazed steak and serve up steaming mashed potatoes on the side. The potatoes derive their creamy richness from low-fat yogurt, not butter and whole milk. Add steamed broccoli and carrots for a substantial "Sunday dinner" sort of meal.

BRAISED PORK WITH SUN-DRIED TOMATOES

Serves: 4
Working time: 30 minutes
Total time: 30 minutes

12 sun-dried (not oil-packed) tomato halves

¾ pound well-trimmed pork tenderloin, cut into 1-inch-wide strips

1½ teaspoons balsamic vinegar

1 teaspoon olive oil

4 cups small broccoli florets

1 red onion, diced

1 cup reduced-sodium chicken broth, defatted

1 cup dry white wine

1 clove garlic, minced

¼ teaspoon salt

⅔ cup pastina or other tiny pasta

2 teaspoons capers, rinsed and drained

1. With kitchen scissors or a small sharp knife, cut the sun-dried tomatoes into thin strips. Set aside. In a medium bowl, toss the pork with the vinegar. Set aside.

2. In a large nonstick saucepan, heat the oil until hot but not smoking over medium heat. Add the broccoli and onion and cook, stirring occasionally, until the onion is softened, about 5 minutes. Add the broth, wine, ½ cup of water, the sun-dried tomatoes, garlic, and salt. Bring to a simmer, cover, and cook for 3 minutes to reduce slightly and blend the flavors.

3. Add the pastina, capers, and reserved pork mixture. Cover and cook until the pasta is just tender and the pork is cooked through, about 5 minutes. Divide the mixture among 4 plates and serve.

Helpful hint: It's usually necessary to soak sun-dried tomatoes to soften them, but when they cook in liquid (as in step 2 of this recipe), you can eliminate the soaking.

Fat: 5g/13%
Calories: 337
Saturated Fat: 1.2g
Carbohydrate: 37g
Protein: 29g
Cholesterol: 55mg
Sodium: 423mg

Sun-dried tomatoes have a powerful essence-of-tomato flavor, with a concentrated fruitiness akin to the flavor of raisins or figs. Oil-packed tomatoes are plumper and softer, but they're swimming in fat, so we prefer to use the dry-packed variety. The pastina (tiny pasta shapes) cooked with the pork are commonly served in broth; here, they serve as a built-in starchy "side dish."

Mexican-Style Beef Stew

SERVES: 4
WORKING TIME: 30 MINUTES
TOTAL TIME: 45 MINUTES

This eye-catching stew bears a certain resemblance to chili, but chick-peas and green peas take the place of beans. And rather than blazing with the heat of chili powder, this stew glows with the vibrant flavors of cumin, oregano, and turmeric. The green chilies add a little heat, but there is nothing here to intimidate those with tender palates.

1 teaspoon ground cumin

1 teaspoon dried oregano

½ teaspoon freshly ground black pepper

½ teaspoon salt

2 tablespoons flour

¾ pound well-trimmed top round of beef, cut into 1-inch cubes

1 tablespoon olive oil

1 large onion, coarsely chopped

3 cloves garlic, slivered

2 red bell peppers, cut into 1-inch squares

4½-ounce can chopped mild green chilies, drained

½ teaspoon turmeric

⅔ cup reduced-sodium chicken broth, defatted

19-ounce can chick-peas, rinsed and drained

1 cup frozen peas

2 tablespoons fresh lemon juice

¼ cup chopped fresh parsley

1. On a sheet of waxed paper, combine ½ teaspoon of the cumin, ½ teaspoon of the oregano, ¼ teaspoon of the black pepper, and ¼ teaspoon of the salt. Place the flour on a second sheet of wax paper. Add the beef to the spice mixture, rubbing the mixture into the meat. Dredge the beef in the flour, shaking off the excess.

2. In a Dutch oven or large saucepan, heat 2 teaspoons of the oil until hot but not smoking over medium heat. Add the beef and cook until lightly browned, about 4 minutes. With a slotted spoon, transfer the beef to a plate. Set aside.

3. Add the remaining 1 teaspoon oil to the pan along with the onion and garlic and cook, stirring frequently, until the onion is softened, about 5 minutes. Add the bell peppers and cook, stirring frequently, until crisp-tender, about 4 minutes. Add the green chilies, turmeric, and the remaining ½ teaspoon cumin, ½ teaspoon oregano, ¼ teaspoon black pepper, and ¼ teaspoon salt, stirring to combine. Add the broth, bring to a boil, and stir in the chick-peas. Reduce to a simmer, cover, and cook for 10 minutes to blend the flavors.

4. Return the beef to the pan along with the peas and cook just until the beef is cooked through and the peas are hot, about 3 minutes. Stir in the lemon juice and parsley and serve.

FAT: 9G/25%
CALORIES: 325
SATURATED FAT: 1.5G
CARBOHYDRATE: 33G
PROTEIN: 29G
CHOLESTEROL: 49MG
SODIUM: 815MG

PEPPER STEAK STIR-FRY

SERVES: 4
WORKING TIME: 30 MINUTES
TOTAL TIME: 30 MINUTES

A trendy restaurant menu might style this dish "four-pepper steak" as it's made with black and white ground pepper as well as red and green bell peppers. An appealing example of "fusion cuisine," this stir-fry is a blend of Asian techniques and Western flavors (the creamy Cognac-mustard sauce is unmistakably French) served with a Middle Eastern pasta.

¾ cup couscous
1½ cups boiling water
¾ teaspoon salt
1 tablespoon flour
¼ teaspoon freshly ground black pepper
¼ teaspoon freshly ground white pepper
½ pound well-trimmed sirloin, cut into 2-by-⅛-inch strips
1 tablespoon vegetable oil
1 red onion, sliced
1 clove garlic, minced
2 red bell peppers, cut into thin strips
1 green bell pepper, cut into thin strips
¾ cup reduced-sodium chicken broth, defatted
1 tablespoon Cognac
2 tablespoons reduced-fat sour cream
1 tablespoon Dijon mustard

1. In a large bowl, combine the couscous, boiling water, and ¼ teaspoon of the salt. Cover and let sit for 5 minutes, or until the liquid has been absorbed. Fluff the couscous with a fork.

2. Meanwhile, in a sturdy plastic bag, combine the flour, black pepper, and white pepper. Add the beef to the bag, shaking to coat with the flour mixture. In a large nonstick skillet or wok, heat 2 teaspoons of the oil over medium-high heat. Add the beef and stir-fry until browned, 3 to 4 minutes. With a slotted spoon, transfer the beef to a plate.

3. Add the remaining 1 teaspoon oil to the skillet. Add the onion and garlic and stir-fry until the onion is just beginning to brown, about 2 minutes. Add the bell peppers, broth, and the remaining ½ teaspoon salt. Bring to a boil, reduce to a simmer, and cook until the bell peppers are tender, about 3 minutes.

4. Stir in the Cognac and cook for 30 seconds. Stir in the sour cream and mustard. Return the beef to the skillet and cook until heated through, about 1 minute. Serve with the couscous.

Helpful hints: Any other type of brandy may be substituted for Cognac, which is the finest (and costliest) of French brandies. You can substitute additional freshly ground black pepper for the white pepper, if you like.

FAT: 7G/21%
CALORIES: 303
SATURATED FAT: 1.8G
CARBOHYDRATE: 37G
PROTEIN: 19G
CHOLESTEROL: 37MG
SODIUM: 669MG

LAMB AND BARLEY SOUP

SERVES: 4
WORKING TIME: 30 MINUTES
TOTAL TIME: 50 MINUTES

Barley, one of the world's first domesticated crops, may qualify as the original comfort food. A simmering pot of barley soup—especially one made with savory lamb, garlic, and pungent rosemary—fills the kitchen with an enticing fragrance, piquing the appetite of anyone within range. A salad with a tart citrus dressing would be a pleasant contrast to the richness of the stew.

1 teaspoon olive oil
1 onion, coarsely diced
3 cloves garlic, minced
3 carrots, thinly sliced
10 ounces well-trimmed lamb shoulder, cut into bite-size pieces
2 tomatoes, coarsely chopped
1 large baking potato (8 ounces), peeled and cut into ½-inch dice
1 large turnip (6 ounces), peeled and cut into ½-inch dice
½ teaspoon dried rosemary
½ teaspoon ground ginger
¾ teaspoon salt
⅔ cup quick-cooking barley

1. In a nonstick Dutch oven, heat the oil until hot but not smoking over medium heat. Add the onion and garlic and cook, stirring frequently, until the onion is lightly browned, about 7 minutes. Add the carrots and cook, stirring frequently, until crisp-tender, about 4 minutes.

2. Add the lamb and cook until no longer pink, about 3 minutes. Stir in the tomatoes, potato, turnip, rosemary, ginger, salt, and 5 cups of water and bring to a boil. Add the barley, reduce the heat to a simmer, cover, and cook until the barley is tender, about 15 minutes.

Helpful hint: Lamb shoulder is great for soups and stews; slow-cooking brings out its excellent flavor and softens this somewhat tough cut. Be sure to get boneless shoulder for this recipe.

FAT: 7G/21%
CALORIES: 303
SATURATED FAT: 1.9G
CARBOHYDRATE: 42G
PROTEIN: 20G
CHOLESTEROL: 47MG
SODIUM: 514MG

With its Spanish, French, African, and Native American influences, Louisiana cooking is one of this country's most fascinating regional cuisines. It tends to be quite rich, but thanks to the bold use of herbs and spices, the robust flavors in this beef stir-fry are wonderful on their own, without high-fat enrichments like butter and cream.

LOUISIANA-STYLE BEEF STIR-FRY

SERVES: 4
WORKING TIME: 40 MINUTES
TOTAL TIME: 40 MINUTES

1 cup long-grain rice

¾ teaspoon salt

1 tablespoon flour

½ pound well-trimmed sirloin, cut into 2-by-⅛-inch strips

1 tablespoon vegetable oil

2 ribs celery, sliced

1 green bell pepper, coarsely diced

1 onion, coarsely diced

1 clove garlic, minced

1 cup reduced-sodium chicken broth, defatted

2 tomatoes, coarsely diced

2 tablespoons ketchup

1 teaspoon fennel seeds, crushed (see tip), or ½ teaspoon ground fennel

1 teaspoon dried oregano

¼ teaspoon red pepper flakes

10-ounce package frozen sliced okra, thawed

2 tablespoons chopped green olives

1 tablespoon chopped fresh parsley (optional)

1. In a medium saucepan, bring 2¼ cups of water to a boil. Add the rice and ¼ teaspoon of the salt, reduce to a simmer, cover, and cook until the rice is tender, about 17 minutes.

2. Meanwhile, place the flour in a sturdy plastic bag. Add the beef to the bag, shaking to coat with the flour. In a large nonstick skillet or wok, heat 2 teaspoons of the oil until hot but not smoking over medium-high heat. Add the beef and stir-fry until browned, 3 to 4 minutes. With a slotted spoon, transfer the beef to a plate.

3. Add the remaining 1 teaspoon oil to the skillet. Add the celery, bell pepper, onion, and garlic and stir-fry until the onion is beginning to brown, about 2 minutes. Add the broth, tomatoes, ketchup, fennel seeds, oregano, red pepper flakes, and the remaining ½ teaspoon salt. Cook, stirring occasionally, until the vegetables are tender, about 3 minutes.

4. Return the beef to the pan and stir in the okra. Cook until heated through, about 1 minute. Stir in the olives. Divide the rice among 4 plates and sprinkle the parsley over. Spoon the beef alongside the rice and serve.

Helpful hint: Either pitted or stuffed green olives will work well in this recipe.

FAT: 7G/18%
CALORIES: 360
SATURATED FAT: 1.5G
CARBOHYDRATE: 55G
PROTEIN: 19G
CHOLESTEROL: 35MG
SODIUM: 827MG

TIP

Although fennel can be purchased in pre-ground form, its flavor will be more intense if you buy fennel seeds and crush them with a mortar and pestle—the traditional kitchen tool for grinding spices at home. This set is marble; porcelain mortar-and-pestle sets, in a variety of sizes, are also widely available. You can use a mortar and pestle for other whole spices too—cumin, cloves, coriander, anise, and the like.

If you've ever aspired to master the French culinary classics, you've probably made boeuf à la bourguignonne. Traditional recipes call for salt pork or fatty bacon, but we've updated the wine-sauced beef stew so that you need only a few teaspoons of oil; we've also substituted frozen pearl onions for fresh to save you a nice chunk of time.

BEEF BURGUNDY

SERVES: 4
WORKING TIME: 25 MINUTES
TOTAL TIME: 40 MINUTES

2 tablespoons flour

½ teaspoon salt

½ teaspoon freshly ground black pepper

¾ pound well-trimmed bottom round of beef, cut into ¾-inch cubes

2 teaspoons olive oil

1½ cups frozen pearl onions

6 cloves garlic, peeled and halved

3 carrots, halved lengthwise and cut into 1-inch pieces

¾ pound small mushrooms

1 cup dry red wine

⅔ cup reduced-sodium beef broth

2 tablespoons no-salt-added tomato paste

Three 3 x ½-inch strips of orange zest (see tip)

½ teaspoon dried thyme

1 bay leaf

1 zucchini, halved lengthwise and thinly sliced

¼ cup chopped fresh parsley

1. On a sheet of waxed paper, combine the flour, ¼ teaspoon of the salt, and ¼ teaspoon of the pepper. Dredge the beef in the flour mixture, shaking off and reserving the excess.

2. In a nonstick Dutch oven or flameproof casserole, heat the oil until hot but not smoking over medium heat. Add the beef and cook until golden brown, about 4 minutes. With a slotted spoon, transfer the beef to a plate. Set aside.

3. Add the pearl onions and garlic to the pan and cook, stirring frequently, until golden, about 2 minutes. Add the carrots and mushrooms and cook, stirring frequently, until lightly colored, about 4 minutes. Add the wine, increase the heat to high, and cook until reduced by half, about 3 minutes. Stir in the broth, tomato paste, orange zest, thyme, bay leaf, and the remaining ¼ teaspoon salt and remaining ¼ teaspoon pepper. Bring to a boil, reduce to a simmer, cover, and cook until the vegetables are tender, about 8 minutes.

4. In a small bowl, stir together the reserved dredging mixture and ⅓ cup of water. Stir the flour mixture into the pan, bring to a boil, and cook, stirring, until slightly thickened, about 3 minutes. Return the beef to the pan, add the zucchini, and simmer gently until the beef is just cooked through, about 2 minutes. Discard the orange zest and bay leaf. Stir in the parsley, divide the mixture among 4 bowls, and serve.

FAT: 8G/24%
CALORIES: 296
SATURATED FAT: 2G
CARBOHYDRATE: 25G
PROTEIN: 24G
CHOLESTEROL: 50MG
SODIUM: 469MG

TIP

To remove a strip of zest from an orange, use a swivel-bladed vegetable peeler to cut off a piece of the outer colored rind, avoiding the bitter white pith underneath. The zest contains the intensely flavored oil found in the skin.

PORK AND RED BEAN CHILI

SERVES: 4
WORKING TIME: 20 MINUTES
TOTAL TIME: 30 MINUTES

Chili—the Southwest's favorite "bowl of red"—is an earthy, sustaining meal that's subject to fascinating variations. This one is mostly red, with just a touch of green in the mild chilies that flavor it. It's made with sizeable chunks of pork rather than ground meat and is sure to be a stick-to-the-ribs dinner.

2 teaspoons vegetable oil

¾ pound well-trimmed pork tenderloin, cut into ¾-inch chunks

1 onion, coarsely chopped

1 clove garlic, minced

1 tablespoon chili powder

1 teaspoon fennel seeds

19-ounce can red kidney beans, rinsed and drained

15-ounce can no-salt-added tomatoes

7-ounce jar roasted red peppers, drained and diced

4½-ounce can chopped mild green chilies, drained

½ teaspoon salt

1. In medium nonstick saucepan, heat 1 teaspoon of the oil until hot but not smoking over medium heat. Add the pork and cook until browned, about 5 minutes. With a slotted spoon, transfer the pork to a plate.

2. Add the remaining 1 teaspoon oil to the pan along with the onion and garlic. Cook, stirring, until the onion is softened, about 4 minutes. Stir in the chili powder and fennel seeds and cook until fragrant, about 1 minute. Add the beans, tomatoes, roasted red peppers, green chilies, and salt. Bring to a boil, reduce to a simmer, and cook, breaking up the tomatoes with the back of a spoon, until slightly thickened, about 10 minutes.

3. Return the pork to the pan and cook until warmed through, about 1 minute. Transfer to a large tureen or serving bowl and serve.

Helpful hint: Veteran chili-lovers may want to substitute canned jalapeños for the mild green chilies to increase the heat in this dish. Feel free to add more chili powder as well.

FAT: 7G/22%
CALORIES: 289
SATURATED FAT: 1.4G
CARBOHYDRATE: 30G
PROTEIN: 27G
CHOLESTEROL: 55MG
SODIUM: 818MG

HONEYED BEEF STIR-FRY

SERVES: 4
WORKING TIME: 35 MINUTES
TOTAL TIME: 35 MINUTES

Chinese cuisine is often based on the balance of yin and yang, concepts that represent complementary opposites. In cooking, this is expressed in contrasts of hot and cold, crisp and soft, dark and light. The sauce for this stir-fry of sirloin and vegetables is made with equal amounts of lime juice and honey for an appealing balance of sweet and sour.

1 cup long-grain rice

¾ teaspoon salt

1 tablespoon vegetable oil

½ pound well-trimmed sirloin, cut into 2-by-⅛-inch strips

1 tablespoon minced fresh ginger

1 clove garlic, minced

1 red bell pepper, cut into thin strips

½ pound sugar snap peas or snow peas, strings removed

1 zucchini, cut into 2-by-⅛-inch strips

1 cup reduced-sodium chicken broth, defatted

2 teaspoons cornstarch

2 tablespoons reduced-sodium soy sauce

2 tablespoons fresh lime juice

2 tablespoons honey

8-ounce can sliced water chestnuts, drained

2 cups packed watercress, tough stems removed

1. In a medium saucepan, bring 2¼ cups of water to a boil. Add the rice and ¼ teaspoon of the salt, reduce to a simmer, cover, and cook until the rice is tender, about 17 minutes.

2. Meanwhile, in a large nonstick skillet, heat 2 teaspoons of the oil until hot but not smoking over medium-high heat. Add the beef and stir-fry until browned, 3 to 4 minutes. With a slotted spoon, transfer the beef to a plate.

3. Add the remaining 1 teaspoon oil to the skillet. Add the ginger and garlic and stir-fry until fragrant, about 1 minute. Add the bell pepper, sugar snap peas, zucchini, broth, and the remaining ½ teaspoon salt. Cook until the vegetables are crisp-tender, about 2 minutes.

4. In a small bowl, combine the cornstarch, soy sauce, lime juice, and honey. Stir the mixture into the skillet along with the water chestnuts and watercress. Cook, stirring, until the sauce is slightly thickened and the watercress is wilted, about 1 minute. Return the beef to the pan and cook until heated through, about 1 minute. Serve with the rice.

Helpful hint: If the sugar snap peas are on the large side, be sure to pull the strings from both the front and back of the pod as they will both be quite tough.

FAT: 6G/14%
CALORIES: 385
SATURATED FAT: 1.4G
CARBOHYDRATE: 62G
PROTEIN: 20G
CHOLESTEROL: 35MG
SODIUM: 984MG

PORK AND BUTTERNUT SQUASH SAUTÉ

SERVES: 4
WORKING TIME: 25 MINUTES
TOTAL TIME: 40 MINUTES

¾ pound small red potatoes, cut into ½-inch dice

2 tablespoons flour

½ teaspoon salt

¼ teaspoon freshly ground black pepper

½ pound lean boneless pork loin, cut into 2-by-¼-inch strips

2 teaspoons olive oil

3 cups peeled, seeded, and cut butternut squash (½-inch chunks)

3 turnips, cut into ½-inch-thick wedges

3 carrots, cut into ½-inch-thick slices

⅔ cup reduced-sodium chicken broth, defatted

¼ cup cider vinegar

½ teaspoon rubbed sage

½ teaspoon ground ginger

2 tablespoons chopped fresh parsley

1. In a large saucepan of boiling water, cook the potatoes until almost tender, about 5 minutes. Drain well and set aside.

2. Meanwhile, on a sheet of waxed paper, combine the flour, ¼ teaspoon of the salt, and ⅛ teaspoon of the pepper. Dredge the pork in the flour mixture, shaking off the excess. In a large skillet, heat the oil until hot but not smoking over medium heat. Add the pork and cook, stirring frequently, until lightly browned, about 3 minutes. With a slotted spoon, transfer the pork to a plate. Set aside.

3. Add the potatoes, squash, turnips, and carrots to the skillet, stirring to coat. Stir in the broth, vinegar, sage, ginger, remaining ¼ teaspoon salt, and remaining ⅛ teaspoon pepper. Bring to a boil, reduce to a simmer, cover, and cook until the vegetables are tender, about 10 minutes.

4. Return the pork to the pan and cook, uncovered, just until the pork is cooked through, about 3 minutes longer. Stir in the parsley and serve.

Suggested accompaniments: Crusty rolls, followed by fresh blueberries swirled into lemon nonfat yogurt.

FAT: 6G/19%
CALORIES: 284
SATURATED FAT: 1.4G
CARBOHYDRATE: 43G
PROTEIN: 17G
CHOLESTEROL: 33MG
SODIUM: 499MG

Sage and ground ginger are the perfect seasonings to highlight the sweetness of the butternut squash and root vegetables in this hearty fall dish, and the cider vinegar accents the richness of the pork. As a bonus, this dish tastes just as good—if not better—if prepared a day ahead. Reheat, covered, on the stovetop over low heat or in the microwave.

A julienne of turnip, parsnip, carrot, and leek goes into this unusual stir-fry. Cutting vegetables into julienne strips is a standard technique in both Eastern and Western cuisines; the "matchstick" pieces cook quickly and uniformly. Here, the vegetables, tossed with juicy strips of sirloin steak, are served with couscous, the grain-like North African pasta.

STIR-FRIED BEEF AND ROOT VEGETABLES

SERVES: 4
WORKING TIME: 45 MINUTES
TOTAL TIME: 45 MINUTES

¾ cup couscous

1½ cups boiling water

¾ teaspoon salt

1 tablespoon vegetable oil

½ pound well-trimmed sirloin, cut into 2-by-⅛-inch strips

1 leek, white and light green parts only, or 2 scallions, cut into 2-by-¼-inch julienne strips

2 carrots, cut into 2-by-¼-inch julienne strips (see tip)

2 parsnips, cut into 2-by-¼-inch julienne strips

1 turnip, cut into 2-by-¼-inch julienne strips

13¾-ounce can reduced-sodium chicken broth, defatted

2 tablespoons no-salt-added tomato paste

½ teaspoon dried thyme

¼ teaspoon freshly ground black pepper

¼ cup chopped fresh parsley

1. In a large bowl, combine the couscous, boiling water, and ¼ teaspoon of the salt. Cover and let sit for 5 minutes, or until the liquid has been absorbed. Fluff the couscous with a fork.

2. Meanwhile, in a large nonstick skillet or wok, heat 2 teaspoons of the oil until hot but not smoking over medium-high heat. Add the beef and stir-fry until browned, 3 to 4 minutes. With a slotted spoon, transfer the beef to a plate.

3. Add the remaining 1 teaspoon oil to the skillet. Add the leek, carrots, parsnips, and turnip and stir-fry until the vegetables begin to brown, about 2 minutes. Stir in the broth, tomato paste, thyme, pepper, and the remaining ½ teaspoon salt. Bring to a boil, reduce to a simmer, cover, and cook until the vegetables are tender, 3 to 4 minutes.

4. Return the beef to the skillet. Add the parsley and cook until the beef is heated through, about 1 minute. Divide the couscous among 4 plates, spoon the beef mixture alongside, and serve.

Helpful hint: Rice-shaped orzo or another small pasta, cooked according to the package directions, could be substituted for the couscous.

TIP

To cut a carrot into julienne strips, first cut it crosswise into shorter lengths (2 inches for this recipe), then thinly slice each piece lengthwise. Stack the slices and cut them lengthwise into matchsticks.

FAT: 7G/19%
CALORIES: 334
SATURATED FAT: 1.4G
CARBOHYDRATE: 49G
PROTEIN: 20G
CHOLESTEROL: 35MG
SODIUM: 772MG

Sicilian-Style Ragout of Beef

SERVES: 4
WORKING TIME: 20 MINUTES
TOTAL TIME: 30 MINUTES

Sicilian cuisine upholds an ancient tradition of accenting savory dishes with sweet ingredients: Raisins, oranges, honey, and sweet Marsala wine go into many Sicilian meat, fish, or poultry dishes. This delicious beef ragout, served over golden ribbons of fettuccine, is simmered in a broth flavored with orange juice, raisins, ginger, and fennel seeds.

¼ cup golden raisins
½ cup hot water
2 tablespoons flour
½ teaspoon salt
¼ teaspoon freshly ground black pepper
¾ pound well-trimmed top round of beef, cut into ½-inch cubes
1 tablespoon olive oil
1 large onion, coarsely chopped
4 cloves garlic, minced
6 ounces fettuccine
2 large tomatoes, coarsely chopped
⅓ cup orange juice
½ cup reduced-sodium chicken broth, defatted
½ teaspoon fennel seeds
¼ teaspoon ground ginger

1. Start heating a large pot of water to boiling for the pasta. In a small bowl, combine the raisins and hot water and set aside to soften. On a sheet of waxed paper, combine the flour, ¼ teaspoon of the salt, and the pepper. Dredge the beef in the flour mixture, shaking off the excess.

2. In a Dutch oven or flameproof casserole, heat 2 teaspoons of the oil until hot but not smoking over medium heat. Add the beef and cook until lightly browned, about 4 minutes. With a slotted spoon, transfer the beef to a plate and set aside. Add the remaining 1 teaspoon oil to the pan along with the onion and garlic and cook, stirring frequently, until the onion is lightly golden, about 5 minutes.

3. Cook the fettuccine in the boiling water until just tender. Drain well.

4. Meanwhile, stir the tomatoes, orange juice, and the raisins and their soaking liquid into the stew and bring to a boil. Stir in the broth, fennel seeds, ginger, and the remaining ¼ teaspoon salt and return to a boil. Reduce to a simmer, cover, and cook until the flavors are blended, about 7 minutes. Uncover, return the beef to the pan, and cook until the beef is just cooked through, about 2 minutes. Divide the fettuccine among 4 plates, spoon the beef mixture alongside, and serve.

FAT: 8G/18%
CALORIES: 396
SATURATED FAT: 1.8G
CARBOHYDRATE: 52G
PROTEIN: 28G
CHOLESTEROL: 89MG
SODIUM: 418MG

BARBECUE-SAUCED STEAK WITH VEGETABLE KEBABS

SERVES: 8
WORKING TIME: 30 MINUTES
TOTAL TIME: 1 HOUR 15 MINUTES

2 cloves garlic, peeled

Two 8-ounce cans tomato sauce

3 tablespoons tomato paste

3 tablespoons Worcestershire sauce

3 tablespoons firmly packed dark brown sugar

2 tablespoons cider vinegar

1 tablespoon chili powder

1 teaspoon dry mustard

½ teaspoon salt

¼ teaspoon cayenne pepper

1½ pounds flank steak, trimmed

3 acorn squash, halved, seeded, and cut into 2-inch pieces

3 red bell peppers, each cut into 8 pieces

1. In a blender or food processor, purée the garlic, tomato sauce, tomato paste, Worcestershire sauce, brown sugar, vinegar, chili powder, mustard, salt, and cayenne until smooth. Transfer 1 cup of the sauce to a shallow glass dish and add the steak, turning to coat. Cover and refrigerate the steak while you prepare the vegetables. Set aside the remaining sauce.

2. In a large pot of boiling water, cook the squash until just tender, about 20 minutes. Drain well and set aside to cool. Meanwhile, preheat the broiler or prepare the grill. Alternately thread the squash and bell peppers on 8 metal skewers and set aside.

3. Place the steak on the broiler or grill rack, discarding the sauce in the dish, and brush with some of the reserved sauce. Broil or grill 4 inches from the heat for 4 to 6 minutes per side for medium, or until desired doneness. Transfer the steak to a serving platter and let stand while you cook the vegetables.

4. Brush the vegetables with some more of the sauce and broil or grill for 4 to 6 minutes per side, or until the vegetables are lightly glazed. Cut the steak into thin diagonal slices, spoon the remaining sauce on top, and serve with the vegetable kebabs.

Suggested accompaniment: A hollowed-out watermelon half filled with assorted melon balls and sprinkled with lime juice and chopped mint.

FAT: 7G/26%
CALORIES: 245
SATURATED FAT: 2.8G
CARBOHYDRATE: 28G
PROTEIN: 20G
CHOLESTEROL: 43MG
SODIUM: 659MG

Herald the grilling season with an American classic—this juicy flank steak dinner. Our easy barbecue sauce does double duty for the steak and vegetables. For even more flavor, marinate the meat in the refrigerator overnight. And to save time, cook the squash a day ahead. An advantage of this meal is that it will wait for your guests—it's equally good at room (or patio) temperature.

STIR-FRIED BEEF WITH MUSHROOMS AND PEANUTS

Serves: 4
Working time: 35 minutes
Total time: 35 minutes

1 cup long-grain rice
¾ teaspoon salt
1 tablespoon vegetable oil
½ pound well-trimmed top round of beef, cut into 2-by-⅛-inch strips
1 red onion, sliced
2 carrots, thinly sliced
½ pound mushrooms, stemmed and quartered
1 tablespoon minced fresh ginger
1 cup reduced-sodium chicken broth, defatted
2 teaspoons cornstarch
2 tablespoons reduced-sodium soy sauce
1 teaspoon dark Oriental sesame oil
8-ounce can sliced water chestnuts, drained
2 tablespoons coarsely chopped peanuts

1. In a medium saucepan, bring 2¼ cups of water to a boil. Add the rice and ¼ teaspoon of the salt, reduce to a simmer, cover, and cook until the rice is tender, about 17 minutes.

2. Meanwhile, in a large nonstick skillet or wok, heat 2 teaspoons of the oil until hot but not smoking over medium heat. Add the beef and stir-fry until browned, 3 to 4 minutes. With a slotted spoon, transfer the beef to a plate.

3. Add the remaining 1 teaspoon oil to the skillet. Add the onion, carrots, mushrooms, and ginger and stir-fry until the carrots are crisp-tender, 2 to 3 minutes. Stir in ½ cup of the broth, reduce to a simmer, and cook until the vegetables are tender, 2 to 3 minutes.

4. Meanwhile, in a small bowl, combine the cornstarch, soy sauce, sesame oil, the remaining ½ cup broth, and the remaining ½ teaspoon salt. Add the broth mixture to the skillet along with the water chestnuts and peanuts. Cook, stirring, until slightly thickened, about 1 minute. Return the beef to the skillet and cook until heated through, about 1 minute. Divide the rice among 4 plates, top with the beef mixture, and serve.

Helpful hint: For an extra touch of color, sprinkle the finished dish with chopped fresh parsley.

Fat: 9g/21%
Calories: 387
Saturated Fat: 1.7g
Carbohydrate: 55g
Protein: 21g
Cholesterol: 32mg
Sodium: 929mg

212

Variety of texture is a feature of many stir-fries: In this dish, delicately crisp vegetables, tender beef, and smooth sauce are all combined with velvety mushrooms and crunchy water chestnuts and peanuts to provide even more variety than usual. Accompany the main dish with a salad of greens, cucumbers, and tomatoes.

SEAFOOD

Left, Sautéed Swordfish with Fresh Tomato Sauce (p. 235).
Above, Southern-Style Shrimp Boil (p. 230).

HERBED STUFFED SWORDFISH

SERVES: 4
WORKING TIME: 25 MINUTES
TOTAL TIME: 30 MINUTES

The dense flesh of swordfish (pesce spada in Italian) can actually be pounded like veal scallopini. And the flavor of swordfish is robust enough to be partnered with a tangy, aromatic mixture of marmalade, rosemary, oregano, and red wine vinegar. A salad made with arugula, which has a uniquely assertive flavor of its own, rounds out the meal.

½ cup chopped fresh parsley
¼ cup plain dried bread crumbs
½ teaspoon grated orange zest
½ teaspoon dried oregano
½ teaspoon dried rosemary
¾ teaspoon salt
4 swordfish steaks, cut
½ inch thick (about 1¼ pounds total)
½ cup orange juice
2 tablespoons orange marmalade
2 tablespoons red wine vinegar
2 teaspoons extra-virgin olive oil
½ cup finely diced jarred roasted red pepper
1 small red onion, finely diced
1 rib celery, finely diced

1. Preheat the oven to 400°. Spray a 9-inch square baking dish with nonstick cooking spray.

2. In a small bowl, combine ¼ cup of the parsley, the bread crumbs, orange zest, oregano, rosemary, and ½ teaspoon of the salt.

3. Place the swordfish steaks between 2 sheets of waxed paper and, with the flat side of a small skillet or meat pounder, pound the swordfish to a ¼-inch thickness. Lay the swordfish flat and sprinkle with ¼ cup of the orange juice. Spoon the parsley mixture over the fish and, starting from a short side, neatly roll up each piece. Place the fish, seam-side down, in the prepared baking dish, cover with foil, and bake for 7 minutes, or until the rolls are just opaque in the center.

4. Meanwhile, in a medium bowl, combine the remaining ¼ cup orange juice, the marmalade, vinegar, oil, red pepper, onion, celery, the remaining ¼ cup parsley, and the remaining ¼ teaspoon salt. Place the fish rolls on 4 plates, spoon the sauce on top, and serve.

Helpful hint: Although meat pounders come in various shapes—some look like mallets, others like long-stemmed mushrooms—their one essential quality is weight.

FAT: 8G/27%
CALORIES: 263
SATURATED FAT: 1.8G
CARBOHYDRATE: 20G
PROTEIN: 27G
CHOLESTEROL: 49MG
SODIUM: 640MG

SESAME-LEMON SHRIMP STIR-FRY

SERVES: 4
WORKING TIME: 35 MINUTES
TOTAL TIME: 35 MINUTES PLUS MARINATING TIME

3 tablespoons reduced-sodium soy sauce

3 tablespoons fresh lemon juice

1 teaspoon dark Oriental sesame oil

1 teaspoon cornstarch

1 teaspoon sugar

1 pound medium shrimp, shelled and deveined

1 tablespoon vegetable oil

4 scallions, cut into 1-inch lengths

2 cloves garlic, finely chopped

1 tablespoon chopped fresh ginger

½ pound green beans, cut on the diagonal into 1-inch lengths

½ pound mushrooms, quartered

¼ teaspoon salt

½ cup canned sliced water chestnuts

¾ teaspoon grated lemon zest

1. In a medium bowl, combine the soy sauce, lemon juice, sesame oil, cornstarch, and sugar. Add the shrimp, tossing to coat well. Cover and refrigerate for at least 30 minutes or for up to 2 hours.

2. In a large nonstick skillet, heat the vegetable oil until hot but not smoking over medium heat. Add the scallions, garlic, and ginger and stir-fry until softened, about 1 minute. Add the green beans, mushrooms, and salt and stir-fry until the green beans are crisp-tender, about 4 minutes.

3. Reserving the marinade, add the shrimp to the pan along with the water chestnuts and lemon zest and stir-fry until the shrimp are almost opaque, about 4 minutes. Add the marinade and cook, stirring, until the shrimp are opaque throughout and the sauce is slightly thickened, about 1 minute.

Helpful hint: Don't marinate the shrimp for more than two hours in the hope that it will intensify the flavor. The acid in the lemon juice will turn the shrimp mushy if it soaks in it too long.

FAT: 6G/27%
CALORIES: 204
SATURATED FAT: 0.9G
CARBOHYDRATE: 16G
PROTEIN: 22G
CHOLESTEROL: 140MG
SODIUM: 732MG

Chinese methods of cooking shrimp range from the simple to the highly complex. Somewhere in between are tempting stir-fries like this one: The shrimp are marinated in a tangy sauce, then stir-fried with gentle spices and crunchy green beans and water chestnuts. Accompany the dish with rice, or break with tradition and serve a sliced baguette or breadsticks.

CIOPPINO

SERVES: 4
WORKING TIME: 25 MINUTES
TOTAL TIME: 35 MINUTES

The varied ethnic populations of the city of San Francisco have contributed tremendously to the local cuisine. Cioppino was a creation of Italian-American fisherman and has been served in San Francisco restaurants since the turn of the century. Accompany this seafood stew with generous slabs of herbed garlic bread or warm Italian bread.

1 tablespoon olive oil

2 red bell peppers, cut into ½-inch squares

2 carrots, thinly sliced

4 cloves garlic, minced

1 cup dry red wine

2 large tomatoes, coarsely chopped

2 tablespoons no-salt-added tomato paste

1 cup bottled clam juice

½ teaspoon dried oregano

¼ teaspoon salt

¼ teaspoon red pepper flakes

16 littleneck clams or other small hard-shell clams, well scrubbed

½ pound large shrimp, shelled and deveined

½ pound flounder fillet, cut into 1-inch chunks

1. In a large skillet, heat the oil until hot but not smoking over medium heat. Add the bell peppers, carrots, and garlic and cook, stirring frequently, until the peppers are crisp-tender, about 4 minutes. Add the wine, bring to a boil, and cook until evaporated by half, about 4 minutes.

2. Stir in the tomatoes, tomato paste, clam juice, 1 cup of water, the oregano, salt, and red pepper flakes. Bring to a boil, add the clams, cover, and cook until the clams have opened, about 5 minutes. Remove the clams as they open and transfer them to 4 soup bowls; discard any that do not open.

3. Add the shrimp, cover, and cook for 2 minutes. Add the flounder, cover, and cook until the shrimp and flounder are just opaque, about 2 minutes. Transfer the shrimp and fish to the soup bowls, spoon in the broth and vegetables, and serve.

Helpful hint: On the East Coast, the smallest clams are properly called "little necks" (two words); clams of about the same size harvested in the West are called littlenecks (one word); Pacific littlenecks are also called rock clams. Any small hard-shell clam will work well in this recipe.

FAT: 6G/23%
CALORIES: 234
SATURATED FAT: 0.9G
CARBOHYDRATE: 15G
PROTEIN: 30G
CHOLESTEROL: 118MG
SODIUM: 441MG

*C*ooling slices of cucumber temper fiery black and cayenne pepper and pungent fresh ginger, and the large, meaty shrimp soak up all the different flavors. To lightly thicken the sauce, we've used the classic stir-fry method, mixing cornstarch with water and stirring it in for the final step. Avoid overcooking or the cornstarch will lose its thickening power.

Hot and Tangy Shrimp

Serves: 4
Working time: 25 minutes
Total time: 40 minutes

½ teaspoon freshly ground black pepper

½ teaspoon ground ginger

½ teaspoon salt

⅛ teaspoon ground allspice

⅛ teaspoon cayenne pepper

1½ pounds large shrimp, shelled and deveined

2 teaspoons olive oil

½ cup minced scallions

4 cloves garlic, slivered

1 tablespoon minced fresh ginger

¾ pound sweet potatoes, peeled and cut into ½-inch dice

1 red bell pepper, cut into ½-inch dice

1 cup reduced-sodium chicken broth, defatted

1 cucumber, peeled, halved lengthwise, seeded, and cut into ½-inch-thick slices (see tip)

2 teaspoons cornstarch

2 tablespoons fresh lime juice

1. In a large bowl, combine the black pepper, ground ginger, salt, allspice, and cayenne and stir to blend. Add the shrimp, rubbing in the spices until well coated. Set aside.

2. Spray a large nonstick skillet with nonstick cooking spray, add the oil, and heat until hot but not smoking over medium heat. Add the scallions, garlic, and fresh ginger and cook, stirring frequently, until the mixture is fragrant, about 2 minutes. Stir in the sweet potatoes and bell pepper and cook, stirring frequently, until the pepper is crisp-tender, about 4 minutes.

3. Stir in the broth and bring to a boil. Reduce to a simmer, cover, and cook until the sweet potatoes are tender, about 10 minutes. Stir in the cucumber and shrimp, cover again, and cook until the shrimp are almost opaque, about 3 minutes.

4. In a cup, combine the cornstarch and 1 tablespoon of water and stir to blend. Bring the shrimp mixture to a boil over medium-high heat, stir in the cornstarch mixture along with the lime juice, and cook, stirring constantly, until the mixture is slightly thickened and the shrimp are just opaque, about 1 minute longer. Spoon the shrimp and vegetables onto a platter and serve.

Suggested accompaniment: Fat-free toasted pound cake slices topped with mandarin orange sections marinated in Marsala wine.

Fat: 5G/17%
Calories: 268
Saturated Fat: .8G
Carbohydrate: 24G
Protein: 31G
Cholesterol: 210MG
Sodium: 654MG

TIP

To remove the seeds from a cucumber, first cut the peeled cucumber in half lengthwise. Holding a half in one hand, scoop out the seeds with a spoon, leaving the cucumber shell intact.

PEPPERY FISH AND CORN CHOWDER

SERVES: 4
WORKING TIME: 20 MINUTES
TOTAL TIME: 30 MINUTES

*W*e've used Canadian bacon here for old-fashioned flavor, and lots of vegetables. Red snapper or halibut could easily replace the cod.

2 teaspoons olive oil

2 ounces Canadian bacon, diced

2 ribs celery, thinly sliced

1 red bell pepper, diced

1 green bell pepper, diced

¾ pound baking potatoes, peeled and cut into ½-inch dice

8-ounce bottle clam juice

1 cup low-fat (1%) milk

1 pound cod fillets, any visible bones removed, cut into 1-inch pieces

1 cup frozen corn kernels, thawed

1 teaspoon hot pepper sauce

½ teaspoon freshly ground black pepper

¼ teaspoon salt

1 tablespoon cornstarch

3 tablespoons chopped fresh parsley

1. In a Dutch oven, heat the oil until hot but not smoking over medium heat. Add the bacon and cook until lightly crisped, about 1 minute. Stir in the celery and bell peppers and cook, stirring frequently, until the vegetables are just tender, about 5 minutes.

2. Add the potatoes, stirring to coat. Add the clam juice, milk, and 1 cup of water. Bring to a boil, reduce to a simmer, cover, and cook until the potatoes are almost tender, about 7 minutes.

3. Stir in the cod, corn, hot pepper sauce, black pepper, and salt, cover again, and simmer until the cod is just opaque, about 4 minutes.

4. In a cup, combine the cornstarch and 1 tablespoon of water and stir to blend. Return the cod mixture to a boil over medium heat, stir in the cornstarch mixture, and cook, stirring constantly, until the chowder is slightly thickened, about 1 minute longer. Stir in the parsley and serve.

Suggested accompaniments: Oyster crackers, and a tossed green salad with buttermilk dressing. For the finale, blueberries garnished with lemon zest and a dollop of vanilla nonfat yogurt.

FAT: 5G/17%
CALORIES: 271
SATURATED FAT: 1.2G
CARBOHYDRATE: 28G
PROTEIN: 28G
CHOLESTEROL: 58MG
SODIUM: 606MG

SHRIMP-FRIED RICE

SERVES: 4
WORKING TIME: 35 MINUTES
TOTAL TIME: 50 MINUTES

1 cup long-grain rice

½ teaspoon salt

2 egg whites

1 whole egg, lightly beaten

3 tablespoons reduced-sodium soy sauce

1 tablespoon rice vinegar

1 tablespoon vegetable oil

3 cups thinly sliced leeks, white and tender green parts only

3 ribs celery, thinly sliced on the diagonal

1 red bell pepper, cut into ¼-inch squares

2 tablespoons minced fresh ginger

2 cloves garlic, minced

½ pound medium shrimp, shelled, deveined, and halved crosswise

½ pound snow peas, halved on the diagonal

¼ cup reduced-sodium chicken broth, defatted

1. In a medium saucepan, bring 2¼ cups of water to a boil. Add the rice and ¼ teaspoon of the salt, reduce to a simmer, cover, and cook until the rice is tender, about 17 minutes.

2. In a small bowl, beat together the egg whites, whole egg, soy sauce, vinegar, and the remaining ¼ teaspoon salt. Set aside.

3. In a large nonstick skillet or wok, heat 2 teaspoons of the oil until hot but not smoking over medium-high heat. Add the leeks, celery, bell pepper, ginger, and garlic and stir-fry until the vegetables are crisp-tender, 3 to 4 minutes. With a slotted spoon, transfer the vegetables to a plate. Add the remaining 1 teaspoon oil to the skillet. Add the shrimp and snow peas and stir-fry until the shrimp are just beginning to turn pink, 2 to 3 minutes.

4. Stir the egg mixture into the skillet and cook, stirring, until the egg mixture is set, about 1 minute. Return the vegetables to the skillet along with the cooked rice and the broth. Cook, stirring, until the ingredients are well combined and the shrimp are opaque throughout, about 1 minute. Divide among 4 bowls and serve.

Helpful hint: Thinly sliced scallions (both the white and green parts) can be substituted for the leeks.

FAT: 6G/15%
CALORIES: 370
SATURATED FAT: 1.1G
CARBOHYDRATE: 58G
PROTEIN: 20G
CHOLESTEROL: 124MG
SODIUM: 923MG

*W*e've cut the fat from traditional fried rice here by omitting two egg yolks and using just 1 tablespoon of oil.

TUNA-NOODLE BAKE

SERVES: 4
WORKING TIME: 25 MINUTES
TOTAL TIME: 50 MINUTES

6 ounces yolk-free egg noodles

½ cup plus 2 tablespoons skim milk

2 tablespoons flour

¾ teaspoon dry mustard

2 teaspoons olive oil

3 scallions, chopped

1 rib celery, chopped

1 red bell pepper, diced

1 cup sliced mushrooms

¼ teaspoon dried thyme

¾ cup evaporated skimmed milk

6⅛-ounce can water-packed tuna, rinsed, drained, and flaked

1½ ounces white Cheddar cheese, shredded (about ⅓ cup)

¼ teaspoon hot pepper sauce

¼ teaspoon salt

3 tablespoons low-fat wheat cracker crumbs or plain dried bread crumbs

1. Preheat the oven to 375°. In a large saucepan of boiling water, cook the noodles until just tender. Drain well and set aside.

2. Meanwhile, in a jar with a tight-fitting lid, shake together the skim milk, flour, and mustard until smooth. Set aside. In a nonstick Dutch oven, heat the oil until hot but not smoking over medium-high heat. Add the scallions, celery, bell pepper, mushrooms, and thyme and cook, stirring frequently, until the vegetables are just tender, about 8 minutes.

3. Stir in the skim milk mixture along with the evaporated milk and bring to a boil, stirring constantly. Reduce to a simmer and cook, stirring occasionally, until the mixture is slightly thickened, about 4 minutes. Remove from the heat and stir in the tuna, Cheddar, hot pepper sauce, and salt. Add the noodles and toss to combine.

4. Spray a 1½-quart baking dish with nonstick cooking spray. Spoon the tuna-noodle mixture into the prepared baking dish, sprinkle the cracker crumbs on top, and bake for 20 to 25 minutes, or until the crumbs are golden brown and the casserole is piping hot.

Suggested accompaniment: For dessert, vanilla ice milk mixed with mashed bananas and a sprinkling of chopped peanuts.

FAT: 8G/19%
CALORIES: 364
SATURATED FAT: 3G
CARBOHYDRATE: 47G
PROTEIN: 27G
CHOLESTEROL: 30MG
SODIUM: 487MG

This rich, homey casserole belies its low-fat components: yolk-free egg noodles, skim milk and evaporated skimmed milk for the sauce, water-packed tuna, and crumbled low-fat wheat crackers for the topping. You may assemble the dish earlier in the day to avoid last-minute fretting, but sprinkle on the cracker crumbs just before baking.

Whether for a casual get-together or a special dinner party, this great-tasting stew, borrowed from the classic San Francisco cioppino, is a rainbow of colors and flavors. Buy the shellfish from a reliable fishmonger to guarantee absolute freshness. If good-quality fresh is not available, use canned clams (about ½ cup) and frozen shrimp.

MIXED SHELLFISH STEW

SERVES: 4
WORKING TIME: 30 MINUTES
TOTAL TIME: 55 MINUTES

1 tablespoon olive oil

⅔ cup minced shallots or red onion

5 cloves garlic, minced

1 red bell pepper, diced

¾ pound small red potatoes, quartered

½ cup chopped fresh parsley

½ cup dry white wine

½ teaspoon salt

12 littleneck or other hard-shell clams, well scrubbed (see tip)

1 pound medium shrimp, shelled and deveined

¼ cup snipped fresh chives or 2 scallions, thinly sliced

1. In a Dutch oven, heat the oil until hot but not smoking over medium heat. Add the shallots and garlic and cook, stirring frequently, until the mixture has softened, about 5 minutes. Stir in the bell pepper and cook until the pepper is crisp-tender, about 4 minutes.

2. Add the potatoes and parsley, stirring to coat. Stir in the wine, ½ cup of water, and the salt. Bring to a boil, reduce to a simmer, cover, and cook until the potatoes are almost tender, about 15 minutes.

3. Add the clams, increase the heat to medium-high, cover, and cook just until the clams have opened, about 4 minutes. Discard any clams that do not open. Stir in the shrimp, cover again, and cook until the shrimp are just opaque, about 4 minutes longer. Sprinkle the chives on top and serve.

Suggested accompaniments: Sourdough bread, and a Bibb lettuce and watercress salad with a citrus vinaigrette. Follow with Bartlett or Anjou pear halves simmered in a raspberry sugar syrup for dessert.

FAT: 6G/19%
CALORIES: 285
SATURATED FAT: .8G
CARBOHYDRATE: 26G
PROTEIN: 27G
CHOLESTEROL: 155MG
SODIUM: 451MG

TIP

Before cooking, check to see that the clams are alive. Hard-shelled clams should be tightly closed or, if the shells are open, they should immediately close when lightly tapped.

SOUTHERN-STYLE SHRIMP BOIL

SERVES: 8
WORKING TIME: 10 MINUTES
TOTAL TIME: 45 MINUTES

4 bay leaves

½ teaspoon whole allspice

½ teaspoon coriander seeds

½ teaspoon yellow mustard seeds

2 cups bottled clam juice or reduced-sodium chicken broth, defatted

1 cup sliced scallions

½ cup sliced celery

¾ teaspoon salt

½ teaspoon red pepper flakes

2 pounds small red potatoes, halved if large

4 ears corn, husks removed, cut in half

3 pounds large unpeeled shrimp

8 cups coarsely torn spinach leaves

1. Make a bouquet garni by combining the bay leaves, allspice, coriander, and mustard seeds on a square of cheesecloth, gathering the cheesecloth ends, and tying with string. In a large pot, combine the bouquet garni, clam juice, 6 cups of water, the scallions, celery, salt, and red pepper flakes. Bring to a boil over high heat.

2. Add the potatoes and return to a boil. Reduce to a simmer, cover, and cook until the potatoes are tender, about 25 minutes.

3. Stir in the corn, shrimp, and spinach. Cover again and cook until the shrimp are just opaque and the corn is tender, about 7 minutes longer. Discard the bouquet garni and serve.

Suggested accompaniments: Limeade, herbed biscuits, and chocolate or vanilla ice milk for dessert.

FAT: 3G/10%
CALORIES: 299
SATURATED FAT: .6G
CARBOHYDRATE: 34G
PROTEIN: 34G
CHOLESTEROL: 210MG
SODIUM: 608MG

Try to use the more mildly flavored Turkish bay leaves for the best taste in this wonderfully informal dish. If you have ground spices rather than seeds in the cupboard, skip the bouquet garni and add the ground allspice and coriander directly to the pot, omitting the mustard seeds. Cooking the shrimp in their shells enriches the broth—be sure to furnish plenty of napkins.

SALMON, POTATO, AND GREEN BEAN SALAD

SERVES: 4
WORKING TIME: 15 MINUTES
TOTAL TIME: 30 MINUTES

In this quick variation on salade niçoise, the potatoes, green beans, and fish are tossed together in a bowl rather than arranged on a platter. The warm vegetables readily soak up the mustardy dressing and taste wonderful, and the salmon makes a nice change from the usual tuna. Bring the salad to the table with a ficelle (a long, skinny loaf of French bread) or bread sticks.

1 pound small red potatoes, halved

¾ pound green beans, halved

⅓ cup reduced-sodium chicken broth, defatted

3 tablespoons reduced-fat mayonnaise

3 tablespoons cider vinegar

1 tablespoon Dijon mustard

¾ teaspoon dried marjoram

1 red onion, diced

2 ribs celery, thinly sliced

3 cups torn red leaf lettuce

14¾-ounce can pink salmon, drained and flaked

1. In a large pot of boiling water, cook the potatoes until almost tender, about 10 minutes. Add the green beans and cook until the beans are crisp-tender and the potatoes are cooked through, about 2 minutes. Drain well.

2. Meanwhile, in a large bowl, combine the broth, mayonnaise, vinegar, mustard, and marjoram. Add the cooked potatoes and beans, the onion, and celery, tossing to combine. Add the lettuce and toss again. Divide the salad among 4 plates, scatter the salmon on top, and serve.

Helpful hint: Chicken broth is used to make this mayonnaise-based dressing pourable and savory without adding fat. You can use this same trick to "stretch" a vinaigrette dressing by replacing some of the oil called for in the traditional recipe with chicken broth.

FAT: 8G/24%
CALORIES: 305
SATURATED FAT: 1.7G
CARBOHYDRATE: 36G
PROTEIN: 24G
CHOLESTEROL: 34MG
SODIUM: 695MG

SAUTÉED SWORDFISH WITH FRESH TOMATO SAUCE

SERVES: 4
WORKING TIME: 30 MINUTES
TOTAL TIME: 35 MINUTES

Not every type of fish would be suited to a robust tomato sauce, but swordfish, with its firm, beefy texture, is the perfect partner for this fresh-tomato topping. The chunky sauce is dotted with capers and flavored with garlic and orange zest. We serve the fish with orzo, but you can use another pasta shape if you like. Or serve the swordfish with grains, such as a mix of white and wild rice.

8 ounces orzo pasta

1 tablespoon flour

1 teaspoon fennel seeds, crushed, or ½ teaspoon ground fennel

½ teaspoon ground coriander

¾ teaspoon salt

⅛ teaspoon cayenne pepper

4 small swordfish steaks (about 4 ounces each)

1 tablespoon vegetable oil

2 shallots, finely chopped, or ⅓ cup chopped scallion whites

2 cloves garlic, minced

2 tomatoes, coarsely diced

¼ cup reduced-sodium chicken broth, defatted

2 tablespoons capers, rinsed, drained, and chopped

½ teaspoon grated orange zest

¼ teaspoon sugar

1. In a medium pot of boiling water, cook the pasta until just tender. Drain well.

2. Meanwhile, on a sheet of waxed paper, combine the flour, fennel, coriander, ¼ teaspoon of the salt, and the cayenne. Dredge the swordfish in the flour mixture, shaking off the excess. In a large nonstick skillet, heat 2 teaspoons of the oil until hot but not smoking over medium-high heat. Add the swordfish and cook until just opaque throughout, about 3 minutes per side. Transfer the swordfish to a plate and cover loosely with foil to keep warm.

3. Add the remaining 1 teaspoon oil to the skillet. Add the shallots and garlic and cook, stirring, until the shallots begin to brown, about 1 minute. Stir in the tomatoes, broth, capers, orange zest, sugar, and the remaining ½ teaspoon salt. Cook until the liquid is slightly reduced and the tomatoes have softened, about 3 minutes.

4. Divide the orzo among 4 plates. Place the swordfish alongside, top with the sauce, and serve.

Helpful hints: Use a mortar and pestle to crush whole fennel seeds. Tuna steaks can be substituted for the swordfish, if you like.

FAT: 9G/21%
CALORIES: 392
SATURATED FAT: 1.7G
CARBOHYDRATE: 49G
PROTEIN: 28G
CHOLESTEROL: 39MG
SODIUM: 664MG

SALMON STEAKS WITH CUCUMBER-DILL SAUCE

SERVES: 4
WORKING TIME: 15 MINUTES
TOTAL TIME: 30 MINUTES

Fresh salmon, with its tempting orangy-pink color, always seems festive; this broiled salmon dish also boasts a rich flavor that needs little enhancement. We've created a super-quick, fresh-tasting sauce with nonfat yogurt, lemon, diced cucumber, Dijon mustard, onion, and lots of fresh dill. Pair the salmon with steamed asparagus and serve with lemon wedges.

1½ cups plain nonfat yogurt

¾ teaspoon grated lemon zest

¼ cup plus 1½ teaspoons fresh lemon juice

1 tablespoon plus 1½ teaspoons Dijon mustard

¾ teaspoon salt

2 medium cucumbers, peeled, seeded, and diced

1 large red onion, diced

¾ cup snipped fresh dill

4 salmon steaks (about 1½ pounds total)

1. Preheat the broiler. In a large bowl, combine the yogurt, lemon zest, lemon juice, mustard, and ½ teaspoon of the salt. Add the cucumbers, onion, and dill to the yogurt mixture and refrigerate until serving time.

2. Sprinkle the salmon with the remaining ¼ teaspoon salt and broil 6 inches from the heat, turning once, for 6 minutes, or until just opaque. Divide the fish among 4 plates and serve with the sauce.

Helpful hints: The easiest way to mince a large amount of dill is by snipping the leaves with kitchen shears. Snip the dill right over the measuring cup. To seed a cucumber, halve the cucumber lengthwise and scoop out the seeds with the tip of a small spoon.

FAT: 10G/28%
CALORIES: 318
SATURATED FAT: 1.6G
CARBOHYDRATE: 18G
PROTEIN: 36G
CHOLESTEROL: 84MG
SODIUM: 640MG

CRAB CAKES WITH SPICY MANGO-MUSTARD SAUCE

SERVES: 4
WORKING TIME: 30 MINUTES
TOTAL TIME: 35 MINUTES

The use of mango chutney makes these crab cakes unique. Serve them with sautéed zucchini sticks—a healthy alternative to fries.

¾ pound lump crabmeat, picked over to remove any cartilage
6 tablespoons flour
¾ cup finely diced red bell pepper
¼ cup fresh lemon juice
¼ cup mango chutney
1 tablespoon plus 2 teaspoons Dijon mustard
1 teaspoon curry powder
½ teaspoon Worcestershire sauce
2 egg whites, lightly beaten
1 tablespoon olive oil
⅓ cup canned crushed pineapple
⅛ teaspoon cayenne pepper

1. In a medium bowl, combine the crabmeat, 2 tablespoons of the flour, ½ cup of the bell pepper, 1 tablespoon of the lemon juice, 1 tablespoon of the chutney, 2 teaspoons of the mustard, the curry powder, and Worcestershire sauce. Fold in the egg whites. Shape the mixture into 4 patties. Place the remaining ¼ cup flour on a sheet of waxed paper. Dredge the crab cakes in the flour, shaking off the excess.

2. In a large nonstick skillet, heat the oil until hot but not smoking over medium heat. Add the crab cakes, reduce the heat to medium-low, and cook until golden brown and cooked through, about 4 minutes per side.

3. Meanwhile, in a small bowl, combine the pineapple, cayenne, the remaining 3 tablespoons chutney, remaining 3 tablespoons lemon juice, remaining ¼ cup bell pepper, and remaining 1 tablespoon mustard. Divide the crab cakes among 4 plates. Top with the mango-mustard sauce and serve.

Helpful hint: Lump crabmeat consists of large, meaty chunks of cooked meat. It is available both fresh and canned. You can use either variety for this recipe, although fresh is preferable.

FAT: 5G/18%
CALORIES: 247
SATURATED FAT: 0.7G
CARBOHYDRATE: 27G
PROTEIN: 21G
CHOLESTEROL: 85MG
SODIUM: 600MG

GREEK-STYLE COD AND LEMON SOUP

SERVES: 4
WORKING TIME: 20 MINUTES
TOTAL TIME: 30 MINUTES

2 cups reduced-sodium chicken broth, defatted

½ teaspoon grated lemon zest

¼ cup fresh lemon juice

½ cup chopped fresh mint

4 scallions, finely chopped

2 cloves garlic, minced

½ teaspoon dried oregano

½ teaspoon salt

½ cup orzo or other small pasta shape

1 yellow summer squash, halved lengthwise and thinly sliced

1½ pounds skinless cod fillets, cut into large pieces

1 teaspoon cornstarch mixed with 1 tablespoon water

1. In a large nonaluminum saucepan, combine 4 cups of water, the broth, lemon zest, lemon juice, mint, scallions, garlic, oregano, and salt. Bring to a boil over medium heat and cook for 5 minutes to blend the flavors.

2. Add the orzo and yellow squash to the pan and cook for 5 minutes. Reduce to a simmer, add the fish, and cook until just opaque, about 4 minutes. Bring to a boil, add the cornstarch mixture, and cook, stirring constantly, until the soup is slightly thickened, about 1 minute. Divide the soup among 4 bowls and serve.

Helpful hint: The soup can be completed through step 1 up to 8 hours in advance. Return to a boil before proceeding.

FAT: 2G/7%
CALORIES: 267
SATURATED FAT: 0.3G
CARBOHYDRATE: 25G
PROTEIN: 36G
CHOLESTEROL: 73MG
SODIUM: 693MG

Lemony soups made with rice (or rice-like orzo pasta) are typically Greek. The fresh lemon taste is perfect with fish.

NEW ORLEANS SPICY SHRIMP STEW

SERVES: 4
WORKING TIME: 25 MINUTES
TOTAL TIME: 40 MINUTES

1 tablespoon olive oil

1 red bell pepper, cut into ½-inch squares

1 green bell pepper, cut into ½-inch squares

4 scallions, thinly sliced

3 cloves garlic, minced

1 cup reduced-sodium chicken broth, defatted

1 teaspoon dried thyme

½ teaspoon salt

½ teaspoon hot pepper sauce

¼ teaspoon freshly ground black pepper

10-ounce package frozen cut okra

1 pound large shrimp, shelled and deveined

1½ cups frozen corn kernels

1½ teaspoons cornstarch mixed with 1 tablespoon water

1. In a Dutch oven, heat the oil until hot but not smoking over medium heat. Add the bell peppers, scallions, and garlic and cook, stirring frequently, until the peppers are tender, about 5 minutes.

2. Add the broth, thyme, salt, hot pepper sauce, and black pepper and bring to a boil. Add the okra, reduce the heat to a simmer, cover, and cook until the okra is tender, about 7 minutes. Add the shrimp and corn, cover, and cook until the shrimp are just opaque, about 3 minutes. Return to a boil, add the cornstarch mixture, and cook, stirring constantly, until slightly thickened, about 1 minute.

Helpful hints: When you buy a pound of large shrimp, you should get about 16 to 20 shrimp. If you can handle a little more spice, feel free to add an additional ¼ teaspoon hot pepper sauce in step 2.

FAT: 6G/24%
CALORIES: 230
SATURATED FAT: 0.9G
CARBOHYDRATE: 24G
PROTEIN: 23G
CHOLESTEROL: 140MG
SODIUM: 599MG

The food-loving city of New Orleans is surrounded by water; it's set in the Mississippi delta, with Lake Pontchartrain to the north, the Gulf of Mexico to the east, and bayous all around. So it's understandable that shellfish—notably shrimp, oysters, crabs, and crayfish—are favorite foods. This peppery Creole-style stew features lots of tasty shrimp along with okra, corn, and peppers.

BAKED STUFFED SOLE WITH OLIVES AND TOMATOES

SERVES: 4
WORKING TIME: 20 MINUTES
TOTAL TIME: 40 MINUTES

In late summer, when locally grown beefsteak tomatoes are plentiful and cheap, try them in this unusual dish. The hefty tomato slices form the base for rolled fish fillets with a lemony olive stuffing. If you have a handsome ceramic baking dish, bring the sizzling fish straight from the oven to the table. Braised leeks make a delicate side dish for this assertively flavored entrée.

⅓ cup plus 1 tablespoon chopped fresh parsley

⅓ cup Calamata or other brine-cured olives, pitted and chopped

3 cloves garlic, minced

2 tablespoons plain dried bread crumbs

½ teaspoon grated lemon zest

2 tablespoons fresh lemon juice

¾ teaspoon dried oregano

4 sole or flounder fillets, any visible bones removed (about 1½ pounds total)

8 thick slices of tomato

¼ teaspoon salt

2 teaspoons olive oil

½ teaspoon paprika

1. Preheat the oven to 400°. In a small bowl, combine ⅓ cup of the parsley, the olives, garlic, bread crumbs, lemon zest, lemon juice, and oregano.

2. Lay the fillets flat, skinned-sides down. Spoon the parsley mixture over the fillets and, starting from a short side, roll up each fillet. Lay the tomato slices in a 9-inch square baking dish, slightly overlapping them. Sprinkle with the salt. Place the fillets, seam-sides down, on top of the tomatoes. Drizzle the fish rolls with the oil and sprinkle with the paprika. Cover with foil and bake for 20 minutes, or until the fish is just opaque in the center.

3. Divide the tomatoes among 4 plates. Top the tomatoes with the fish rolls, spoon the pan juices over the fish, sprinkle with the remaining 1 tablespoon parsley, and serve.

Helpful hint: Flounder has many names: Some types are identified as "sole" in supermarkets. Depending on where you live, you can buy various types of flounder called lemon sole, gray sole, rex sole, petrale, winter or summer flounder, starry flounder, witch flounder, fluke, or sand dab.

FAT: 8G/29%
CALORIES: 249
SATURATED FAT: 1.2G
CARBOHYDRATE: 10G
PROTEIN: 34G
CHOLESTEROL: 82MG
SODIUM: 513MG

SAUTÉED BAY SCALLOPS ASIAN-STYLE

SERVES: 4
WORKING TIME: 10 MINUTES
TOTAL TIME: 30 MINUTES

1 cup long-grain rice

¼ teaspoon salt

2 teaspoons vegetable or olive oil

3 scallions, thinly sliced

3 cloves garlic, minced

¾ teaspoon ground ginger

1 zucchini, quartered lengthwise and thinly sliced

½ cup canned sliced water chestnuts

1 cup cherry tomatoes

1½ teaspoons cornstarch

½ cup reduced-sodium chicken broth, defatted

3 tablespoons reduced-sodium soy sauce

3 tablespoons sherry

1 teaspoon sugar

1¼ pounds bay scallops or quartered sea scallops

1. In a medium saucepan, bring 2¼ cups of water to a boil. Add the rice and salt, reduce to a simmer, cover, and cook until the rice is tender, about 17 minutes.

2. Meanwhile, in a large nonstick skillet, heat the oil until hot but not smoking over medium heat. Add the scallions, garlic, and ginger and cook, stirring frequently, until the scallions are crisp-tender, about 1 minute. Add the zucchini and water chestnuts and cook, stirring occasionally, until the zucchini is crisp-tender, about 3 minutes. Add the cherry tomatoes and cook until heated through, about 1 minute.

3. In a small bowl, combine the cornstarch, broth, soy sauce, sherry, and sugar. Add the mixture to the skillet and bring to a boil. Add the scallops, reduce the heat to a simmer, and cook until the scallops are just opaque, about 2 minutes. Divide the scallop mixture among 4 plates, spoon the rice alongside, and serve.

Helpful hint: Canned water chestnuts are available both whole and sliced. Whole water chestnuts can be sliced, but they are quite small and unwieldy. To save yourself time, buy the sliced variety.

FAT: 4G/10%
CALORIES: 379
SATURATED FAT: 0.5G
CARBOHYDRATE: 52G
PROTEIN: 30G
CHOLESTEROL: 47MG
SODIUM: 907MG

Bay scallops, those succulent thimble-sized morsels, are the closest thing to "instant" seafood: Here, it takes just two minutes to cook them through. The crisp contrast of water chestnuts and zucchini—along with vivid cherry tomatoes and the bold seasoning trio of garlic, scallions, and ginger—makes this a tantalizing dinner dish.

The fifteen minutes or so needed for preparing the sauce here fits perfectly into the cooking time for the rice—and that's one of the simple secrets of quick cooking. Scarlet cherry tomatoes add a cheerful dash of color to the sautéed shrimp and rice. You can also use yellow or orange cherry tomatoes—or similar-sized pear-shaped tomatoes—if you like.

SAUTÉED SHRIMP WITH HERBED CHERRY TOMATOES

SERVES: 4
WORKING TIME: 20 MINUTES
TOTAL TIME: 30 MINUTES

1 cup long-grain rice

¾ teaspoon salt

2 teaspoons olive oil

2 scallions, thinly sliced

3 cloves garlic, slivered

*1 pound large shrimp, shelled
and deveined (see tip)*

2 cups halved cherry tomatoes

¼ cup chopped fresh basil

¼ cup chopped fresh mint

*¼ teaspoon freshly ground black
pepper*

*½ cup reduced-sodium chicken
broth, defatted*

*1 teaspoon cornstarch mixed
with 1 tablespoon water*

1. In a medium saucepan, bring 2¼ cups of water to a boil. Add the rice and ¼ teaspoon of the salt, reduce to a simmer, cover, and cook until the rice is tender, about 17 minutes.

2. Meanwhile, in a large nonstick skillet, heat the oil until hot but not smoking over medium heat. Add the scallions and garlic and cook until the scallions are slightly softened, about 1 minute. Add the shrimp and cook until opaque on the outside but still a bit translucent in the center, about 3 minutes. With a slotted spoon, transfer the shrimp to a plate.

3. Add the cherry tomatoes, basil, mint, pepper, and the remaining ½ teaspoon salt to the pan and cook until the tomatoes are softened and begin to get juicy, about 4 minutes. Add the broth and bring to a boil. Stir in the cornstarch mixture and cook, stirring, until slightly thickened, about 1 minute. Return the shrimp to the skillet and stir until opaque throughout, about 1 minute. Divide the rice among 4 plates, spoon the shrimp mixture alongside, and serve.

Helpful hint: You'll get about 16 to 20 large shrimp when you buy a pound; medium shrimp come 21 to 25 per pound.

FAT: 4G/12%
CALORIES: 311
SATURATED FAT: 0.7G
CARBOHYDRATE: 43G
PROTEIN: 23G
CHOLESTEROL: 140MG
SODIUM: 637MG

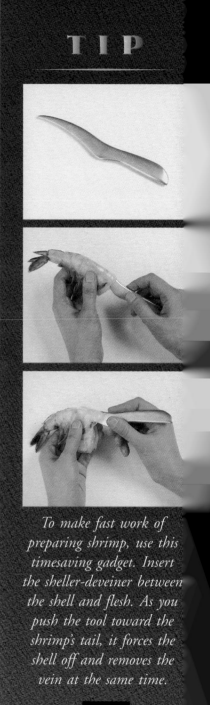

TIP

To make fast work of preparing shrimp, use this timesaving gadget. Insert the sheller-deveiner between the shell and flesh. As you push the tool toward the shrimp's tail, it forces the shell off and removes the vein at the same time.

247

*A*ny firm white fish will simmer well in our hearty version of the popular Mediterranean fish stew—haddock, hake, or halibut are all good stand-ins for the cod. The roasted red pepper purée, assertively laced with red pepper flakes and garlic, infuses the stew with rich, deep flavor as well as color.

BOUILLABAISSE

SERVES: 4
WORKING TIME: 25 MINUTES
TOTAL TIME: 50 MINUTES

9 thin slices (½ ounce each) French or Italian bread

1 clove garlic, halved, plus 5 cloves garlic, minced

½ cup jarred roasted red peppers, drained

¼ teaspoon red pepper flakes

1 tablespoon olive oil

1 large onion, coarsely chopped

1 cup cut fennel or celery (1-inch chunks; see tip)

⅓ cup dry white wine

⅓ cup orange juice

½ teaspoon grated orange zest

½ teaspoon fennel seeds

2 cups chopped tomatoes

¼ teaspoon salt

½ pound cod or red snapper fillets, any visible bones removed, cut into 4 pieces

½ pound sea scallops

6 ounces lump crabmeat

⅓ cup chopped fresh parsley

1. Preheat the oven to 400°. Rub the bread with the cut sides of the halved garlic clove. Reserve the garlic halves. Bake the bread for 5 to 7 minutes, or until toasted and crisp. Transfer 1 slice of the toast to a food processor or blender. Add the red peppers, red pepper flakes, reserved garlic halves, and 1 teaspoon of the oil and purée until smooth; set aside. Reserve the remaining toasts.

2. In a Dutch oven, heat the remaining 2 teaspoons oil until hot but not smoking over medium heat. Add the onion and minced garlic and cook, stirring frequently, until the onion has softened, about 7 minutes. Stir in the fennel and cook, stirring frequently, until the fennel is tender, about 5 minutes. Stir in the wine, orange juice, orange zest, and fennel seeds. Increase the heat to high, bring to a boil, and cook until the liquid has reduced by half, about 5 minutes. Stir in the tomatoes and salt and cook until the mixture is slightly thickened, about 5 minutes longer.

3. Stir in 1½ cups of water and return to a boil. Add the cod, scallops, and crabmeat, reduce the heat to medium, cover, and cook until the seafood is just opaque, about 4 minutes longer. Stir in the parsley and half of the red pepper purée. Ladle the bouillabaisse into 4 bowls. Spread the remaining red pepper purée over the reserved toasts and serve with the bouillabaisse.

Suggested accompaniment: Follow with sliced plums poached in red wine.

FAT: 6G/16%
CALORIES: 340
SATURATED FAT: .9G
CARBOHYDRATE: 33G
PROTEIN: 33G
CHOLESTEROL: 86MG
SODIUM: 647MG

TIP

To prepare fresh fennel, cut the stalks from the bulb, and trim the stem end and any tough outer sections from the bulb. Cut the bulb crosswise into 1-inch-thick slices, then cut the slices into 1-inch chunks.

A surprisingly simple dish to prepare, this is special enough for a pull-out-all-the-stops dinner party. We pair the salmon with its natural flavor partners, dill and lemon, and then display the fish on a bed of colorful vegetables. Baking the salmon with the skin on allows it to hold its shape (for presentation, we remove the skin just before serving).

BAKED SALMON ON A BED OF VEGETABLES

SERVES: 4
WORKING TIME: 30 MINUTES
TOTAL TIME: 1 HOUR 10 MINUTES

¼ cup plus 1 tablespoon snipped fresh dill

2 tablespoons fresh lemon juice

¼ teaspoon salt

¼ teaspoon freshly ground black pepper

2 salmon fillets with skin (about 10 ounces each), any visible bones removed

4 carrots, cut into 2-inch julienne strips

3 leeks (white and light green parts only), cut into 2-inch julienne strips

1 pound baking potatoes, peeled and cut into 2-inch julienne strips

2 teaspoons olive oil

1. Preheat the oven to 400°. In a small bowl, combine ¼ cup of the dill, the lemon juice, ⅛ teaspoon of the salt, and ⅛ teaspoon of the pepper. Lay the salmon fillets flat, skin-side down. Spoon half of the dill mixture on top of each fillet. Carefully press the dill-covered sides of the salmon together. Set aside.

2. In a large bowl, combine the carrots, leeks, and potatoes. Add the oil, remaining 1 tablespoon dill, remaining ⅛ teaspoon salt, and remaining ⅛ teaspoon pepper and toss well to combine. Spread the vegetables in a 14 x 10-inch roasting pan. Place the salmon on top, keeping the dill-covered sides together, cover with foil, and bake for 20 minutes.

3. Remove the foil and gently stir the vegetables. Replace the foil and continue to bake for 20 minutes longer, or until the salmon is just opaque and the vegetables are tender.

4. Transfer the salmon to a cutting board and separate the fillets. Remove and discard the skin (see tip; top photo), turn the salmon dill-covered side up, then cut each fillet crosswise in half (bottom photo). Divide the vegetable mixture among 4 plates and place the salmon on top, dill-covered side up. Drizzle any pan juices over the salmon and serve.

Suggested accompaniment: End with reduced-fat cherry cheesecake.

FAT: 12G/28%
CALORIES: 376
SATURATED FAT: 1.8G
CARBOHYDRATE: 36G
PROTEIN: 32G
CHOLESTEROL: 78MG
SODIUM: 247MG

TIP

Using a small, sharp paring knife, carefully trim off the salmon skin, keeping the blade as close to the skin as possible. Turn the salmon, dill-covered side up, and cut each fillet crosswise in half to make four generous servings.

251

SPANISH-STYLE HALIBUT STEAKS

SERVES: 4
WORKING TIME: 20 MINUTES
TOTAL TIME: 25 MINUTES

G reen olives, along with tomatoes and roasted red peppers, give these meaty fish steaks a typically Spanish flavor. Most of the green olives sold in this country are imported from Spain, where a large proportion of the world's table olives are grown. Accompany the halibut with strips or half-rounds of zucchini and carrots, cooked crisp-tender in flavored broth, and a basket of warm rolls.

2 teaspoons olive oil

1 small onion, finely chopped

2 cloves garlic, minced

1 small pickled jalapeño pepper, finely chopped

¼ cup fresh lime juice

1½ teaspoons mild chili powder

1 teaspoon dried oregano

Four halibut steaks (about 1½ pounds total)

14½-ounce can no-salt-added stewed tomatoes

½ cup jarred roasted red peppers, rinsed, drained, and cut into thick strips

¼ cup green olives, pitted and coarsely chopped

1 tablespoon capers, rinsed and drained

1. Preheat the broiler. In a large nonstick skillet, heat the oil until hot but not smoking over medium heat. Add the onion and garlic and cook, stirring occasionally, until the onion is softened, about 5 minutes. Add the jalapeño, stirring to mix.

2. Meanwhile, in a small bowl, combine the lime juice, chili powder, and oregano. Place the halibut on the broiler rack and sprinkle with 2 tablespoons of the lime juice mixture. Broil 6 inches from the heat, turning once, for 6 minutes, or until the halibut is just opaque.

3. Add the tomatoes, roasted red peppers, olives, capers, and the remaining lime juice mixture to the skillet and bring to a boil. Reduce the heat to a simmer and cook, stirring occasionally, until the sauce is slightly thickened and the flavors are blended, about 5 minutes. Place the fish on 4 plates, spoon the sauce on top, and serve.

Helpful hint: Either plain or stuffed green olives would be fine for this recipe. The pimientos with which the stuffed olives are filled taste very much like the roasted red peppers used here.

FAT: 7G/27%
CALORIES: 237
SATURATED FAT: 0.9G
CARBOHYDRATE: 13G
PROTEIN: 31G
CHOLESTEROL: 44MG
SODIUM: 442MG

EXTRA-QUICK

Left, Caribbean Pork with Pineapple Salsa (p. 311).
Above, Chicken Cobb Salad (p. 280)

These moist, tasty patties—deliciously seasoned with sage, mustard, and ketchup—will satisfy even the most ardent burger lover. For a final touch, we've stirred together our low-fat version of Russian dressing made with reduced-fat sour cream. Dilled potato salad is a perfect accompaniment.

BROILED CHICKEN BURGERS

SERVES: 4
WORKING TIME: 15 MINUTES
TOTAL TIME: 25 MINUTES

1 pound skinless, boneless chicken breast , cut into small chunks

3 tablespoons ketchup

1 tablespoon Dijon mustard

½ teaspoon dried sage

½ teaspoon salt

½ teaspoon freshly ground black pepper

2 slices (1 ounce each) white sandwich bread, torn into small pieces

3 tablespoons low-fat (1%) milk

3 tablespoons reduced-fat sour cream

4 hamburger buns

4 romaine lettuce leaves

12 tomato slices

1. In a food processor, process the chicken until coarsely ground (see tip). Transfer to a large bowl and stir in 2 tablespoons of the ketchup, 2 teaspoons of the mustard, the sage, salt, and pepper. In a small bowl, combine the bread and the milk, stirring to evenly moisten the bread. Add the bread mixture to the chicken along with 2 tablespoons of the sour cream, mixing well to combine. Shape into 4 burgers.

2. Preheat the broiler or prepare the grill. Broil or grill the burgers 6 inches from the heat, turning once, for 8 minutes, or until cooked through but still juicy. Transfer the burgers to a plate and set aside. Place the buns on the rack and broil or grill for 30 seconds, or until lightly toasted.

3. Meanwhile, in a small bowl, stir together the remaining 1 teaspoon mustard, remaining 1 tablespoon ketchup, and remaining 1 table-spoon sour cream. Place the toasted buns on 4 plates. Top each with a lettuce leaf, a burger, 3 tomato slices, and a dollop of the ketchup-sour cream mixture, and serve.

Helpful hints: The chicken patties can be prepared up to 1 day ahead and refrigerated, or they can be frozen between sheets of waxed paper and wrapped in foil. For a slightly nuttier taste, replace the white bread used in the burger mixture with whole-wheat or one of the multi-grained breads.

FAT: 6G/14%
CALORIES: 376
SATURATED FAT: 1.6G
CARBOHYDRATE: 42G
PROTEIN: 35G
CHOLESTEROL: 70MG
SODIUM: 972MG

TIP

To coarsely grind the chicken, drop small pieces through the feed tube of a food processor while pulsing the machine with on-and-off motions. Do not overprocess; the chicken should still have some texture and not be completely puréed.

SAUTÉED PORK SCALLOPINI ON A BED OF GREENS

SERVES: 4
WORKING TIME: 20 MINUTES
TOTAL TIME: 25 MINUTES

1¼ pounds small red potatoes, quartered

¾ teaspoon salt

2 tablespoons balsamic vinegar

2 teaspoons olive oil

1 teaspoon Dijon mustard

¾ teaspoon firmly packed brown sugar

½ teaspoon freshly ground black pepper

2 cups watercress or arugula leaves

2 tomatoes, cut into small wedges

1 Belgian endive, cut into 1-inch pieces, or 2 cups torn Boston lettuce

¾ pound well-trimmed center-cut pork loin, cut into 8 slices

2 tablespoons flour

1. In a large pot of boiling water, cook the potatoes with ¼ teaspoon of the salt until tender, about 15 minutes. Drain well.

2. Meanwhile, in a large bowl, combine the vinegar, 1 teaspoon of the oil, the mustard, brown sugar, ¼ teaspoon of the remaining salt, and ¼ teaspoon of the pepper. Place the watercress, tomatoes, and endive on top of the dressing, but do not toss. When the potatoes are done, add them to the salad. Set aside.

3. Place the pork slices between 2 sheets of waxed paper, and with the flat side of a small skillet or meat pounder, pound the pork to a ¼-inch thickness. On another sheet of waxed paper, combine the flour, the remaining ¼ teaspoon salt, and the remaining ¼ teaspoon pepper. Dredge the pork in the flour mixture, shaking off the excess.

4. In a large nonstick skillet, heat the remaining 1 teaspoon oil until hot but not smoking over medium-high heat. Add the pork and cook until browned and cooked through, about 2 minutes per side. Toss the salad mixture together, spoon onto 4 plates, top with the pork cutlets, and serve.

Helpful hint: Belgian endive discolors and turns bitter when exposed to light, so it's wrapped in paper within its shipping box. When shopping for Belgian endive, dig to the bottom of the box for small, pale heads that have been protected from the light.

FAT: 7G/22%
CALORIES: 291
SATURATED FAT: 1.8G
CARBOHYDRATE: 33G
PROTEIN: 23G
CHOLESTEROL: 54MG
SODIUM: 457MG

For this innovative one-dish meal, tender pork cutlets are served on a warm potato-and-greens salad. The slight bitterness of the watercress and endive is balanced by the delicate sweetness of the mustard and brown sugar vinaigrette. Serve this satisfying entrée with a basket of Italian bread.

SHRIMP ALL'ARRABBIATA

SERVES: 4
WORKING TIME: 25 MINUTES
TOTAL TIME: 25 MINUTES

In Italian, arrabbiata means "angry," and appropriately, the shrimp in this dish are bathed in a fiery tomato sauce. The sauce, seasoned with red pepper flakes, oregano, ginger, and rosemary, is brightened with bits of bell pepper and olives. For a colorful side dish, toss together a salad of radicchio, baby spinach, and other tender greens.

1 teaspoon olive oil
1 red bell pepper, diced
2 cloves garlic, minced
¾ cup bottled clam juice
1 tomato, chopped
¼ cup Calamata or other brine-cured black olives, pitted and slivered
¾ teaspoon dried oregano
½ teaspoon ground ginger
½ teaspoon dried rosemary
¼ teaspoon red pepper flakes
¼ teaspoon salt
1 pound medium shrimp, shelled and deveined
¾ teaspoon cornstarch mixed with 1 teaspoon water

1. In a large nonstick skillet, heat the oil until hot but not smoking over medium heat. Add the bell pepper and garlic and cook, stirring, until well coated, about 1 minute. Add ¼ cup of the clam juice and cook until the pepper is softened, about 3 minutes. Stir in the remaining ½ cup clam juice, the tomato, olives, oregano, ginger, rosemary, red pepper flakes, and salt and cook for 3 minutes to reduce slightly.

2. Add the shrimp to the pan and cook until the shrimp are just opaque, about 2 minutes. Bring to a boil, stir in the cornstarch mixture, and cook, stirring, until slightly thickened, about 1 minute. Divide the shrimp mixture among 4 plates and serve.

Helpful hint: Clam juice is ideal for seafood sauces, but you can substitute chicken broth if necessary.

FAT: 4G/26%
CALORIES: 139
SATURATED FAT: .6G
CARBOHYDRATE: 5G
PROTEIN: 19G
CHOLESTEROL: 140MG
SODIUM: 448MG

The vibrant mingling of sweet mango and spicy chili sauce, sharpened with a splash of lime juice, adds a Caribbean accent to this colorful salad. Make it up to a day ahead of time or serve it immediately. To cut preparation time as well as cleanup, microwave the sweet potato cubes, covered, at full power (100 percent) for four to five minutes, stirring once or twice.

CARIBBEAN CHICKEN SALAD

SERVES: 4
WORKING TIME: 15 MINUTES
TOTAL TIME: 25 MINUTES

¾ pound sweet potatoes, peeled and cut into 1-inch cubes

¾ cup chili sauce

¼ cup fresh lime juice

6 drops hot pepper sauce

1 pound skinless, boneless chicken breasts

1 cucumber, peeled, halved lengthwise, seeded, and diced

1 mango, halved, pitted, and cut into ½-inch pieces (see tip)

2 tablespoons minced scallion

1 tablespoon olive oil

3 cups ½-inch-wide shredded romaine lettuce

4 teaspoons coarsely chopped unsalted dry-roasted peanuts

1. In a medium saucepan, combine the sweet potatoes with water to cover. Bring to a boil over high heat, reduce to a simmer, cover, and cook until the potatoes are tender, about 10 minutes. Drain and cool.

2. Meanwhile, preheat the broiler. In a large bowl, combine the chili sauce, lime juice, and hot pepper sauce. Remove 3 tablespoons of this chili sauce mixture and set aside the remaining sauce. Place the chicken on the broiler rack and brush with the 3 tablespoons chili sauce mixture. Broil the chicken 4 inches from the heat for about 4 minutes per side, or until the chicken is just cooked through. Transfer the chicken to a cutting board and cut the chicken into thin diagonal slices.

3. Add the sweet potatoes, cucumber, mango, scallion, oil, and chicken slices to the reserved chili sauce mixture and toss to coat. Cover and refrigerate if not serving immediately.

4. Place the lettuce on 4 plates and spoon the chicken salad on top. Sprinkle with the peanuts and serve.

Suggested accompaniments: Sesame flat breads, and sliced bananas sprinkled with dark rum for dessert.

FAT: 7G/21%
CALORIES: 304
SATURATED FAT: 1.1G
CARBOHYDRATE: 32G
PROTEIN: 30G
CHOLESTEROL: 66MG
SODIUM: 423MG

TIP

Score each mango half into squares, cutting to, but not through, the skin. Turn the mango half inside out to pop the cut pieces outward. Cut the pieces away from the skin.

CHICKEN BREASTS WITH PINEAPPLE-PEPPER RELISH

SERVES: 4
WORKING TIME: 10 MINUTES
TOTAL TIME: 20 MINUTES

Red pepper flakes and chili sauce provide the heat for this relish. For a flavor twist, substitute cantaloupe or mango for the pineapple.

16-ounce can crushed pineapple in juice, drained

1 red bell pepper, diced

1 scallion, finely chopped

¼ cup plus 2 tablespoons chili sauce

¼ cup plus 1 tablespoon thawed frozen pineapple juice concentrate

2 tablespoons honey

2 teaspoons red wine vinegar

¼ teaspoon red pepper flakes

4 skinless, boneless chicken breast halves (about 1 pound total)

1. Preheat the broiler or prepare the grill. If using a broiler, line the broiler pan with foil. In a medium bowl, combine the pineapple, bell pepper, scallion, 2 tablespoons of the chili sauce, 1 tablespoon of the pineapple juice concentrate, 1 tablespoon of the honey, the vinegar, and pepper flakes and stir to blend. Let the pineapple-pepper relish stand while you prepare the chicken.

2. In a small bowl, combine the remaining ¼ cup chili sauce, remaining ¼ cup pineapple juice concentrate, and remaining 1 tablespoon honey and stir to blend. Brush the chicken with half of this chili sauce mixture and broil or grill 4 inches from the heat for 4 minutes. Turn the chicken, brush with the remaining chili sauce mixture, and broil or grill for about 4 minutes longer, or until the chicken is just cooked through.

3. Place the chicken on 4 plates, spoon the pineapple-pepper relish on the side, and serve.

Suggested accompaniments: Warm corn tortillas, a green salad with sliced cucumbers and a garlic vinaigrette, and fresh pineapple wedges.

FAT: 2G/6%
CALORIES: 299
SATURATED FAT: .4G
CARBOHYDRATE: 44G
PROTEIN: 28G
CHOLESTEROL: 66MG
SODIUM: 419MG

Spanish-Style Chicken

Serves: 4
Working time: 15 minutes
Total time: 25 minutes

4-ounce jar roasted red peppers or pimientos, rinsed and drained

Two 4-ounce cans mild green chilies, rinsed and drained

2 slices firm white sandwich bread, toasted and coarsely torn

¼ cup reduced-sodium chicken broth, defatted

¼ cup dark raisins

2 tablespoons slivered blanched almonds

½ teaspoon seeded, chopped pickled jalapeño pepper

½ teaspoon salt

1 tablespoon flour

¼ teaspoon freshly ground black pepper

4 skinless, boneless chicken breast halves (about 1 pound total)

2 teaspoons vegetable oil

Four 6-inch flour tortillas

2 tablespoons thinly sliced scallion

1. Remove a red pepper half, cut into thin strips, and set aside. In a food processor or blender, combine the remaining red peppers, the chilies, bread, broth, 2 tablespoons of the raisins, 1 tablespoon of the almonds, the jalapeño pepper, and ¼ teaspoon of the salt and purée until smooth.

2. On a plate, combine the flour, the remaining ¼ teaspoon salt, and the black pepper. Dredge the chicken in the flour mixture, shaking off the excess. In a large nonstick skillet, heat the oil until hot but not smoking over medium heat. Add the chicken and cook, turning once, until golden brown, about 5 minutes. Add the pepper purée, bring to a boil over medium-high heat, reduce to a simmer, and cover. Cook until the chicken is cooked through, about 8 minutes longer.

3. Meanwhile, preheat the oven to 350°. Wrap the tortillas in foil and heat for 5 minutes, or until the tortillas are heated through.

4. With a slotted spoon, transfer the chicken to a cutting board and cut the chicken into diagonal slices. Place the tortillas on 4 plates and spoon the chicken and sauce on top. Sprinkle with the remaining 2 tablespoons raisins, remaining 1 tablespoon almonds, reserved pepper strips, and scallion and serve.

Suggested accompaniment: Green seedless grapes and sliced kiwi and nectarine garnished with a sprig of watercress.

Fat: 8g/23%
Calories: 319
Saturated Fat: 1.2g
Carbohydrate: 30g
Protein: 31g
Cholesterol: 66mg
Sodium: 663mg

Thickening the sauce with bread is a centuries-old Catalan technique that lends subtle flavor and body without fat.

CHICKEN STIR-FRY WITH BROCCOLI, GARLIC, AND BASIL

SERVES: 4
WORKING TIME: 20 MINUTES
TOTAL TIME: 20 MINUTES

Tomato-vegetable juice adds a rich undertone to this intriguing dish—be sure to keep some on hand since it's a great flavor shortcut. As with all stir-fries, cooking is very quick so it's important to have all the ingredients cut and measured beforehand. Also, remember to cut meats and vegetables into small, uniform pieces to ensure even cooking.

2 teaspoons vegetable oil

1 pound skinless, boneless chicken breasts, cut into 2-inch chunks

3 cloves garlic, minced

¼ cup finely chopped scallions

1 tablespoon minced fresh ginger

3 cups broccoli florets

1 cup peeled, thinly sliced broccoli stems

1 cucumber, halved lengthwise and thinly sliced

1 cup cherry tomatoes

5½-ounce can reduced-sodium tomato-vegetable juice

¾ teaspoon salt

3 tablespoons chopped fresh basil

1. In a large nonstick skillet, heat the oil until hot but not smoking over medium heat. Add the chicken and cook, stirring frequently, until the chicken is no longer pink, about 2 minutes.

2. Add the garlic, scallions, and ginger and cook, stirring constantly, until fragrant, about 30 seconds. Add the broccoli florets and stems, the cucumber, tomatoes, tomato-vegetable juice, and salt. Cook, stirring frequently, until the chicken is cooked through and the broccoli is crisp-tender, about 5 minutes longer.

3. Stir in the basil. Spoon the chicken and vegetables onto 4 plates and serve.

Suggested accompaniments: Steamed white rice, followed by fresh cherries marinated in red wine.

FAT: 4G/18%
CALORIES: 201
SATURATED FAT: .7G
CARBOHYDRATE: 11G
PROTEIN: 30G
CHOLESTEROL: 66MG
SODIUM: 545MG

BUFFALO CHICKEN STRIPS

SERVES: 4
WORKING TIME: 15 MINUTES
TOTAL TIME: 25 MINUTES

½ cup low-fat (1%) milk

½ teaspoon honey

1 pound skinless, boneless chicken breasts, cut into 1-inch-wide strips

1 cup crushed cornflakes (about 2 cups uncrushed)

¼ teaspoon ground ginger

¼ teaspoon dried thyme

¼ teaspoon dried rosemary

1 cup plain nonfat yogurt

2 ounces blue cheese, crumbled

½ cup minced scallions

6 drops hot pepper sauce

2 carrots, cut into sticks

2 ribs celery with leaves, cut into sticks

1. Preheat the oven to 400°. Line a baking sheet with foil and spray with nonstick cooking spray. In a shallow bowl, combine the milk and honey and stir to blend. Add the chicken strips, stir to coat, and let stand for 10 minutes.

2. Meanwhile, on a plate, combine the cornflakes, ginger, thyme, and rosemary. Dip the chicken strips into the cornflake mixture to coat thoroughly, gently pressing cornflakes into the chicken. Place the chicken on the prepared baking sheet and bake for 8 minutes, or until the chicken is crisp, golden, and cooked through.

3. In a medium bowl, combine the yogurt, blue cheese, scallions, and hot pepper sauce and stir to blend. Place the chicken and the carrot and celery sticks on 4 plates and serve with the blue cheese dip.

Suggested accompaniments: Iced herbal tea, and a dessert of raspberry sorbet served with miniature nonfat cookies.

FAT: 6G/15%
CALORIES: 357
SATURATED FAT: 3.3G
CARBOHYDRATE: 37G
PROTEIN: 37G
CHOLESTEROL: 79MG
SODIUM: 716MG

For this popular finger food, we've substituted lean chicken breast for the usual wings and then soaked the strips in low-fat milk and honey for extra tenderness. The creamy base for the dip is nonfat yogurt rather than sour cream. To crush cornflakes, place them in a resealable plastic bag, seal, and run a rolling pin or heavy glass over the bag.

THAI-STYLE CHICKEN AND VEGETABLES

SERVES: 4
WORKING TIME: 25 MINUTES
TOTAL TIME: 25 MINUTES

A finishing flourish of fresh herbs is typically Thai. Here, basil and mint are the last ingredients added to a colorful stir-fry of chicken, squash, and red bell pepper. Garlic, scallions, soy sauce, and chili sauce supply the dish with savory depth; the herbs, along with some just-squeezed lime juice, provide a tantalizing, bright note.

2 tablespoons plus 2 teaspoons cornstarch
¼ teaspoon salt
1 pound skinless, boneless chicken breasts, cut into 1-inch chunks
1 tablespoon olive oil
3 cloves garlic, finely chopped
4 scallions, thinly sliced
1 red bell pepper, cut into 1-inch squares
2 yellow summer squash, halved lengthwise and cut crosswise into ¼-inch-wide slices
¼ cup fresh lime juice
¼ cup chili sauce
2 tablespoons reduced-sodium soy sauce
¾ teaspoon firmly packed brown sugar
⅓ cup chopped fresh basil
¼ cup chopped fresh mint

1. In a sturdy plastic bag, combine 2 tablespoons of the cornstarch and the salt. Add the chicken to the bag, shaking to coat with the cornstarch mixture.

2. In a large nonstick skillet or wok, heat the oil until hot but not smoking over medium heat. Add the chicken and stir-fry until golden brown and just cooked through, about 3 minutes. With a slotted spoon, transfer the chicken to a plate.

3. Add the garlic and scallions to the pan and stir-fry just until fragrant, about 1 minute. Add the bell pepper and stir-fry for 2 minutes. Add the squash and stir-fry until the bell pepper and squash are crisp-tender, about 2 minutes.

4. In a small bowl, combine the lime juice, chili sauce, soy sauce, brown sugar, and the remaining 2 teaspoons cornstarch. Stir the mixture into the skillet and bring to a boil. Return the chicken to the skillet and stir in the basil and mint. Cook, stirring, just until heated through, about 1 minute.

Helpful hint: Coating the chicken (and thickening the sauce) with cornstarch rather than flour gives the sauce a delicate, translucent consistency. Cornstarch is often used for this purpose in Asian cooking.

FAT: 5G/19%
CALORIES: 239
SATURATED FAT: 0.9G
CARBOHYDRATE: 20G
PROTEIN: 29G
CHOLESTEROL: 66MG
SODIUM: 743MG

*T*his recipe is so quick you'll want to start your side dish before putting the turkey under the broiler. Julienned carrots and zucchini, steamed until tender and sprinkled with lemon juice and fresh herbs, are an appetizing partner for the crumb-crusted turkey cutlets. Green beans, asparagus, or broiled tomatoes would partner well, too.

Broiled Turkey Breast Dijonnaise

SERVES: 4
WORKING TIME: 5 MINUTES
TOTAL TIME: 15 MINUTES

3 tablespoons reduced-fat mayonnaise

1 tablespoon Dijon mustard

1 tablespoon fresh lemon juice

½ teaspoon dried sage

½ teaspoon salt

¼ teaspoon freshly ground black pepper

4 turkey cutlets (about 1 pound total)

⅓ cup plain dried bread crumbs

1. Preheat the broiler. In a small bowl, combine the mayonnaise, mustard, lemon juice, sage, salt, and pepper.

2. Spread the mayonnaise mixture over one side of the cutlets. Broil the turkey cutlets, topping-side up, 6 inches from the heat for 4 minutes, or until the cutlets are cooked through. Sprinkle with the bread crumbs and cook for 30 seconds to lightly brown the topping. Place the cutlets on 4 plates and serve.

Helpful hint: You can prepare the mayonnaise mixture up to 1 day in advance and refrigerate it in a covered container until needed.

TIP

Turkey cutlets, available from your butcher or grocery store, are convenient single-portion pieces cut crosswise from a boneless turkey breast half. They usually weigh about 4 ounces each. They may be cooked as is, or pounded like scallopini.

FAT: 4G/18%
CALORIES: 196
SATURATED FAT: 0.7G
CARBOHYDRATE: 9G
PROTEIN: 29G
CHOLESTEROL: 70MG
SODIUM: 586MG

Hot and Tangy Barbecued Chicken with Noodles

Serves: 4
Working time: 15 minutes
Total time: 25 minutes

This wonderfully flavorful chicken gets its sweetness from ketchup and brown sugar, spiciness from hot pepper sauce, and subtle tanginess from mild rice vinegar. Since vegetables figure heavily in this dish and noodles form the base, there really is no need for any accompaniment, except a simple offering for dessert.

⅔ cup low-sodium ketchup

2 tablespoons rice wine vinegar or cider vinegar

2 teaspoons firmly packed dark brown sugar

½ teaspoon ground coriander

4 cups ¼-inch-thick shredded green cabbage

2 carrots, shredded

6 drops hot pepper sauce

4 skinless, boneless chicken breast halves (about 1 pound total)

4 ounces capellini noodles

⅓ cup finely chopped scallions

2 tablespoons chopped fresh cilantro or mint

1. Preheat the broiler or prepare the grill. If using a broiler, line the broiler pan with foil. Start heating a large pot of water to boiling for the noodles.

2. In a large bowl, combine the ketchup, vinegar, brown sugar, and coriander and stir to blend. Remove 3 tablespoons of the ketchup mixture and set aside. Add the cabbage, carrots, hot pepper sauce, and 2 tablespoons of water to the remaining ketchup mixture in the bowl and toss to coat thoroughly.

3. Brush the chicken with the 3 tablespoons ketchup mixture and broil or grill 4 inches from the heat for about 4 minutes per side, or until the chicken is just cooked through.

4. Cook the noodles in the boiling water until just tender. Drain well. Place the noodles on 4 plates and spoon the cabbage mixture and the chicken on top. Sprinkle with the scallions and cilantro and serve.

Suggested accompaniment: Hazelnut coffee with almond biscotti or meringue cookies.

Fat: 2g/6%
Calories: 301
Saturated Fat: .5g
Carbohydrate: 38g
Protein: 32g
Cholesterol: 66mg
Sodium: 405mg

TURKEY WITH CHUNKY HONEY-MUSTARD SAUCE

SERVES: 4
WORKING TIME: 25 MINUTES
TOTAL TIME: 25 MINUTES

We don't know who first thought of mixing honey with mustard, but millions of happy eaters have since enjoyed the combination. We've sharpened the hot-sweet contrast (and given the dish a South-of-the-Border slant) by rubbing the turkey cutlets with chili powder and lime juice. Roasted or oven-fried potatoes would be a tasty accompaniment.

1 tablespoon fresh lime juice
1½ teaspoons chili powder
4 thinly sliced turkey cutlets (about 1 pound total)
2 tablespoons flour
½ teaspoon salt
¼ teaspoon freshly ground black pepper
4 teaspoons olive oil
1 red bell pepper, cut into ½-inch squares
3 scallions, thinly sliced
1 cup frozen corn kernels
⅔ cup reduced-sodium chicken broth, defatted
1 tablespoon honey
1 tablespoon Dijon mustard
2 teaspoons cornstarch mixed with 1 tablespoon water

1. In a small bowl, combine the lime juice and chili powder. Brush the mixture over both sides of the turkey cutlets. On a sheet of waxed paper, combine the flour, salt, and black pepper. Dredge the turkey in the flour mixture, shaking off the excess. In a large non-stick skillet, heat 1 tablespoon of the oil until hot but not smoking over medium heat. Add the turkey and cook until golden brown and just cooked through, about 1 minute per side. With a slotted spoon, transfer the turkey to a plate.

2. Add the remaining 1 teaspoon oil, the bell pepper, and scallions to the skillet and cook, stirring, until crisp-tender, about 4 minutes. Stir in the corn and cook until heated through, about 1 minute.

3. In a small bowl, combine the broth, honey, and mustard. Add the mixture to the pan and bring to a boil. Stir in the cornstarch mixture, return to a boil, and cook, stirring, until slightly thickened, about 1 minute. Reduce to a simmer, return the turkey to the pan, and cook until just heated through, about 1 minute. Divide the turkey among 4 plates, spoon the sauce over, and serve.

Helpful hint: If your market doesn't offer thinly sliced turkey cutlets, pound regular cutlets yourself: Place the cutlets between two sheets of waxed paper and using the flat side of small skillet or a meat pounder, pound the cutlets to a ¼-inch thickness.

FAT: 6G/21%
CALORIES: 257
SATURATED FAT: 0.9G
CARBOHYDRATE: 20G
PROTEIN: 31G
CHOLESTEROL: 70MG
SODIUM: 540MG

For classic veal Milanese, veal scallopini are dipped in whole beaten eggs, coated with bread crumbs and Parmesan, and fried in butter. For this trimmed-down version, chicken breasts are dipped in Parmesan, egg whites, and bread crumbs, then baked in the oven with a mere drizzling of olive oil. Round out the meal with roasted new potatoes and Italian green beans.

CHICKEN MILANESE

SERVES: 4
WORKING TIME: 15 MINUTES
TOTAL TIME: 25 MINUTES

½ cup plain dried bread crumbs

¼ cup grated Parmesan cheese

1 egg white beaten with
1 tablespoon water

4 skinless, boneless chicken breast
halves (about 1 pound total)

2 teaspoons olive oil

⅔ cup dry white wine

½ cup reduced-sodium chicken
broth, defatted

2 tablespoons balsamic vinegar

3 cloves garlic, minced

2 teaspoons anchovy paste

½ teaspoon dried rosemary

1 teaspoon cornstarch mixed
with 1 tablespoon water

2 tablespoons chopped fresh
parsley

1. Preheat the oven to 400°. Line a large baking sheet with foil.

2. Place the bread crumbs, Parmesan, and egg white mixture in 3 shallow bowls. Dip the chicken into the Parmesan (see tip, top photo), then into the egg white (middle photo), and finally into the bread crumbs (bottom photo). Place the chicken on the prepared baking sheet and drizzle with the oil. Bake for 10 minutes, or until the chicken is cooked through and golden brown.

3. Meanwhile, in a large skillet, combine the wine, broth, vinegar, garlic, anchovy paste, and rosemary and bring to a boil over medium heat. Boil, stirring occasionally, until the garlic is tender and the sauce is slightly reduced, about 4 minutes. Stir in the cornstarch mixture and cook, stirring, until slightly thickened, about 1 minute. Add the parsley, stirring to combine. Add the chicken and turn to coat with the sauce. Place the chicken on 4 plates and serve.

Helpful hint: Anchovy paste comes in tubes, making it a convenient way to keep anchovies on hand. Keep the tube tightly capped and store it in the refrigerator. Anchovy paste will keep for 6 months or longer.

FAT: 6G/20%
CALORIES: 268
SATURATED FAT: 1.9G
CARBOHYDRATE: 12G
PROTEIN: 32G
CHOLESTEROL: 71MG
SODIUM: 491MG

T I P

CHICKEN COBB SALAD

SERVES: 4
WORKING TIME: 15 MINUTES
TOTAL TIME: 20 MINUTES

The secret ingredient here is mango chutney, which pairs beautifully with the tart apple. Piquant blue cheese is the Cobb salad signature.

1 pound skinless, boneless chicken breasts

⅔ cup plain nonfat yogurt

3 tablespoons mango chutney

2 tablespoons reduced-fat mayonnaise

1 tablespoon fresh lemon juice

½ teaspoon salt

2 apples, preferably 1 Granny Smith and 1 McIntosh, cored and diced

1 rib celery, finely diced

2 tablespoons minced scallion

12 leaves Boston lettuce

1 ounce blue cheese, crumbled

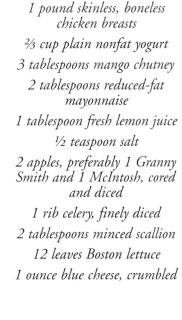

1. Preheat the broiler. Place the chicken on the broiler rack and broil 4 inches from the heat for about 4 minutes per side, or until just cooked through. Transfer the chicken to a cutting board and cut the chicken into ¾-inch chunks.

2. In a large bowl, combine the yogurt, chutney, mayonnaise, lemon juice, and salt and stir to blend. Add the apples, celery, and scallion. Fold in the chicken until well coated.

3. Arrange the lettuce leaves on 4 plates and spoon the chicken salad on top. Sprinkle with the blue cheese and serve.

Suggested accompaniments: Dark pumpernickel bread, and fresh fruit.

FAT: 6G/20%
CALORIES: 268
SATURATED FAT: 2.2G
CARBOHYDRATE: 22G
PROTEIN: 30G
CHOLESTEROL: 74MG
SODIUM: 654MG

ORIENTAL CHICKEN SOUP

SERVES: 4
WORKING TIME: 15 MINUTES
TOTAL TIME: 25 MINUTES

2 cups reduced-sodium chicken broth, defatted

1¼ pounds whole chicken legs, split and skinned

2 cloves garlic, minced

2 red bell peppers, diced

3 tablespoons cider vinegar

1 tablespoon reduced-sodium soy sauce

¾ teaspoon ground ginger

¼ teaspoon salt

3 cups ½-inch-wide shredded cabbage

3 ounces capellini noodles, broken into small pieces

¼ pound snow peas, cut into ½-inch diagonal pieces

2 scallions, finely chopped

¼ pound firm tofu, cut into ½-inch chunks

¼ teaspoon sesame oil

1. In a medium saucepan, combine the broth, 3½ cups of water, chicken, and garlic. Bring to a boil over high heat, reduce to a simmer, cover, and cook until the chicken is cooked through, about 15 minutes. With a slotted spoon, transfer the chicken to a cutting board. Strip the chicken meat from the bones and dice the chicken. Skim the fat from the broth.

2. Return the broth to a boil. Add the bell peppers, vinegar, soy sauce, ginger, and salt and cook for 2 minutes. Stir in the cabbage, capellini, snow peas, scallions, diced chicken, and more water to cover, if necessary. Cook until the capellini is tender, about 2 minutes longer. Stir in the tofu and sesame oil, ladle the soup into 4 bowls, and serve.

Suggested accompaniments: Thin bread sticks, and chilled red and green seedless grapes.

FAT: 7G/23%
CALORIES: 274
SATURATED FAT: 1.2G
CARBOHYDRATE: 27G
PROTEIN: 27G
CHOLESTEROL: 64MG
SODIUM: 693MG

This intriguing noodle soup wonderfully showcases the contrasting textures and tastes characteristic of Oriental cooking.

F*resh-squeezed lemon juice is a deliciously classic seasoning for asparagus. We've turned this delicate spring vegetable into a substantial main dish here by adding chicken, water chestnuts, and a creamy lemon-dill sauce. If you have a handsome skillet or wok, you can bring this dish directly from the stove to the table.*

CHICKEN, ASPARAGUS, AND LEMON CREAM STIR-FRY

SERVES: 4
WORKING TIME: 25 MINUTES
TOTAL TIME: 25 MINUTES

1 pound asparagus, tough ends trimmed (see tip), cut on the diagonal into 2-inch lengths

2 teaspoons olive oil

½ cup finely chopped shallots or scallion whites

1 pound skinless, boneless chicken breasts, cut crosswise into ½-inch-wide strips

½ cup canned sliced water chestnuts, drained

¾ cup reduced-sodium chicken broth, defatted

½ teaspoon grated lemon zest

1 tablespoon fresh lemon juice

1 tablespoon flour

3 tablespoons reduced-fat sour cream

½ teaspoon salt

½ cup snipped fresh dill

1. In a large pot of boiling water, cook the asparagus for 2 minutes to blanch. Drain, rinse under cold water, and drain again.

2. In a large nonstick skillet or wok, heat the oil until hot but not smoking over medium heat. Add the shallots and stir-fry until softened, about 4 minutes. Add the chicken and water chestnuts and stir-fry until the chicken is almost cooked through, about 4 minutes. Stir in the asparagus and stir-fry until just heated through, about 1 minute.

3. In a small jar with a tight-fitting lid, combine the broth, lemon zest, lemon juice, flour, sour cream, and salt and shake until smooth. Add to the skillet and cook, stirring frequently, until slightly thickened, about 2 minutes. Stir in the dill and serve.

Helpful hint: Choose shallots as you do garlic: The cloves should be firm, the skin dry; there should be no green sprouts poking from their tips.

TIP

To prepare asparagus for cooking, hold each spear in your hands and bend it until the stem snaps off; it should break naturally where the woody base merges into the more tender part of the stalk.

FAT: 5G/20%
CALORIES: 225
SATURATED FAT: 1.5G
CARBOHYDRATE: 13G
PROTEIN: 32G
CHOLESTEROL: 70MG
SODIUM: 484MG

CHICKEN WITH CHILI CORN SAUCE

SERVES: 4
WORKING TIME: 15 MINUTES
TOTAL TIME: 25 MINUTES

2 teaspoons medium-hot chili powder

½ teaspoon salt

¼ teaspoon sugar

4 skinless, boneless chicken breast halves (about 1 pound total)

¾ cup reduced-sodium chicken broth, defatted

1 red bell pepper, diced

1 green bell pepper, diced

¾ cup frozen corn kernels

2 tablespoons finely chopped scallion

2 tablespoons fresh lime juice

2 tablespoons light sour cream

1. Preheat the broiler or prepare the grill. In a cup, combine ½ teaspoon of the chili powder, ¼ teaspoon of the salt, and the sugar. Rub the chicken with the chili mixture and let stand while you prepare the chili corn sauce.

2. In a large nonstick skillet, combine the broth, bell peppers, corn, scallion, lime juice, the remaining 1½ teaspoons chili powder, and remaining ¼ teaspoon salt. Bring to a boil over medium-high heat, reduce to a simmer, and cook until the bell peppers are tender and the sauce is slightly thickened, about 7 minutes. Set aside.

3. Broil or grill the chicken 4 inches from the heat for about 4 minutes per side, or until the chicken is just cooked through.

4. Gently rewarm the corn mixture over low heat. Remove from the heat and stir in the sour cream. Place the chicken on 4 plates, spoon the chili corn sauce on top, and serve.

Suggested accompaniments: Grilled French bread. For dessert, applesauce with currants and a dusting of ground nutmeg.

Just a touch of sour cream nicely cools the slightly spicy corn sauce for these chili-rubbed chicken breasts. For easier last-minute preparation, fix the sauce ahead, without the sour cream, and then gently reheat just before serving. Stir in the sour cream off the heat to prevent curdling.

FAT: 3G/14%
CALORIES: 187
SATURATED FAT: .9G
CARBOHYDRATE: 11G
PROTEIN: 29G
CHOLESTEROL: 68MG
SODIUM: 482MG

BROILED ORANGE CHICKEN

SERVES: 4
WORKING TIME: 10 MINUTES
TOTAL TIME: 20 MINUTES

A spice rub and a fruity glaze combine to give these skinless chicken breasts a lovely finish and a fabulous flavor. If you have some extra time, you could intensify the ginger taste by adding a tablespoon of grated fresh ginger to the orange juice mixture. Serve this with a tossed salad, along with rice or roasted potatoes, for a simple, yet elegant meal.

1 teaspoon paprika

1 teaspoon dried tarragon

½ teaspoon ground ginger

4 skinless, boneless chicken breast halves (about 1 pound total)

½ cup orange juice

2 tablespoons red wine vinegar

1 tablespoon firmly packed light brown sugar

½ teaspoon salt

½ teaspoon olive oil

2 cloves garlic, minced

1 green bell pepper, cut into 1-inch squares

1 teaspoon cornstarch mixed with 1 tablespoon water

1. Preheat the broiler. In a small bowl, combine the paprika, tarragon, and ginger. Rub the mixture onto the chicken. Place the chicken on the broiler rack and sprinkle with 2 tablespoons of the orange juice. Broil the chicken 6 inches from the heat, turning once, for 8 minutes, or until just cooked through.

2. Meanwhile, in a medium saucepan, combine the remaining 6 tablespoons orange juice, the vinegar, brown sugar, salt, oil, garlic, and bell pepper. Bring to a boil over medium heat and cook until the bell pepper is crisp-tender, about 2 minutes. Stir in the cornstarch mixture and cook, stirring, until slightly thickened, about 1 minute. Place the chicken on 4 plates, spoon the sauce over, and serve.

Helpful hint: If you have any leftover chicken, use it for sandwiches the next day. Slice the chicken and serve it on French bread with Boston lettuce; add a little chutney, if you have it on hand.

FAT: 2G/11%
CALORIES: 171
SATURATED FAT: 0.5G
CARBOHYDRATE: 10G
PROTEIN: 27G
CHOLESTEROL: 66MG
SODIUM: 350MG

SAUTÉED RED SNAPPER WITH ONION RELISH

SERVES: 4
WORKING TIME: 20 MINUTES
TOTAL TIME: 20 MINUTES

1 red onion, diced

1 red or yellow bell pepper, diced

*6 pimiento-stuffed green olives
(1 ounce), chopped*

2 tablespoons chopped fresh mint

¼ cup fresh lime juice

4 teaspoons honey

1 tablespoon balsamic vinegar

½ teaspoon salt

*4 skinless red snapper fillets
(about 6 ounces each), any
visible bones removed*

1 teaspoon paprika

2 tablespoons flour

1 tablespoon olive oil

1. In a small bowl, combine the onion and ice water to cover. In a medium bowl, combine the bell pepper, olives, mint, 3 tablespoons of the lime juice, the honey, vinegar, and ¼ teaspoon of the salt. Set both bowls aside while you prepare the fish.

2. Sprinkle both sides of the snapper with the remaining 1 tablespoon lime juice, the paprika, and the remaining ¼ teaspoon salt. Place the flour on a sheet of waxed paper. Dredge the fillets in the flour, shaking off the excess.

3. In a large nonstick skillet, heat the oil until hot but not smoking over medium heat. Add the snapper and cook until lightly browned and just cooked through, about 2 minutes per side.

4. Meanwhile, drain the onion, pat dry, and add to the bowl with the bell pepper mixture; stir to combine. Serve the snapper with the relish.

Helpful hints: Brief soaking in ice water tames the onion's bite—a point to remember whenever you're using raw onions for salads or sandwiches. You can substitute any firm-fleshed white fish, such as striped bass or sole, for the red snapper, if you like.

FAT: 7G/23%
CALORIES: 273
SATURATED FAT: 1G
CARBOHYDRATE: 16G
PROTEIN: 36G
CHOLESTEROL: 63MG
SODIUM: 558MG

When you're sautéing fish fillets, it helps to dredge them in flour—otherwise it's all too easy for the fish to stick to the pan. A dusting of flour also produces just a suggestion of a crisp crust, which offers a pleasing contrast to the tender fish. These meaty snapper fillets are topped with a sweet-and-tangy relish of diced bell pepper, onion, and green olives.

ASIAN CHICKEN AND VEGETABLE SALAD

SERVES: 4
WORKING TIME: 15 MINUTES
TOTAL TIME: 25 MINUTES

*F*ast-food restaurants offer an approximation of this Asian-style salad, but those can't compare with this homemade version. Our salad boasts thick, tender slices of sesame-soy-basted chicken breasts, fresh bell peppers, sugar snap peas, and crisp-tender turnip wedges—all tossed with greens, scallions, and a light, tangy dressing. A basket of bakery-fresh rolls rounds out the meal.

3 tablespoons reduced-sodium soy sauce

2 tablespoons firmly packed light brown sugar

2 tablespoons rice vinegar or cider vinegar

2 teaspoons dark Oriental sesame oil

2 teaspoons Dijon mustard

½ teaspoon ground ginger

1 pound skinless, boneless chicken breasts

1 turnip, peeled and cut into 16 wedges

2 red bell peppers, cut into thin strips

½ pound sugar snap peas

3 scallions, cut into julienne strips

4 cups torn Boston lettuce

1. Preheat the broiler. In a large bowl, combine the soy sauce, brown sugar, vinegar, sesame oil, mustard, and ginger. Coat the chicken with 2 tablespoons of the soy mixture. Broil the chicken 6 inches from the heat, turning once, for 8 minutes, or until browned and cooked through. Let the chicken cool slightly, then cut crosswise into ½-inch-wide strips. Set aside.

2. Meanwhile, in a large pot of boiling water, cook the turnip for 2 minutes. Add the bell peppers and sugar snap peas and cook for 30 seconds to blanch. Drain well. Transfer the vegetables to the soy sauce mixture remaining in the large bowl. Add the chicken, scallions, and lettuce, tossing well to combine. Divide the salad among 4 bowls and serve warm or at room temperature.

Helpful hint: Sugar snap peas are edible, pod and all, but you do need to stem and string them before cooking. Using your fingers, snap off the stem and use it to pull the string off the pod. It's a classic kitchen job for helpful kids.

FAT: 4G/15%
CALORIES: 245
SATURATED FAT: 0.7G
CARBOHYDRATE: 22G
PROTEIN: 30G
CHOLESTEROL: 66MG
SODIUM: 672MG

SALSA-MARINATED CHICKEN

SERVES: 4
WORKING TIME: 15 MINUTES
TOTAL TIME: 20 MINUTES

This recipe is a good example of how an already excellent store-bought product can become "homemade" with a few simple touches. Jarred salsa is mixed with tomato paste for a no-cook poultry marinade. Then, by adding corn and bell pepper for texture, and lime juice and cilantro for zing, we've created a full-flavored vegetable salsa to serve on the side.

1½ cups good-quality prepared salsa

2 tablespoons no-salt-added tomato paste

4 skinless, boneless chicken breast halves (about 1 pound total)

1 green bell pepper, cut into thin strips

⅔ cup frozen corn kernels, thawed

3 tablespoons finely chopped scallion

2 tablespoons fresh lime juice

2 tablespoons chopped fresh cilantro or parsley

1. Preheat the broiler or prepare the grill. In a shallow bowl, combine ½ cup of the salsa and the tomato paste and stir to blend. Add the chicken, turn to coat, and let stand while you prepare the vegetable salsa.

2. In a medium bowl, combine the remaining 1 cup salsa, the bell pepper, corn, scallion, lime juice, and cilantro.

3. Broil or grill the chicken 4 inches from the heat for about 4 minutes per side, or until the chicken is just cooked through. Place the chicken on 4 plates, spoon the vegetable salsa on the side, and serve.

Suggested accompaniments: Mixed greens with diced avocado sprinkled with a balsamic vinaigrette. For dessert, reduced-calorie vanilla pudding dusted with unsweetened cocoa powder.

FAT: 2G/10%
CALORIES: 182
SATURATED FAT: .4G
CARBOHYDRATE: 14G
PROTEIN: 27G
CHOLESTEROL: 66MG
SODIUM: 530MG

*T*he enticing colors are just the beginning of this stir-fry's appeal, which includes the crunch of water chestnuts and lightly cooked bell peppers and snow peas, sharply underscored with the fresh tastes of ginger and orange. Teriyaki sauce, available in the Oriental foods section of the supermarket, gives the chicken a tasty glaze.

STIR-FRIED CHICKEN WITH PEPPERS AND SNOW PEAS

SERVES: 4
WORKING TIME: 20 MINUTES
TOTAL TIME: 20 MINUTES

2 teaspoons Oriental sesame oil

1 pound skinless, boneless
chicken breasts, cut into
½-inch-wide strips

1 large onion, halved and cut
into thin strips

1 red bell pepper, cut into
½-inch strips

1 green bell pepper, cut into
½-inch strips

3 cloves garlic, minced

2 strips orange zest, each about
3 inches long

1 tablespoon minced fresh
ginger

½ teaspoon salt

½ pound snow peas, trimmed
and cut diagonally in half
(see tip)

8-ounce can sliced water
chestnuts, rinsed and drained

2 teaspoons teriyaki sauce

1. In a large nonstick skillet, heat the oil until hot but not smoking
   over medium heat. Add the chicken and cook, stirring frequently,
   for 2 minutes. Add the onion, bell peppers, garlic, orange zest,
   ginger, and salt and cook, stirring frequently, until the chicken is
   lightly browned, about 3 minutes.

2. Stir in the snow peas, water chestnuts, teriyaki sauce, and 3 tablespoons of water. Increase the heat to high and cook, stirring frequently, until the chicken is cooked through and the vegetables
   are crisp-tender, about 3 minutes longer. Spoon the chicken and
   vegetables onto 4 plates and serve.

Suggested accompaniments: Steamed brown rice, and fresh kumquats.

TIP

*To prepare snow peas for
cooking, trim the stem end
and pull off the string
along the straight side. For
best results, cook snow peas
just until they are crisp-
tender and a vibrant
green.*

FAT: 4G/16%
CALORIES: 231
SATURATED FAT: .7G
CARBOHYDRATE: 19G
PROTEIN: 29G
CHOLESTEROL: 66MG
SODIUM: 472MG

STIR-FRIED SWORDFISH TERIYAKI

SERVES: 4
WORKING TIME: 25 MINUTES
TOTAL TIME: 25 MINUTES

*T*eriyaki marinade, a lightly sweetened mixture of wine and soy sauce, flavors the fish and vegetables in this delectable stir-fry.

1 cup long-grain rice
¼ teaspoon salt
¼ cup dry white wine or dry sherry
3 tablespoons reduced-sodium soy sauce
2 tablespoons fresh lemon juice
1 tablespoon firmly packed light brown sugar
1 teaspoon cornstarch
1 tablespoon dark Oriental sesame oil
4 scallions, cut into 1-inch lengths
2 cloves garlic, finely chopped
1 tablespoon finely chopped fresh ginger
2 cups mushrooms, halved
1 large carrot, cut into 2-by-⅛-inch julienne strips
1 pound swordfish steaks, skinned and cut into 1-inch chunks
¼ pound snow peas, cut lengthwise into thin strips

1. In a medium saucepan, bring 2¼ cups of water to a boil. Add the rice and salt, reduce to a simmer, cover, and cook until the rice is tender, about 17 minutes.

2. Meanwhile, in a small bowl, combine the wine, soy sauce, lemon juice, brown sugar, and cornstarch. In a large nonstick skillet or wok, heat the oil until hot but not smoking over medium heat. Add the scallions, garlic, and ginger and stir-fry until the scallions are softened, about 2 minutes. Add the mushrooms and carrot and stir-fry until the carrot is crisp-tender, about 4 minutes.

3. Add the swordfish to the skillet and stir-fry until almost opaque throughout, about 3 minutes. Stir the soy mixture to recombine and add to the skillet along with the snow peas. Cook, stirring, until the swordfish is cooked through and the snow peas are crisp-tender, about 1 minute. Divide the rice among 4 plates, spoon the swordfish over, and serve.

Helpful hint: You can make the teriyaki sauce up to 12 hours in advance; store it in a covered jar in the refrigerator and shake it before adding it to the skillet.

FAT: 8G/18%
CALORIES: 395
SATURATED FAT: 1.7G
CARBOHYDRATE: 51G
PROTEIN: 26G
CHOLESTEROL: 39MG
SODIUM: 695MG

RED SNAPPER WITH CHILI-CORN SALSA

SERVES: 4
WORKING TIME: 20 MINUTES
TOTAL TIME: 25 MINUTES

2 teaspoons chili powder

1 teaspoon ground cumin

1 teaspoon ground coriander

½ teaspoon salt

1½ cups frozen corn kernels, thawed

1 tomato, diced

3 scallions, thinly sliced

1 pickled jalapeño pepper, seeded and finely chopped

2 tablespoons balsamic or red wine vinegar

4 skinless red snapper fillets (about 6 ounces each), any visible bones removed

2 tablespoons flour

1 tablespoon olive oil

1. In a medium bowl, combine the chili powder, cumin, coriander, and salt. Remove 2 teaspoons of the mixture and set aside. Stir the corn, tomato, scallions, jalapeño, and vinegar into the mixture remaining in the bowl.

2. Rub the reserved spice mixture onto both sides of the red snapper fillets. Place the flour on a sheet of waxed paper. Dredge the snapper in the flour, shaking off the excess. In a large nonstick skillet, heat the oil until hot but not smoking over medium heat. Add the snapper and cook until lightly browned and just opaque, about 3 minutes per side. Divide the snapper among 4 plates, spoon the salsa over, and serve.

Helpful hints: You can substitute any firm-fleshed white fish, such as flounder or sole, for the red snapper. If you like the blend of chili powder, cumin, and coriander, try mixing up some extra to rub on chicken breasts, turkey cutlets, and other meats and poultry before sautéing, broiling, or grilling.

FAT: 7G/22%
CALORIES: 286
SATURATED FAT: 1G
CARBOHYDRATE: 19G
PROTEIN: 38G
CHOLESTEROL: 63MG
SODIUM: 458MG

Toss a salad to serve with this zesty Mexican-style dish. The snapper is rubbed with chili, cumin, and coriander.

FETA-TOPPED BROILED CHICKEN

SERVES: 4
WORKING TIME: 10 MINUTES
TOTAL TIME: 20 MINUTES

Inspired by Mediterranean flavors and topped with sliced ripe tomato and tangy feta cheese, this dish is sure to please. For accompaniments, we suggest herbed orzo, a rice-shaped pasta with an almost creamy texture when cooked, and a cooling salad of red leaf lettuce, sliced cucumbers, and tomatoes.

2 tablespoons no-salt-added tomato paste
1 teaspoon red wine vinegar
½ teaspoon dried rosemary
½ teaspoon dried oregano
½ teaspoon paprika
½ teaspoon salt
¼ teaspoon freshly ground black pepper
4 skinless, boneless chicken breast halves (about 1 pound total)
1 tomato, halved and thinly sliced
½ cup crumbled feta cheese (2 ounces)

1. In a small bowl, stir together the tomato paste, vinegar, rosemary, oregano, paprika, salt, and pepper. Rub the mixture onto the chicken breasts and set aside.

2. Preheat the broiler. Broil the chicken 6 inches from the heat, turning once, for 6 minutes. Top the chicken with the tomato slices and broil for 1 minute. Top with the feta and broil for 1 minute, or until the cheese is melted and the chicken is cooked through. Place the chicken breasts on 4 plates and serve.

Helpful hint: Instead of the feta, you can use goat cheese or, for a milder flavor, shredded Monterey jack.

FAT: 5G/23%
CALORIES: 178
SATURATED FAT: 2.5G
CARBOHYDRATE: 4G
PROTEIN: 29G
CHOLESTEROL: 78MG
SODIUM: 514MG

SPRING VEGETABLE SALAD

SERVES: 4
WORKING TIME: 10 MINUTES
TOTAL TIME: 25 MINUTES

A favorite side dish, this deftly streamlined salad makes a hearty meatless main course when chick-peas are added for protein. In addition, sweet baby carrots, sugar snap peas, green beans, and spinach transform a simple potato salad into something quite special. The Russian dressing is made with nonfat yogurt and reduced-fat mayonnaise, and flavored with tarragon.

1½ pounds small red potatoes, quartered

½ teaspoon salt

2 cups peeled baby carrots

½ pound green beans

½ pound sugar snap peas

½ cup plain nonfat yogurt

3 tablespoons reduced-fat mayonnaise

3 tablespoons ketchup

2 tablespoons fresh lemon juice

½ teaspoon dried tarragon

19-ounce can chick-peas, rinsed and drained

10-ounce bag cleaned spinach, torn

1. In a large pot of boiling water, cook the potatoes with ¼ teaspoon of the salt until almost tender, about 10 minutes. Add the carrots and cook for 2 minutes. Add the green beans and cook for 2 minutes. Add the sugar snap peas and cook for 30 seconds. All of the vegetables should be just barely tender. Drain well.

2. Meanwhile, in a large bowl, combine the yogurt, mayonnaise, ketchup, lemon juice, tarragon, and the remaining ¼ teaspoon salt. Add the drained vegetables and chick-peas, tossing to coat with the dressing. Add the spinach, toss again, and serve.

Helpful hint: Sugar snap peas become more widely available every year; however, if you can't get them (they do have a short season), substitute fresh snow peas.

FAT: 5G/12%
CALORIES: 377
SATURATED FAT: 0.6G
CARBOHYDRATE: 71G
PROTEIN: 15G
CHOLESTEROL: 1MG
SODIUM: 818MG

CHICKEN DIJONNAISE

SERVES: 4
WORKING TIME: 15 MINUTES
TOTAL TIME: 20 MINUTES

The zesty honey-mustard glaze enhances the delicate taste of this chicken, and the cucumber and sweet red pepper relish provides a refreshingly light accent. If you're using a grill, there's no need to heat up the kitchen on a sultry summer evening—all the cooking is done outside.

3 tablespoons Dijon mustard

2 tablespoons honey

4 teaspoons cider vinegar

½ cup finely diced cucumber

½ cup finely diced red bell pepper

½ cup finely diced tomato

3 tablespoons finely chopped scallion

⅛ teaspoon freshly ground black pepper

4 skinless, boneless chicken breast halves (about 1 pound total)

1. Preheat the broiler or prepare the grill. In a 1-cup measure, combine the mustard, honey, and vinegar and stir to blend. Transfer ¼ cup of the honey-mustard mixture to a medium bowl and set aside the remaining mixture.

2. Add the cucumber, bell pepper, tomato, scallion, and black pepper to the ¼ cup honey-mustard mixture and toss to coat.

3. Brush the chicken with the reserved honey-mustard mixture and broil or grill 4 inches from the heat for about 4 minutes per side, or until the chicken is just cooked through. Place the chicken on 4 plates, spoon the cucumber-bell pepper relish on top, and serve.

Suggested accompaniments: Tossed salad with radicchio, cherry tomatoes, and a red wine vinaigrette. For dessert, apple slices sautéed with cranberries and brown sugar.

FAT: 2G/10%
CALORIES: 186
SATURATED FAT: .4G
CARBOHYDRATE: 14G
PROTEIN: 27G
CHOLESTEROL: 66MG
SODIUM: 417MG

BROILED SWORDFISH WITH SPICY HONEY SAUCE

SERVES: 4
WORKING TIME: 10 MINUTES
TOTAL TIME: 15 MINUTES

½ teaspoon grated lemon zest

¼ cup fresh lemon juice

¼ cup honey

1 teaspoon turmeric

¾ teaspoon ground cumin

½ teaspoon ground ginger

½ teaspoon salt

½ teaspoon hot pepper sauce

Four swordfish steaks (about 1½ pounds total)

1 small red bell pepper, finely diced

2 tablespoons chopped fresh parsley

1. Preheat the broiler. In a small bowl, combine the lemon zest, lemon juice, honey, turmeric, cumin, ginger, salt, and hot pepper sauce.

2. Place the swordfish on the rack and sprinkle with 2 tablespoons of the lemon-honey mixture. Broil the swordfish 6 inches from the heat, turning once, for 6 minutes, or until lightly colored and just opaque. Stir the bell pepper and parsley into the remaining honey-lemon mixture. Divide the fish among 4 plates, spoon the sauce over the fish, and serve.

Helpful hint: Depending on the fish's diet, swordfish flesh when raw can vary from pale beige to rosy pink; whatever its original shade, it will turn a cream color when cooked.

FAT: 6G/21%
CALORIES: 261
SATURATED FAT: 1.7G
CARBOHYDRATE: 21G
PROTEIN: 31G
CHOLESTEROL: 59MG
SODIUM: 430MG

A welcome change from steak, swordfish is just as meaty and satisfying. Turmeric in the honey-lemon basting sauce turns the fish a lovely golden color. As a side dish, lightly sauté some pre-shredded coleslaw mix, then toss it with a light, tangy rice-vinegar dressing—or serve store-bought slaw if you're pressed for time.

HAWAIIAN CHICKEN STIR-FRY

SERVES: 4
WORKING TIME: 25 MINUTES
TOTAL TIME: 25 MINUTES

In Hawaii, this flavor-packed stir-fry would be prepared with fresh pineapple, rather than canned. You can use whichever you prefer. The fruit provides a delightful counterpoint to the garlicky, slightly hot chicken; bell peppers give the stir-fry a tasty crunch. All you need to complete this meal is a simple green salad and a basket of crusty rolls.

1 tablespoon olive oil
4 scallions, thinly sliced
2 cloves garlic, finely chopped
1 pound skinless, boneless chicken breasts, cut into 1-inch chunks
¾ teaspoon ground ginger
½ teaspoon salt
⅛ teaspoon cayenne pepper
1 red bell pepper, cut into thin strips
1 green bell pepper, cut into thin strips
20-ounce can juice-packed pineapple chunks, drained, juice reserved
1 tablespoon honey
1 tablespoon red wine vinegar
2 teaspoons cornstarch mixed with 1 tablespoon water

1. In a large nonstick skillet or wok, heat the oil until hot but not smoking over medium heat. Add the scallions and garlic and stir-fry until fragrant, about 1 minute. Add the chicken and sprinkle with the ginger, salt, and cayenne. Stir-fry until the chicken is golden brown, about 3 minutes. Add the bell peppers and stir-fry until the peppers are crisp-tender, about 3 minutes. Stir in the pineapple.

2. In a small bowl, combine ½ cup of the reserved pineapple juice, the honey, and vinegar. Add the juice mixture to the skillet and bring to a boil. Stir in the cornstarch mixture, return to a boil, and cook, stirring, until the sauce is slightly thickened and the chicken is cooked through, about 1 minute. Divide among 4 plates and serve.

Helpful hint: If you'd like to serve this stir-fry with rice, put the water for the rice on to boil before you heat the oil for the stir-fry to be sure it will be ready at serving time.

FAT: 5G/16%
CALORIES: 280
SATURATED FAT: 0.8G
CARBOHYDRATE: 32G
PROTEIN: 28G
CHOLESTEROL: 66MG
SODIUM: 352MG

SAUTÉED CHICKEN WITH TANGY TOMATO SAUCE

SERVES: 4
WORKING TIME: 15 MINUTES
TOTAL TIME: 25 MINUTES

It doesn't take a lot of time to make a scintillating entrée like this one: Beautifully browned chicken breasts and bright bell pepper strips are simmered in a richly herbed tomato sauce— red wine vinegar gives it a nice bite. Serve the chicken with crisp-tender green beans or steamed asparagus.

2 tablespoons flour
½ teaspoon salt
½ teaspoon freshly ground black pepper
4 skinless, boneless chicken breast halves (about 1 pound total)
2 teaspoons olive oil
3 scallions, thinly sliced
2 cloves garlic, minced
¼ cup red wine vinegar
⅔ cup reduced-sodium chicken broth, defatted
1 tomato, coarsely chopped
2 tablespoons no-salt-added tomato paste
1 yellow bell pepper, cut into ½-inch-wide strips
½ teaspoon dried thyme
¼ teaspoon dried rosemary

1. On a sheet of waxed paper, combine the flour, ¼ teaspoon of the salt, and ¼ teaspoon of the black pepper. Dredge the chicken in the flour mixture, shaking off the excess. In a large nonstick skillet, heat the oil until hot but not smoking over medium heat. Add the chicken and cook until golden brown, about 2 minutes per side. Transfer the chicken to a plate. Set aside.

2. Add the scallions and garlic to the pan and cook until the scallions are wilted, about 1 minute. Add the vinegar, increase the heat to high, and cook until slightly evaporated, about 1 minute. Add the broth, tomato, tomato paste, bell pepper, thyme, rosemary, the remaining ¼ teaspoon salt, and remaining ¼ teaspoon black pepper. Bring to a boil, add the chicken, reduce to a simmer, cover, and cook until the chicken is cooked through, about 8 minutes. Divide the chicken and sauce among 4 bowls and serve.

Helpful hint: If you have any leftovers, slice the chicken and reheat it in the sauce over low heat (add a little water if the sauce has thickened). Pile the chicken on hefty slices of Italian bread, top with the sauce, and enjoy tasty open-face chicken sandwiches.

FAT: 4G/19%
CALORIES: 189
SATURATED FAT: 0.7G
CARBOHYDRATE: 9G
PROTEIN: 28G
CHOLESTEROL: 66MG
SODIUM: 466MG

CARIBBEAN PORK WITH PINEAPPLE SALSA

SERVES: 4
WORKING TIME: 20 MINUTES
TOTAL TIME: 20 MINUTES

*G*ive traditional Tex-Mex salsa the evening off: It's time for something more exotic. These succulent pork cutlets are lavished with a most original tropical salsa made with pineapple, tomato, lime juice, and cilantro. To complement the sweetness of the salsa, accompany the chops with sweet potato slices that have been parboiled, then quickly sautéed.

Two 8-ounce cans juice-packed pineapple chunks, drained and coarsely chopped

1 red onion, finely chopped

1 tomato, chopped

¼ cup fresh lime juice

¼ cup chopped fresh cilantro or parsley

2 tablespoons honey

1 pound well-trimmed boneless pork chops

1 teaspoon paprika

1 teaspoon ground ginger

1 teaspoon ground allspice

1 teaspoon cinnamon

¾ teaspoon salt

2 teaspoons vegetable oil

1. In a medium bowl, combine the pineapple, onion, tomato, lime juice, cilantro, and honey. Set aside.

2. Place the pork between 2 sheets of waxed paper and, with the flat side of a small skillet or meat pounder, pound the pork to a ⅛-inch thickness. In a sturdy plastic bag, combine the paprika, ginger, allspice, cinnamon, and salt. Add the pork to the bag, tossing to coat.

3. In a large nonstick skillet, heat the oil until hot but not smoking over medium heat. Add the pork cutlets and cook until browned and cooked through, about 3 minutes per side. Divide the pork cutlets among 4 plates and serve with the pineapple salsa.

Helpful hint: Allspice is not a blend of spices, as many people think. It's the dried berry of a tree that grows in Jamaica and other tropical countries. If you don't have allspice on hand, you can substitute ¼ teaspoon ground cloves and ½ teaspoon ground nutmeg for a similar flavor.

FAT: 9G/26%
CALORIES: 317
SATURATED FAT: 2.5G
CARBOHYDRATE: 35G
PROTEIN: 26G
CHOLESTEROL: 67MG
SODIUM: 481MG

CHICKEN WITH PLUM TOMATO SALSA

SERVES: 4
WORKING TIME: 15 MINUTES
TOTAL TIME: 20 MINUTES

The flavors of several aromatic herbs and spices shine through: cilantro, cumin, and coriander. Both the salsa and chicken can be made up to eight hours ahead and stored separately in the refrigerator. You could also serve the salsa with broiled or grilled fish such as salmon or tuna, or mix it with low-fat cottage cheese for a zesty snack.

½ teaspoon dried oregano
¼ teaspoon ground cumin
¼ teaspoon ground coriander
½ teaspoon salt
4 skinless, boneless chicken breast halves (about 1 pound total)
2 teaspoons olive oil
¾ pound plum tomatoes (about 3), coarsely chopped
½ cup peeled, seeded, and diced cucumber
3 tablespoons chopped fresh cilantro or parsley
2 tablespoons red wine vinegar
⅛ teaspoon cayenne pepper

1. Preheat the broiler or prepare the grill. In a cup, combine the oregano, cumin, coriander, and ¼ teaspoon of the salt. Rub the chicken with the spice mixture, drizzle with the oil, and let stand while you prepare the plum tomato salsa.

2. In a medium bowl, combine the tomatoes, cucumber, cilantro, vinegar, the remaining ¼ teaspoon salt, and the cayenne pepper.

3. Broil or grill the chicken 4 inches from the heat for about 4 minutes per side, or until the chicken is just cooked through. Place the chicken on 4 plates, spoon the plum tomato salsa on top, and serve.

Suggested accompaniments: Couscous with a sprinkling of toasted pine nuts. For dessert, cubed cantaloupe or honeydew melon tossed with lime juice and dusted with crushed amaretti cookies.

FAT: 4G/21%
CALORIES: 173
SATURATED FAT: .7G
CARBOHYDRATE: 6G
PROTEIN: 27G
CHOLESTEROL: 66MG
SODIUM: 360MG

GRILLED CHICKEN WITH PARSLEY PESTO

SERVES: 4
WORKING TIME: 15 MINUTES
TOTAL TIME: 25 MINUTES

*T*he pesto served on top of this mouth-watering chicken is loaded with flavor, yet it has almost no fat. Serve with a green salad.

3 tablespoons reduced-sodium soy sauce

2 tablespoons honey

2 cloves garlic, minced

½ teaspoon ground ginger

¼ teaspoon cinnamon

¼ teaspoon red pepper flakes

4 skinless, boneless chicken breast halves (about 1 pound total)

1 cup fresh parsley leaves

⅓ cup reduced-sodium chicken broth, defatted

1 slice (1 ounce) white sandwich bread, torn into small pieces

1. In a small bowl, stir together 2 tablespoons of the soy sauce, 1 tablespoon of the honey, the garlic, ¼ teaspoon of the ginger, the cinnamon, and red pepper flakes. Rub the mixture onto the chicken breasts and set aside.

2. Preheat the broiler or prepare the grill. Broil or grill the chicken 6 inches from the heat, turning once, for 8 minutes, or until cooked through.

3. Meanwhile, in a food processor or blender, combine the parsley, broth, bread, the remaining ¼ teaspoon ginger, remaining 1 tablespoon soy sauce, and remaining 1 tablespoon honey. Process until smooth. Place the chicken on 4 plates, spoon the pesto over, and serve.

Helpful hints: You can make the pesto earlier in the day, or even the day before. Just bring it to room temperature before spooning over the chicken. You can also use a dollop of it to spice up steamed vegetables.

FAT: 2G/8%
CALORIES: 193
SATURATED FAT: 0.4G
CARBOHYDRATE: 15G
PROTEIN: 28G
CHOLESTEROL: 66MG
SODIUM: 622MG

Creamy Sole with Potatoes and Mushrooms

Serves: 4
Working time: 15 minutes
Total time: 25 minutes

1 baking potato, peeled and thinly sliced

½ teaspoon dried marjoram

½ teaspoon paprika

4 sole or flounder fillets, any visible bones removed (about 1½ pounds total)

2 teaspoons olive oil

2 cloves garlic, slivered

½ pound mushrooms, trimmed and thinly sliced

1 cup reduced-sodium chicken broth, defatted

½ teaspoon salt

2 tablespoons flour

⅔ cup evaporated low-fat milk

6 tablespoons shredded Cheddar cheese (1½ ounces)

1. In a medium pot of boiling water, cook the potato until almost tender, about 5 minutes. Drain well. Meanwhile, sprinkle the marjoram and paprika over the sole fillets and roll the fillets up. Set aside.

2. In a large nonstick skillet, heat the oil until hot but not smoking over medium heat. Add the garlic and mushrooms and cook until the mushrooms are almost tender, about 4 minutes.

3. Stir in the potato slices, broth, and salt and bring to a boil. Whisk in the flour and evaporated milk and return to a boil. Reduce the heat to a simmer, place the fish on top of the vegetables, cover, and cook until the fish rolls are just opaque in the center, about 7 minutes. Sprinkle the cheese over the fish and cook, uncovered, until just melted, about 1 minute. Divide the fish rolls and potato mixture among 4 plates and serve.

Helpful hint: If you're in a real hurry, you can buy sliced mushrooms from a supermarket salad bar, but don't buy them more than a day in advance or they'll turn dark brown.

Fat: 9g/25%
Calories: 323
Saturated Fat: 3.1g
Carbohydrate: 18g
Protein: 41g
Cholesterol: 100mg
Sodium: 687mg

Here's a wonderfully soothing meal of skillet-scalloped potatoes, herbed steamed fish, and a cheese topping.

EAST-WEST CHICKEN STIR-FRY

SERVES: 4
WORKING TIME: 20 MINUTES
TOTAL TIME: 20 MINUTES

or this stir-fry, the pepperiness of watercress, a typical Western ingredient, blends delightfully with the crispness of the water chestnuts, while hot pepper sauce adds just enough heat. Oriental sesame oil, with a deep nutty taste, is used sparingly as a flavor accent.

1 teaspoon Oriental sesame oil

2 red bell peppers, diced

¼ pound mushrooms, cut into quarters

1 pound skinless, boneless chicken breasts, cut into 2-inch chunks

3 cloves garlic, minced

½ cup thinly sliced scallions

2 cups watercress, thick stems trimmed

⅔ cup sliced water chestnuts, rinsed and drained

6 drops hot pepper sauce

½ teaspoon salt

1. In a large nonstick skillet, heat the oil until hot but not smoking over medium heat. Add the bell peppers and mushrooms and cook, stirring frequently, until the vegetables begin to soften, about 2 minutes. Add the chicken and cook, stirring frequently, until the chicken is lightly browned and almost cooked through, about 5 minutes.

2. Stir in the garlic and scallions and cook, stirring frequently, until fragrant, about 1 minute. Add the watercress, water chestnuts, pepper sauce, and salt and stir to coat thoroughly. Cover and cook until the chicken is cooked through and the watercress has wilted, about 2 minutes longer. Spoon the chicken and vegetables onto 4 plates and serve.

Suggested accompaniments: Jasmine tea and thin noodles. For dessert, fresh pineapple wedges sprinkled with brown sugar and broiled.

FAT: 3G/14%
CALORIES: 190
SATURATED FAT: .5G
CARBOHYDRATE: 13G
PROTEIN: 28G
CHOLESTEROL: 66MG
SODIUM: 367MG

TANDOORI CHICKEN

SERVES: 4
WORKING TIME: 15 MINUTES
TOTAL TIME: 25 MINUTES

2 teaspoons curry powder

1 teaspoon turmeric

1 teaspoon paprika

¾ teaspoon ground ginger

½ teaspoon salt

¼ teaspoon freshly ground black pepper

1 tablespoon fresh lemon juice

1 tablespoon plus 1 teaspoon honey

1 cup plain nonfat yogurt

1 red bell pepper, finely chopped

2 scallions, thinly sliced

3 tablespoons chopped dried apricots

4 skinless, boneless chicken breast halves (about 1 pound total)

1. In a large bowl, stir together the curry powder, turmeric, paprika, ginger, salt, and black pepper. Stir in the lemon juice and 1 tablespoon of the honey until well combined. Remove 1 tablespoon of the mixture and set aside.

2. Add the yogurt, the remaining 1 teaspoon honey, and all but 1 tablespoon each of the bell pepper, scallions, and apricots to the remaining spice mixture, stirring to combine. Refrigerate the yogurt sauce while you cook the chicken.

3. Preheat the broiler or prepare the grill. Brush the chicken with the reserved spice mixture and broil or grill 6 inches from the heat, turning once, for 8 minutes, or until cooked through and golden brown. Cut the chicken into thin diagonal slices, and divide among 4 plates. Top the chicken slices with yogurt sauce, sprinkle with the reserved bell pepper, scallions, and apricots, and serve.

Helpful hints: For an even more intense flavor, rub the marinade on the chicken up to 8 hours in advance. You can also prepare the yogurt mixture up to 1 day ahead.

FAT: 2G/8%
CALORIES: 203
SATURATED FAT: 0.5G
CARBOHYDRATE: 16G
PROTEIN: 30G
CHOLESTEROL: 67MG
SODIUM: 394MG

*A*s *you will note, this dish takes practically no time at all to prepare. Yet in spite of this apparent simplicity, the results are deliciously complex—the fragrant spiciness of curry, paprika, and ground ginger is sweetly tempered with honey. For a complete meal, spoon a mound of fluffy white rice on the plate next to the chicken.*

GRILLED BEEF SALAD

SERVES: 4
WORKING TIME: 15 MINUTES
TOTAL TIME: 25 MINUTES

Here's an ideal summertime supper: If you like, you can grill it outdoors over medium heat and never turn on the stove. Ready-shredded cabbage speeds the preparation of the slaw, which is tangy with apple juice, lime juice, hot pepper sauce, and more. Offer a basket of dinner rolls or soft bread sticks with this delightful warm-weather meal.

¼ cup raisins
½ cup boiling water
¼ cup fresh lime juice
3 tablespoons reduced-sodium soy sauce
½ teaspoon dried mint
1 pound well-trimmed top round steak
⅓ cup apple juice
1 tablespoon honey
½ teaspoon celery seed
¼ teaspoon salt
¼ teaspoon hot pepper sauce
4 cups packaged shredded cabbage
1 cup shredded carrots

1. In a small bowl, combine the raisins and boiling water. Set aside to soften.

2. In a medium bowl, combine the lime juice, soy sauce, and mint. Place the steak on a plate. Measure out 3 tablespoons of the lime juice mixture, spoon over the steak, and turn to coat the steak on both sides with the marinade. Set aside to marinate while you make the rest of the salad and preheat the broiler.

3. Preheat the broiler. Add the apple juice, honey, celery seed, salt, and hot pepper sauce to the lime juice mixture remaining in the bowl. Stir in the cabbage and carrots. Drain the raisins and add to the bowl.

4. Broil the steak 5 inches from the heat, turning once, for 10 minutes, or until medium-rare. Transfer the steak to a cutting board and thinly slice. Divide the steak among 4 plates, spoon the cabbage salad alongside, and serve.

Helpful hint: A packaged slaw mix that contains both cabbage and carrots would save you the step of shredding carrots in preparing this recipe.

FAT: 5G/18%
CALORIES: 247
SATURATED FAT: 1.5G
CARBOHYDRATE: 23G
PROTEIN: 29G
CHOLESTEROL: 72MG
SODIUM: 670MG

CHICKEN, CORN, AND ZUCCHINI SAUTÉ

SERVES: 4
WORKING TIME: 15 MINUTES
TOTAL TIME: 20 MINUTES

2 teaspoons olive oil

1 ounce Canadian bacon, diced

1 zucchini, cut into thin rounds

½ pound mushrooms, thinly sliced

1 pound skinless, boneless chicken breasts, cut into large chunks

1 tablespoon flour

½ cup apple cider or natural apple juice

½ teaspoon salt

1 cup frozen corn kernels

2 tablespoons chopped fresh parsley (optional)

1. In a large nonstick skillet, heat the oil until hot but not smoking over medium heat. Add the bacon and cook until lightly crisped, about 2 minutes. Stir in the zucchini and mushrooms, cover, and cook until the vegetables begin to soften, about 5 minutes.

2. Stir in the chicken and flour and cook, uncovered, stirring frequently, until the chicken is lightly browned, about 2 minutes. Add the cider and salt. Bring to a boil over medium-high heat, reduce to a simmer, cover, and cook until the chicken is cooked through, about 4 minutes.

3. Stir in the corn and cook, uncovered, until the corn is just heated through, about 2 minutes longer. Spoon the chicken and vegetables onto 4 plates, sprinkle with the parsley, and serve.

Suggested accompaniments: Boiled red potato halves tossed with cracked black pepper, followed by peach halves baked with maple syrup.

FAT: 5G/19%
CALORIES: 231
SATURATED FAT: .9G
CARBOHYDRATE: 17G
PROTEIN: 31G
CHOLESTEROL: 69MG
SODIUM: 453MG

Chunky with vegetables and accented with apple cider, this recipe exemplifies simple home cooking. Using just a touch of olive oil mixed with a small amount of smoky Canadian bacon enhances the flavor without overloading on fat. To store mushrooms, refrigerate them, unwashed, in a loosely closed brown paper bag for up to one week.

CHINESE CHICKEN SALAD WITH PEANUTS

SERVES: 4
WORKING TIME: 15 MINUTES
TOTAL TIME: 20 MINUTES

The hoisin sauce and apple juice create both a sharp-sweet dressing for this salad and a quick marinade for the chicken breasts. For a peppery variation, substitute alfalfa or radish sprouts for the bean sprouts.

⅓ cup hoisin sauce

¼ cup apple juice

1 teaspoon vegetable oil

¼ teaspoon salt

1 pound skinless, boneless chicken breasts

2 red bell peppers, cut into thin strips

2 carrots, shredded

2 cups bean sprouts

8-ounce can sliced water chestnuts, rinsed and drained

2 tablespoons finely chopped scallion

½ teaspoon ground ginger

3 cups ¼-inch-wide shredded romaine lettuce

1 tablespoon coarsely chopped unsalted dry-roasted peanuts

1. Preheat the broiler. In a large bowl, combine the hoisin sauce, apple juice, oil, and salt. Remove 2 tablespoons of this hoisin sauce mixture and set aside the remaining sauce. Place the chicken on the broiler rack and brush with the 2 tablespoons hoisin sauce mixture. Broil the chicken 4 inches from the heat for 4 minutes per side, or until just cooked through. Transfer the chicken to a cutting board and cut the chicken into thin diagonal slices.

2. Add the chicken slices, bell pepper strips, carrots, sprouts, water chestnuts, scallion, and ginger to the reserved hoisin sauce mixture and toss to coat.

3. Place the lettuce on 4 plates and spoon the chicken salad on top. Sprinkle with the peanuts and serve.

Suggested accompaniments: Rice cakes, and oolong or almond tea with fortune cookies afterward.

FAT: 4G/13%
CALORIES: 275
SATURATED FAT: .7G
CARBOHYDRATE: 29G
PROTEIN: 31G
CHOLESTEROL: 66MG
SODIUM: 914MG

TEX-MEX TURKEY SAUSAGE STEW

SERVES: 4
WORKING TIME: 10 MINUTES
TOTAL TIME: 25 MINUTES

1 cup long-grain rice

½ teaspoon salt

½ pound hot Italian-style turkey sausage, cut into 1-inch pieces

⅓ cup reduced-sodium chicken broth, defatted

1 green bell pepper, cut into 1-inch squares

14½-ounce can no-salt-added stewed tomatoes

4½-ounce can chopped mild green chilies

½ teaspoon ground cumin

½ teaspoon dried oregano

1 cup frozen corn kernels

1. In a medium saucepan, bring 2¼ cups of water to a boil. Add the rice and ¼ teaspoon of the salt, reduce to a simmer, cover, and cook until the rice is tender, about 17 minutes.

2. Meanwhile, spray a large nonstick skillet with nonstick cooking spray. Add the turkey sausage and cook over medium heat just until lightly browned, about 3 minutes. Add the broth and bell pepper and simmer until the pepper is tender, about 4 minutes.

3. Stir the tomatoes, chilies, cumin, oregano, and remaining ¼ teaspoon salt into the skillet. Bring to a boil, reduce to a simmer, and cook until the sausage is cooked through and the sauce is slightly thickened, about 5 minutes. Stir in the corn and cook just until warmed through. Divide the rice among 4 plates, spoon the stew alongside, and serve.

Helpful hint: If your family doesn't go for spicy food, use sweet sausage instead of hot. If, on the other hand, you like things extra hot, add a pinch of cayenne or a few shakes of hot pepper sauce to the stew before serving.

FAT: 7G/18%
CALORIES: 344
SATURATED FAT: 1.8G
CARBOHYDRATE: 57G
PROTEIN: 16G
CHOLESTEROL: 30MG
SODIUM: 915MG

Mexican cooks would make this stew with the spicy pork sausage called chorizo, which is not very widely available here. In its place, we've used Italian-style turkey sausage, which contributes its own wonderful seasonings to the chilies, cumin, and oregano in the dish. Of course, turkey is also lower in fat than pork. Accompany the stew with a lightly dressed salad to refresh the palate.

CUBAN-STYLE BEEF STEW

SERVES: 4
WORKING TIME: 15 MINUTES
TOTAL TIME: 20 MINUTES

*T*his *quick-to-fix stew offers all the body of a long-simmered concoction, thanks to instant taste tricks—jarred salsa and canned green chilies.*

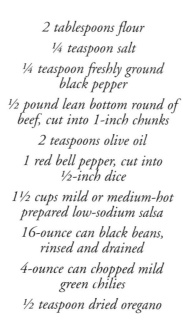

2 tablespoons flour

¼ teaspoon salt

¼ teaspoon freshly ground black pepper

½ pound lean bottom round of beef, cut into 1-inch chunks

2 teaspoons olive oil

1 red bell pepper, cut into ½-inch dice

1½ cups mild or medium-hot prepared low-sodium salsa

16-ounce can black beans, rinsed and drained

4-ounce can chopped mild green chilies

½ teaspoon dried oregano

1. On a sheet of waxed paper, combine the flour, salt, and black pepper. Dredge the beef in the flour mixture, shaking off the excess. In a nonstick Dutch oven, heat the oil until hot but not smoking over medium heat. Add the beef and cook, stirring frequently, until browned, about 5 minutes. With a slotted spoon, transfer the beef to a plate and set aside.

2. Add the bell pepper to the pan and cook, stirring frequently, until the pepper is softened, about 4 minutes. Stir in the salsa, black beans, chilies, and oregano. Bring to a boil, reduce to a simmer, cover, and cook until the flavors have blended, about 5 minutes.

3. Return the beef to the pan and cook, uncovered, until the beef is just cooked through, about 5 minutes longer. Ladle the stew into 4 bowls and serve.

Suggested accompaniments: Romaine and shredded carrot salad with a red wine vinaigrette. For dessert, broiled sliced papaya sprinkled with brown sugar and vanilla.

FAT: 6G/24%
CALORIES: 229
SATURATED FAT: 1.4G
CARBOHYDRATE: 24G
PROTEIN: 19G
CHOLESTEROL: 33MG
SODIUM: 548MG

Soft Turkey Tacos

Serves: 4
Working time: 15 minutes
Total time: 20 minutes

2 teaspoons olive oil

¾ pound turkey cutlets, cut into ½-inch-wide strips

½ teaspoon salt

½ teaspoon chili powder

½ teaspoon ground cumin

1¾ pounds plum tomatoes, coarsely chopped

4½-ounce can chopped mild green chilies with their juice

3 scallions, thinly sliced

1 tablespoon fresh lime juice

Eight 6-inch flour tortillas

2 cups shredded romaine lettuce

2 tablespoons reduced-fat sour cream

1. Preheat the oven to 400°. In a large nonstick skillet, heat the oil until hot but not smoking over medium heat. Add the turkey, sprinkle with ¼ teaspoon of the salt, ¼ teaspoon of the chili powder, and ¼ teaspoon of the cumin and cook, stirring frequently, until just cooked through, about 2 minutes per side. With a slotted spoon, transfer the turkey to a plate.

2. Add the tomatoes, chilies, scallions, the remaining ¼ teaspoon salt, remaining ¼ teaspoon chili powder, and remaining ¼ teaspoon cumin to the skillet. Cook until the sauce is slightly reduced, about 4 minutes. Return the turkey to the pan and cook just until warmed through, about 1 minute. Remove from the heat and stir in the lime juice.

3. Meanwhile, wrap the tortillas in foil and bake until hot but not crisp, about 4 minutes. Divide the tortillas among 4 plates. Spoon the turkey mixture onto the warm tortillas, top with the lettuce and a dollop of the sour cream. Roll up the tortillas or leave open and serve.

Helpful hint: You can serve the tacos with a variety of accompaniments, such as minced scallions, shredded cilantro, extra chopped chilies, or salsa.

Fat: 8g/23%
Calories: 318
Saturated Fat: 1.5g
Carbohydrate: 36g
Protein: 28g
Cholesterol: 55mg
Sodium: 731mg

Roll 'em up and dig in: These soft tacos are overflowing with flavor, and are easier to eat than crisp tacos.

PINEAPPLE CHICKEN

SERVES: 4
WORKING TIME: 25 MINUTES
TOTAL TIME: 25 MINUTES

You may have encountered the pairing of chicken and pineapple in a Cantonese restaurant, where the fruit is often used in a stir-fried chicken dish. Savory chicken is a wonderful foil for sweet, juicy pineapple; here, they're bathed in a sweet-spicy sauce, with cherry tomatoes added for a burst of color and a touch of tartness.

1 tablespoon cider vinegar

2 teaspoons grated fresh ginger

1 pound skinless, boneless chicken breasts, cut into ¾-inch cubes

20-ounce can juice-packed pineapple chunks, juice reserved

½ cup reduced-sodium chicken broth, defatted

2 tablespoons firmly packed light brown sugar

2 teaspoons Worcestershire sauce

½ teaspoon chili powder

⅛ teaspoon ground cloves

1 cup cherry tomatoes

3 scallions, finely chopped

2 teaspoons cornstarch mixed with 1 tablespoon water

1. In a medium bowl, combine the vinegar and ginger. Add the chicken, tossing to coat.

2. In a medium skillet, combine ½ cup of the reserved pineapple juice, the broth, brown sugar, Worcestershire sauce, chili powder, and cloves. Bring to a boil over medium heat. Reduce the heat to a simmer, add the chicken, and cook until the chicken is just cooked through, about 5 minutes. Add the pineapple chunks, tomatoes, scallions, and cornstarch mixture and cook, stirring, until slightly thickened, about 2 minutes. Spoon the chicken onto 4 plates and serve.

Helpful hint: Pineapple packed in fruit juice has about 50 fewer calories per cup than pineapple packed in heavy syrup.

FAT: 2G/7%
CALORIES: 263
SATURATED FAT: 0.4G
CARBOHYDRATE: 35G
PROTEIN: 28G
CHOLESTEROL: 66MG
SODIUM: 194MG

FLOUNDER WITH TOMATO "MAYONNAISE"

SERVES: 4
WORKING TIME: 25 MINUTES
TOTAL TIME: 25 MINUTES

The thick, garlicky "mayonnaise" for this flounder sauté makes a wonderful low-fat alternative to tartar sauce. Studded with bits of fresh tomato and scallion, our sauce is based on a purée of white kidney beans with nonfat yogurt and a little reduced-fat mayo added for creaminess. Round out the meal with a side of roasted potatoes.

1 clove garlic

1 cup canned white kidney beans (cannellini), rinsed and drained

¼ cup plain nonfat yogurt

2 tablespoons reduced-fat mayonnaise

2 tablespoons fresh lemon juice

¾ teaspoon salt

⅛ teaspoon hot pepper sauce

4 plum tomatoes, coarsely diced

1 tablespoon flour

¼ teaspoon freshly ground black pepper

4 flounder fillets (about 4 ounces each), any visible bones removed

1 tablespoon vegetable oil

½ cup sliced scallions

1. In a small saucepan of boiling water, cook the garlic for 1 minute to blanch. Rinse under cold water and remove the skin. Place the garlic in a food processor or blender along with the beans, yogurt, mayonnaise, 1 tablespoon of the lemon juice, ½ teaspoon of the salt, and the hot pepper sauce. Process to a smooth purée. Transfer the mixture to a bowl and stir in half of the diced tomatoes. Set aside.

2. On a sheet of waxed paper, combine the flour, pepper, and the remaining ¼ teaspoon salt. Dredge the fillets in the flour mixture, shaking off the excess. In a large nonstick skillet, heat the oil until hot but not smoking over medium-high heat. Add the fish and cook until just opaque, about 2 minutes per side.

3. Meanwhile, in a small bowl, combine the remaining tomatoes with the scallions. Divide the fish among 4 plates and sprinkle with the remaining 1 tablespoon lemon juice. Top with the tomato "mayonnaise" and tomato-scallion mixture and serve.

Helpful hints: You can make the mayonnaise in advance up to the point of adding the tomatoes: Refrigerate the sauce for up to 12 hours. At serving time, stir in the tomatoes. You can substitute any firm-fleshed white fish, such as striped bass or red snapper, for the flounder, if you like.

FAT: 7G/27%
CALORIES: 233
SATURATED FAT: 1G
CARBOHYDRATE: 16G
PROTEIN: 27G
CHOLESTEROL: 55MG
SODIUM: 671MG

PORK CUTLETS WITH PLUM SAUCE

SERVES: 4
WORKING TIME: 25 MINUTES
TOTAL TIME: 25 MINUTES

The Chinese plum sauce sold in cans and jars is made from fruit, chilies, vinegar, and sugar. Our homemade version, which includes sliced fresh plums, plum jam, fresh ginger, and orange juice, is the perfect complement to sautéed pork and sweet potatoes. A green salad with red onions offers a nice contrast to the plums.

1 pound sweet potatoes, peeled and cut crosswise into ¼-inch-thick slices

4 well-trimmed boneless pork loin chops (about 3 ounces each)

1 tablespoon flour

½ teaspoon salt

½ teaspoon dried sage

¼ teaspoon freshly ground black pepper

1 tablespoon olive oil

¾ pound red or black plums, pitted and cut into ½-inch slices

4 scallions, chopped

½ cup reduced-sodium chicken broth, defatted

⅓ cup orange juice

¼ cup plum jam

1 tablespoon minced fresh ginger

1 teaspoon cornstarch mixed with 2 tablespoons water

1. In a large saucepan of boiling water, cook the sweet potatoes until firm-tender, 4 to 5 minutes. Drain well.

2. Meanwhile, place the pork chops between 2 sheets of waxed paper and, with the flat side of a small skillet or meat pounder, pound the pork to a ¼-inch thickness. On another sheet of waxed paper, combine the flour, salt, sage, and pepper. Dredge the pork in the flour mixture, shaking off the excess. In a large nonstick skillet, heat the oil until hot but not smoking over medium-high heat. Add the pork and cook until golden brown on the outside and no longer pink on the inside, about 2 minutes per side. Transfer the pork to a plate.

3. Add the plums, scallions, broth, orange juice, plum jam, and ginger to the skillet and bring to a boil. Reduce to a simmer and cook until the plums are almost tender, 1 to 2 minutes. Add the cornstarch mixture and cook, stirring, until slightly thickened, about 1 minute.

4. Return the pork to the skillet along with the sweet potatoes, turning to coat with the sauce. Cook until heated through, about 1 minute. Divide among 4 plates and serve.

Helpful hint: You can substitute turkey cutlets for the pork cutlets, if you like. In step 2, cook them until they are cooked through, about 1 minute per side, and continue with the recipe.

FAT: 9G/23%
CALORIES: 357
SATURATED FAT: 2.2G
CARBOHYDRATE: 49G
PROTEIN: 21G
CHOLESTEROL: 50MG
SODIUM: 420MG

Italian-Style Chicken Sauté

SERVES: 4
WORKING TIME: 35 MINUTES
TOTAL TIME: 35 MINUTES

1 tablespoon olive oil

6 cloves garlic, peeled

½ teaspoon dried rosemary

1 small dried chili pepper, or
¼ teaspoon red pepper flakes

2 tablespoons flour

½ teaspoon salt

¼ teaspoon freshly ground black
pepper

4 skinless, boneless chicken breast
halves (about 1 pound total)

½ cup dry red wine

1 tomato, diced

1 cup reduced-sodium chicken
broth, defatted

2 teaspoons anchovy paste

¼ cup chopped fresh basil

2 teaspoons cornstarch mixed
with 1 tablespoon water

1. In a large nonstick skillet, heat the oil until warm over low heat. Add the garlic, rosemary, and chili pepper and cook, turning the garlic as it colors, until the garlic is golden brown, about 4 minutes. Remove and discard the garlic.

2. On a sheet of waxed paper, combine the flour, ¼ teaspoon of the salt, and the black pepper. Dredge the chicken in the flour mixture, shaking off the excess. Increase the heat under the skillet to medium, add the chicken, and cook until golden brown and cooked through, about 5 minutes per side. With a slotted spoon, transfer the chicken to a plate.

3. Add the wine to the skillet, increase the heat to high, and cook, stirring, until slightly reduced, about 1 minute. Stir in the tomato, broth, anchovy paste, basil, and the remaining ¼ teaspoon salt and bring to a boil. Cook until richly flavored, about 3 minutes. Return to a boil, add the cornstarch mixture, and cook, stirring, until slightly thickened, about 1 minute. Reduce the heat to low, return the chicken to the pan, and simmer just until heated through, about 1 minute. Divide the chicken among 4 plates, spoon the sauce over, and serve.

Helpful hint: Contrary to what you might expect, the anchovy paste added to the sauce introduces a richly savory quality, not a fishy taste. You can leave it out, if you like.

FAT: 5G/20%
CALORIES: 223
SATURATED FAT: 0.9G
CARBOHYDRATE: 9G
PROTEIN: 29G
CHOLESTEROL: 68MG
SODIUM: 624MG

A light and spicy tomato sauce, fragrant with rosemary and basil, transforms these boneless chicken breast halves into an entrée with Italian flair. Made with tomato, dried chili pepper, and red wine, the sauce is worlds away from anything you can buy in a jar. Serve the chicken with sautéed zucchini crescents and diced red peppers; for a more substantial meal, add some pasta or rice.

CHICKEN WITH APPLES IN CREAM SAUCE

SERVES: 4
WORKING TIME: 20 MINUTES
TOTAL TIME: 20 MINUTES

*T*hink "fast food," and regional French cuisine is not what comes to mind. But here's a taste of Normandy, a region on France's north coast, known for its apples and apple brandy, as well as its rich dairy products. We've used thick, cream-like evaporated low-fat milk in place of Normandy's high-fat cream. Serve the chicken with a colorful mélange of bell peppers and red onions.

2 teaspoons olive oil

1 pound skinless, boneless chicken breasts, cut into 2-inch chunks

1 Granny Smith apple, cored and cut into 16 wedges

2 tablespoons applejack

½ teaspoon dried sage

½ teaspoon salt

¼ teaspoon freshly ground black pepper

¼ teaspoon ground ginger

1 tablespoon flour

1 cup evaporated low-fat milk

1 teaspoon Dijon mustard

1 teaspoon chopped fresh parsley

1. In a large nonstick skillet, heat the oil until hot but not smoking over medium heat. Add the chicken and apple and cook just until the chicken is no longer pink, about 3 minutes.

2. Remove the pan from the heat and stir in the applejack. Return to the heat and boil for 1 minute. Add the sage, salt, pepper, ginger, and flour, stirring, until well combined. Stir in the evaporated milk and mustard, cover, and cook until the chicken is cooked through and the apple is tender, about 5 minutes. Spoon the chicken and apple wedges onto 4 plates, sprinkle with the parsley, and serve.

Helpful hint: Applejack is the American counterpart of Normandy's great apple brandy, Calvados. Any apple brandy—or, if you prefer, cider—can be used for this recipe.

FAT: 5G/18%
CALORIES: 247
SATURATED FAT: 0.7G
CARBOHYDRATE: 13G
PROTEIN: 31G
CHOLESTEROL: 76MG
SODIUM: 443MG

VEGETABLES & SALADS

Left, Roasted Potatoes with Parmesan and Herbs (p. 343).
Above, Waldorf Salad (p. 350).

ROASTED POTATOES WITH PARMESAN AND HERBS

SERVES: 4
WORKING TIME: 15 MINUTES
TOTAL TIME: 45 MINUTES

When you cook potatoes in the pan along with a roast or bird, the result is undeniably delicious but unfortunately loaded with fat. The potatoes absorb the fat that runs off from the meat. But even with a spoonful of olive oil and a generous sprinkling of Parmesan, these "al forno" (oven-cooked) potatoes are a healthier choice. Try them with sage-rubbed roasted game hens.

1½ pounds small red potatoes
1 tablespoon extra-virgin olive oil
3 cloves garlic, peeled and halved
¾ teaspoon dried rosemary
½ teaspoon dried sage
1½ teaspoons grated lemon zest
½ teaspoon salt
¼ cup grated Parmesan cheese

1. Preheat the oven to 400°. With a vegetable peeler, peel a thin band around the circumference of each potato. In a large pot of boiling water, cook the potatoes for 5 minutes. Drain.

2. In a large roasting pan, combine the oil, garlic, rosemary, and sage. Bake until the garlic is fragrant and the oil is hot, about 4 minutes. Add the potatoes, lemon zest, and salt and bake, turning occasionally, for 20 minutes, or until the potatoes are crisp, golden, and tender. Sprinkle the Parmesan over the potatoes and bake for 2 minutes, or just until the cheese is melted and golden brown.

Helpful hint: If you're in a hurry, you can skip the peeling step and roast the potatoes with their skins on.

FAT: 5G/23%
CALORIES: 193
SATURATED FAT: 1.4G
CARBOHYDRATE: 32G
PROTEIN: 6G
CHOLESTEROL: 4MG
SODIUM: 380MG

ITALIAN GREEN BEANS WITH GARLIC AND TOMATOES

SERVES: 4
WORKING TIME: 20 MINUTES
TOTAL TIME: 30 MINUTES

1 teaspoon olive oil
1 onion, finely chopped
3 cloves garlic, slivered
1½ cups chopped tomatoes
½ cup chopped fresh basil
½ teaspoon salt
1 teaspoon hot pepper sauce
Two 10-ounce packages frozen Italian flat green beans

1. In a large nonstick skillet, heat the oil until hot but not smoking over medium heat. Add the onion and garlic and cook, stirring frequently, until the onion is softened, about 7 minutes.

2. Add the tomatoes, basil, salt, and hot pepper sauce and bring to a boil. Add the beans, reduce the heat to a simmer, and cook until the beans are tender, about 8 minutes.

Helpful hint: If you can get fresh Italian flat green beans, use them in place of the frozen. The cooking times will be approximately the same, depending on the size of the fresh beans. Test them after 8 minutes and if they are still too raw, continue cooking them, with the skillet covered.

This colorful vegetable toss will brighten a meal centered on simple chicken breasts or pork cutlets. The flavors are as bright as the jade-green beans and crimson tomatoes: There's garlic, fresh basil, and peppery heat. Add the hot sauce in small increments to taste—half the amount called for here may be enough for some.

FAT: 2G/19%
CALORIES: 96
SATURATED FAT: .3G
CARBOHYDRATE: 20G
PROTEIN: 4G
CHOLESTEROL: 0MG
SODIUM: 319MG

BOURBON-GLAZED YAMS

MAKES: 4 CUPS
WORKING TIME: 20 MINUTES
TOTAL TIME: 1 HOUR 10 MINUTES

You can't beat the homey goodness of these yams, made sweet, tart, and mellow with brown sugar, pineapple juice, and bourbon.

2 pounds yams or sweet potatoes
2 teaspoons unsalted butter
3 tablespoons firmly packed light brown sugar
¼ cup pineapple juice
1 tablespoon fresh lime juice
½ teaspoon salt
⅛ teaspoon ground allspice
⅛ teaspoon ground nutmeg
3 tablespoons bourbon
¼ cup minced scallions

1. Preheat the oven to 450°. With a fork, prick the yams in several places. Place on a baking sheet and bake for 45 minutes, or until the yams are tender. When cool enough to handle, peel the yams and cut crosswise into 1½-inch slices.

2. In a large skillet, melt the butter over medium heat. Add the brown sugar and stir to blend. Add the pineapple juice, lime juice, salt, allspice, and nutmeg and cook until the mixture is bubbly, about 2 minutes. Stir in the yams and cook, gently turning occasionally, until the yams are glazed and nicely coated, about 10 minutes.

3. Remove the pan from the heat and add the bourbon. Bring the mixture to a boil over high heat and cook until the bourbon has evaporated, about 2 minutes. Stir in the scallions. Spoon the yams into a medium bowl and serve.

Helpful hints: The yams can be prepared 1 day ahead through step 1, then refrigerated. Bring to room temperature before proceeding. Leftovers can be made into a delightful winter soup: Purée the yams in a food processor with a little chicken broth, and then gently reheat, stirring in more broth or skim milk to reach the desired consistency.

VALUES ARE PER ½ CUP
FAT: 1G/6%
CALORIES: 162
SATURATED FAT: 0.6G
CARBOHYDRATE: 34G
PROTEIN: 2G
CHOLESTEROL: 3MG
SODIUM: 158MG

POLENTA WITH TOMATO-MUSHROOM SAUCE

SERVES: 4
WORKING TIME: 20 MINUTES
TOTAL TIME: 40 MINUTES

1 teaspoon olive oil

3 cloves garlic, minced

½ pound mushrooms, thinly sliced

⅔ cup reduced-sodium chicken broth, defatted

8-ounce can no-salt-added tomato sauce

¾ teaspoon salt

¼ teaspoon dried rosemary

¼ teaspoon ground ginger

⅛ teaspoon red pepper flakes

1 cup yellow cornmeal

½ cup crumbled Gorgonzola cheese (2 ounces)

1. In a large nonstick skillet, heat the oil until hot but not smoking over medium heat. Add the garlic and cook until fragrant, about 1 minute. Add the mushrooms and broth and bring to a boil. Reduce to a simmer, cover, and cook until the mushrooms are softened, about 3 minutes. Add the tomato sauce, ¼ teaspoon of the salt, the rosemary, ginger, and red pepper flakes. Cook until the sauce is slightly reduced and the flavors are blended, about 5 minutes. Set aside.

2. In a medium bowl, combine the cornmeal and 1 cup of water. In a medium saucepan, bring 1½ cups of water to a boil over medium heat. Add the remaining ½ teaspoon of salt and reduce to a gentle simmer. Stirring constantly, gradually add the corn-meal mixture. Cook until the mixture is thick and leaves the sides of the pan, about 7 minutes. Add the Gorgonzola and stir until melted.

3. Gently reheat the tomato-mushroom sauce over low heat. Serve the polenta topped with the sauce.

Helpful hints: Although polenta is often cooked and then cooled in a pan, making it stiff enough to slice, this method yields a soft, creamy dish, about as thick as mashed potatoes. If you don't care for blue cheese, you can use shredded Fontina or Monterey jack.

FAT: 7G/28%
CALORIES: 227
SATURATED FAT: 3.2G
CARBOHYDRATE: 35G
PROTEIN: 9G
CHOLESTEROL: 13MG
SODIUM: 731MG

This tasty polenta can take the starring role alongside a simple main dish, such as baked haddock or cod.

CORN PUDDING

MAKES: 5 CUPS
WORKING TIME: 10 MINUTES
TOTAL TIME: 1 HOUR 5 MINUTES

Often the tried-and-true holiday classics remain the best—as is the case with scrumptious corn pudding. Here we've reduced the fat, but have kept in the custardy goodness. This dish works very well for a buffet, since it stays flavorful even at room temperature.

3 tablespoons flour
2 cups low-fat (1%) milk
2 whole eggs
1 egg white
1 tablespoon sugar
¾ teaspoon salt
½ teaspoon dried thyme
½ teaspoon freshly ground black pepper
5 cups frozen corn kernels, thawed and well drained
1 teaspoon chopped fresh parsley

1. Preheat the oven to 325°. Spray a shallow 1½-quart baking dish with nonstick cooking spray.

2. Place the flour in a large saucepan, and gradually whisk in the milk over medium heat until no lumps remain. Bring to a boil, reduce to a simmer and cook, whisking frequently, until the mixture is very slightly thickened, about 2 minutes. Remove from the heat. In a medium bowl, whisk together the whole eggs, egg white, sugar, salt, thyme, and pepper. Gradually whisk about ½ cup of the hot milk mixture into the egg mixture, whisking constantly.

3. Whisk the warmed egg mixture back into the saucepan and cook, whisking constantly, just until the mixture is thick enough to coat the back of a spoon, about 3 minutes. Stir in the corn.

4. Spoon the mixture into the prepared baking dish and place the baking dish in a large roasting pan. Add enough hot water to the roasting pan to come halfway up the sides of the baking dish and bake for 50 to 55 minutes, or until the pudding is just set. Remove the corn pudding from the water, sprinkle the parsley on top, and serve.

Helpful hints: You can prepare the corn pudding 2 hours ahead and hold it at room temperature. Canned corn kernels can be substituted for the frozen. Be sure to drain the corn well to avoid a watery pudding.

VALUES ARE PER ½ CUP
FAT: 2G/16%
CALORIES: 124
SATURATED FAT: 0.7G
CARBOHYDRATE: 23G
PROTEIN: 6G
CHOLESTEROL: 44MG
SODIUM: 210MG

WALDORF SALAD

SERVES: 4
WORKING TIME: 20 MINUTES
TOTAL TIME: 20 MINUTES

1 cup plain nonfat yogurt

2 tablespoons reduced-fat sour cream

2 tablespoons reduced-fat mayonnaise

1 teaspoon grated lemon zest

2 tablespoons fresh lemon juice

¼ teaspoon salt

¼ teaspoon freshly ground black pepper

2 Granny Smith apples, cored and cut into 1-inch chunks

1 Red Delicious apple, cored and cut into 1-inch chunks

2 ribs celery, thinly sliced

1 cup red seedless grapes, halved

1 small head romaine lettuce, cut crosswise into ¼-inch-wide shreds

1 tablespoon coarsely chopped walnuts

1. In a large bowl, combine the yogurt, sour cream, mayonnaise, lemon zest, lemon juice, salt, and pepper and stir to blend. Add the apples, celery, and grapes and toss well to coat.

2. Place the lettuce on 4 salad plates and spoon the apple mixture on top. Garnish with the walnuts and serve.

Helpful hint: To get a jump on the party, toss the apple mixture with the dressing earlier in the day and refrigerate. Just before serving, spoon over the shredded lettuce and then garnish with the walnuts.

FAT: 5G/22%
CALORIES: 190
SATURATED FAT: 1.1G
CARBOHYDRATE: 34G
PROTEIN: 6G
CHOLESTEROL: 4MG
SODIUM: 266MG

Everyone will recognize this favorite, but they won't guess that we've lightened it for the holidays. The dressing is a creamy blend of nonfat yogurt, reduced-fat sour cream, and reduced-fat mayonnaise, sharpened with a touch of lemon juice and zest. Serve as a first course for a sit-down dinner, or in a beautiful wooden bowl as part of a buffet spread.

SHALLOT-TOPPED GARLIC MASHED POTATOES

MAKES: 8 CUPS
WORKING TIME: 30 MINUTES
TOTAL TIME: 50 MINUTES

What sets these sensational mashed potatoes apart is both the garlic and the caramelized shallots, which add a deep, rich flavor.

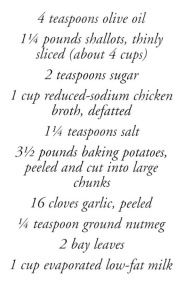

4 teaspoons olive oil

1¼ pounds shallots, thinly sliced (about 4 cups)

2 teaspoons sugar

1 cup reduced-sodium chicken broth, defatted

1¼ teaspoons salt

3½ pounds baking potatoes, peeled and cut into large chunks

16 cloves garlic, peeled

¼ teaspoon ground nutmeg

2 bay leaves

1 cup evaporated low-fat milk

1. In a large nonstick skillet, heat 2 teaspoons of the oil until hot but not smoking over medium heat. Add the shallots, sprinkle with the sugar, and cook, stirring frequently, until the shallots are glazed, 5 to 8 minutes. Add the broth and ¼ teaspoon of the salt and cook, stirring occasionally, until the shallots are tender and golden brown, about 7 minutes longer. Set aside; cover with foil.

2. Meanwhile, in a large pot, combine the potatoes, garlic, nutmeg, bay leaves and enough cold water to cover. Bring to a boil and add ½ teaspoon of the salt. Reduce to a simmer and cook until the potatoes are tender, about 20 minutes. Drain well. Discard the bay leaves.

3. Transfer the potatoes and garlic to a large bowl and mash until the mixture is smooth. Add the evaporated milk, remaining 2 teaspoons oil, and remaining ½ teaspoon of salt and mash until the mixture is thick and creamy. Spoon the mashed potatoes into a medium serving bowl, spoon the shallot mixture on top, and serve.

Helpful hints: You can replace the shallots with 4 large onions, thinly sliced. If you have leftover mashed potatoes, stir in enough chicken broth and/or skim milk to thin for a potato soup. Or, for a brunch dish, stir an egg white into the potatoes, shape into patties, and sauté in a nonstick skillet coated with nonstick cooking spray.

VALUES ARE PER ½ CUP
FAT: 2G/12%
CALORIES: 115
SATURATED FAT: 0.2G
CARBOHYDRATE: 22G
PROTEIN: 4G
CHOLESTEROL: 3MG
SODIUM: 237MG

BRAISED LEEKS

SERVES: 4
WORKING TIME: 15 MINUTES
TOTAL TIME: 45 MINUTES

4 medium leeks

1⅔ cups reduced-sodium tomato-vegetable juice

Three 3 x ½-inch strips of orange zest

⅔ cup orange juice

½ teaspoon dried thyme

¼ teaspoon cinnamon

¼ teaspoon ground allspice

¼ teaspoon cayenne pepper

1 tablespoon extra-virgin olive oil

½ teaspoon salt

2 tablespoons diced yellow or red bell pepper

1. Trim the root ends off each leek, being careful to keep the leeks intact. Trim the tough dark green tops off, then quarter each leek lengthwise up to but not through the root. Swish the leeks in a bowl of lukewarm water, easing the leaves apart to remove the grit. Lift out the leeks, leaving the grit behind; repeat as needed with clean water. Set aside.

2. In a large skillet, combine the tomato-vegetable juice, orange zest, orange juice, thyme, cinnamon, allspice, and cayenne. Bring to a boil over medium heat, reduce to a simmer, and add the leeks. Cover and cook until the leeks are tender, about 30 minutes.

3. With a slotted spoon, transfer the leeks to a serving platter. Add the oil and salt to the sauce in the skillet, return to a boil over high heat, and cook, stirring constantly, for 1 minute. Spoon the sauce over the leeks, sprinkle the bell pepper on top, and serve.

Helpful hints: This can be prepared 1 day ahead and refrigerated—the leeks will absorb even more flavor. Do not add the bell pepper until just before serving. Depending on the rest of the menu, the leeks can be served hot, at room temperature, or chilled.

FAT: 4G/24%
CALORIES: 143
SATURATED FAT: 0.5G
CARBOHYDRATE: 26G
PROTEIN: 3G
CHOLESTEROL: 0MG
SODIUM: 430MG

Simmering the leeks in a deeply fragrant orange-tomato sauce turns a simple vegetable into an extraordinary dish.

CAULIFLOWER WITH CHEDDAR SAUCE

MAKES: 4 CUPS
WORKING TIME: 25 MINUTES
TOTAL TIME: 30 MINUTES

*O*ur version of this vegetable classic tastes as good as the original, even though we've cut way back on the fat. Adding vinegar to the cauliflower cooking water lends a subtle flavor to the vegetable, and also helps to keep it white. For a simple embellishment, garnish with chopped fresh parsley or chives just before serving.

3 tablespoons flour
1½ cups low-fat (1%) milk
1 cup diced onion
1 teaspoon Dijon mustard
½ teaspoon salt
¼ teaspoon cayenne pepper
1 cup finely diced red bell pepper
¼ cup plus 2 tablespoons shredded Cheddar cheese
1 tablespoon distilled white vinegar or cider vinegar
1 head cauliflower, cut into florets

1. Place the flour in a large saucepan, and gradually whisk in the milk over medium heat until no lumps remain. Bring to a boil and stir in the onion, mustard, salt, and cayenne. Reduce to a simmer and cook, stirring frequently, until the sauce is slightly thickened, about 5 minutes.

2. Stir in the bell pepper and Cheddar and cook just until the cheese has melted, about 1 minute longer. Remove from the heat.

3. Meanwhile, bring a large pot of water to a boil, add the vinegar and cauliflower, and cook until the cauliflower is tender, about 5 minutes. Drain well and transfer to a medium serving bowl. Spoon the hot sauce over the cauliflower and serve.

Helpful hint: The sauce can be made earlier in the day and refrigerated. Gently reheat in a double boiler while you cook the cauliflower.

VALUES ARE PER ½ CUP
FAT: 2G/27%
CALORIES: 81
SATURATED FAT: 1.4G
CARBOHYDRATE: 11G
PROTEIN: 5G
CHOLESTEROL: 7MG
SODIUM: 220MG

ORANGE-GLAZED CARROTS

MAKES: 4 CUPS
WORKING TIME: 20 MINUTES
TOTAL TIME: 40 MINUTES

2 pounds carrots, cut lengthwise into thirds, then into 2-inch pieces

¾ teaspoon finely julienned orange zest

1½ cups fresh orange juice

2 cloves garlic, minced

⅓ cup thinly sliced scallion whites

1 tablespoon firmly packed light brown sugar

2 teaspoons unsalted butter

1 teaspoon ground ginger

½ teaspoon salt

¼ cup thinly sliced scallion greens

1. In a large saucepan, combine the carrots, orange zest, orange juice, garlic, scallion whites, brown sugar, butter, ginger, and salt. Bring to a boil over medium heat and cook gently, stirring occasionally, until the carrots are tender and glossy and the liquid is syrupy, about 20 minutes.

2. Stir in the scallion greens until well combined. Spoon the carrots into a medium bowl and serve.

Helpful hints: Plan on buying 5 or 6 oranges for the needed amount of juice. This can be prepared up to 1 day ahead through step 1. To serve, gently reheat, stirring occasionally, on the stovetop over low heat or in a microwave on half power. Mix in the scallion greens just before serving.

VALUES ARE PER ½ CUP
FAT: 1G/13%
CALORIES: 88
SATURATED FAT: 0.6G
CARBOHYDRATE: 19G
PROTEIN: 2G
CHOLESTEROL: 3MG
SODIUM: 179MG

For this simple and appealing side dish, the tartness of orange deliciously underscores the sweetness of carrots. And we've added a subtle Oriental touch by enlivening the taste with a little ginger. These carrots look especially inviting on a big buffet table with other great holiday staples—orange yams, green beans, ruby red cranberry sauce, and a golden bird.

BAKED EGGPLANT WITH HERBS AND LEMON

SERVES: 4
WORKING TIME: 20 MINUTES
TOTAL TIME: 45 MINUTES

B*aking (rather than frying) eggplant minimizes the fat content of this dish: A Parmesan crust and a zesty tomato sauce ensure full flavor.*

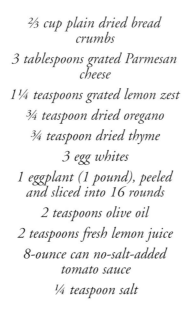

⅔ cup plain dried bread crumbs

3 tablespoons grated Parmesan cheese

1¼ teaspoons grated lemon zest

¾ teaspoon dried oregano

¾ teaspoon dried thyme

3 egg whites

1 eggplant (1 pound), peeled and sliced into 16 rounds

2 teaspoons olive oil

2 teaspoons fresh lemon juice

8-ounce can no-salt-added tomato sauce

¼ teaspoon salt

1. Preheat the oven to 400°. Line a baking sheet with foil.

2. On a plate, combine the bread crumbs, Parmesan cheese, ¾ teaspoon of the lemon zest, ¼ teaspoon of the oregano, and ¼ teaspoon of the thyme. In a shallow bowl, beat the egg whites with 2 tablespoons of water. Dip each eggplant round into the egg whites, then into the bread crumb mixture, and place on the prepared baking sheet.

3. In a small bowl, combine the oil and lemon juice and drizzle the mixture over the eggplant slices. Bake for 25 minutes, or until crisp and golden brown. Transfer the eggplant to a serving platter.

4. Meanwhile, in a small saucepan, combine the tomato sauce, salt, the remaining ½ teaspoon lemon zest, remaining ½ teaspoon oregano, and remaining ½ teaspoon thyme. Bring to a boil over medium heat. Reduce to a simmer and cook for 2 minutes to blend the flavors. Spoon the sauce over the eggplant and serve.

Helpful hint: Although eggplant looks like a sturdy vegetable, it's actually thin-skinned and quite perishable. Use eggplant within 5 days of purchase; as it ages, the vegetable may turn bitter.

FAT: 5G/27%
CALORIES: 168
SATURATED FAT: 1.2G
CARBOHYDRATE: 24G
PROTEIN: 8G
CHOLESTEROL: 3MG
SODIUM: 418MG

Sweet Potato Purée

SERVES: 4
WORKING TIME: 25 MINUTES
TOTAL TIME: 40 MINUTES

1¾ pounds sweet potatoes,
    peeled and thinly sliced

½ pound baking potatoes,
    peeled and thinly sliced

5 cloves garlic, thinly sliced

2 cups reduced-sodium chicken
    broth, defatted, or reduced-
    sodium vegetable broth

¼ cup reduced-fat sour cream

1 tablespoon olive oil

1 teaspoon sugar

¾ teaspoon dried thyme

¾ teaspoon ground ginger

½ teaspoon salt

½ teaspoon freshly ground
    black pepper

1. In a large saucepan, combine the sweet potatoes, baking potatoes, garlic, broth, and 1 cup of water. Bring to a boil, reduce to a simmer, cover, and cook until the potatoes are tender, about 20 minutes. Drain well, reserving the cooking liquid.

2. Transfer the potatoes to a large bowl. Add the sour cream, oil, sugar, thyme, ginger, salt, and pepper. With a potato masher or an electric beater, mash the mixture until smooth, adding enough of the reserved cooking liquid to make a creamy purée. Spoon the purée into a large bowl and serve.

Helpful hint: Turn any leftovers into a satisfying potato soup by reheating the purée over low heat and then stirring in enough reduced-sodium chicken broth to thin.

FAT: 6G/20%
CALORIES: 259
SATURATED FAT: 1.5G
CARBOHYDRATE: 47G
PROTEIN: 6G
CHOLESTEROL: 5MG
SODIUM: 626MG

Vividly orange and enticingly flavorful, these creamy potatoes are deceptively rich, but actually use very little fat.

Italians love artichokes, which in Italy appear in the market in a variety of shapes and sizes. A high-fat sauce often accompanies these velvet-fleshed vegetables, but this luxurious dip is based on reduced-fat mayonnaise and mashed garlic. Stuffed swordfish and rosemary-flavored potatoes would make a lovely meal with the artichokes.

ARTICHOKES WITH GARLIC "MAYONNAISE"

SERVES: 4
WORKING TIME: 20 MINUTES
TOTAL TIME: 45 MINUTES

1 all-purpose potato (6 ounces), peeled and thinly sliced

4 cloves garlic, peeled

¼ cup fresh lemon juice

3 tablespoons reduced-fat mayonnaise

3 tablespoons reduced-sodium chicken broth, defatted

¾ teaspoon dried rosemary

¾ teaspoon dried marjoram

½ teaspoon salt

4 large artichokes (12 ounces each)

3 tablespoons chopped fresh parsley

1. In a small pot of boiling water, cook the potato until tender, about 12 minutes. Add the garlic during the last 3 minutes of cooking. Drain. Transfer to a large bowl and mash until smooth. Add 2 tablespoons of the lemon juice, the mayonnaise, broth, ¼ teaspoon of the rosemary, ¼ teaspoon of the marjoram, and the salt. Set aside.

2. In a large pot, combine 3½ cups of water, the remaining 2 tablespoons lemon juice, the remaining ½ teaspoon rosemary, and remaining ½ teaspoon marjoram. Bring to a boil over high heat.

3. Meanwhile, pull off the tough bottom leaves of the artichoke (see tip; top photo). With kitchen shears, snip the sharp, pointed ends from the remaining leaves (middle photo). With a paring knife, trim off the end of the stem (bottom photo). Add the artichokes to the boiling liquid, cover, and cook until the artichokes are tender, about 25 minutes. Stir the parsley into the garlic "mayonnaise" and serve with the artichokes.

Helpful hint: To eat an artichoke, pull off the outer leaves one at a time and scrape the fleshy base from each leaf by drawing it between your front teeth. When you've finished the leaves, remove the prickly "choke" from the artichoke bottom before eating it.

FAT: 3G/21%
CALORIES: 130
SATURATED FAT: .4G
CARBOHYDRATE: 25G
PROTEIN: 6G
CHOLESTEROL: 0MG
SODIUM: 525MG

PEPPER, ZUCCHINI, AND POTATO TIELLA

SERVES: 4
WORKING TIME: 15 MINUTES
TOTAL TIME: 35 MINUTES

1 pound small red potatoes, halved

1 tablespoon olive oil

2 cloves garlic, peeled and halved

¾ teaspoon dried oregano

½ teaspoon dried rosemary

½ teaspoon dried sage

1 red onion, cut into 1-inch chunks

1 red bell pepper, cut into ½-inch-wide strips

2 zucchini, halved lengthwise and cut into 1-inch pieces

1 tomato, coarsely chopped

½ teaspoon salt

1. Preheat the oven to 400°. In a large pot of boiling water, cook the potatoes for 5 minutes to blanch. Drain well.

2. In a 13-x-9-inch baking dish, combine the oil, garlic, oregano, rosemary, and sage. Bake until the oil is hot and the herbs are fragrant, about 5 minutes. Add the potatoes, onion, bell pepper, zucchini, tomato, and salt, stirring to combine. Bake, stirring occasionally, for 25 minutes, or until the vegetables are tender. Divide among 4 plates and serve hot or at room temperature.

Helpful hint: Any kind of summer squash can go into this casserole. Golden zucchini, patty pan (white or yellow), yellow crookneck, or yellow straightneck would all work well.

FAT: 4G/22%
CALORIES: 166
SATURATED FAT: .5G
CARBOHYDRATE: 30G
PROTEIN: 4G
CHOLESTEROL: 0MG
SODIUM: 293MG

The province of Apulia, which forms the "heel" of the boot-shaped Italian peninsula, is home to the layered casserole called "tiella." The dish is infinitely variable, but is almost always made with potatoes. Peppers, onions, and tomatoes are other common ingredients. In this casual tiella, the vegetables are stirred together rather than layered.

GREEN BEAN SALAD

SERVES: 4
WORKING TIME: 15 MINUTES
TOTAL TIME: 20 MINUTES

These deliciously toothsome green beans, enlivened with dill and lemon juice, are tossed with sliced water chestnuts for a bit of crunch. The dressing is a flavorful mix of broth, lemon juice, and Dijon mustard—but not a bit of oil. This is an ideal dish for entertaining since it looks pretty on a buffet table and will hold up at room temperature.

1¼ pounds green beans

¼ cup reduced-sodium chicken broth, defatted, or reduced-sodium vegetable broth

2 tablespoons fresh lemon juice

1 tablespoon Dijon mustard

¼ teaspoon salt

⅛ teaspoon freshly ground black pepper

1 small red onion, finely chopped

½ cup canned sliced water chestnuts, well drained

⅓ cup snipped fresh dill

1. In a large pot of boiling water, cook the green beans until crisp-tender, about 4 minutes. (The time will vary depending on the age of the beans.) Drain, rinse under cold water, and drain again.

2. In a large serving bowl, whisk together the broth, lemon juice, mustard, salt, and pepper. Add the green beans, onion, water chestnuts, and dill, toss well to combine, and serve.

Helpful hints: This salad is equally good served at room temperature or chilled. If you do decide to serve it chilled, some of the bright green color of the beans will fade, but don't worry, the taste won't.

FAT: 0.2G/3%
CALORIES: 76
SATURATED FAT: 0G
CARBOHYDRATE: 17G
PROTEIN: 4G
CHOLESTEROL: 0MG
SODIUM: 282MG

SAUTÉED SPINACH WITH SUN-DRIED TOMATOES

SERVES: 4
WORKING TIME: 10 MINUTES
TOTAL TIME: 20 MINUTES

*M*ake a lovely meatless meal of a big baked potato and this garlicky spinach; it's sautéed with bits of sweet sun-dried tomatoes.

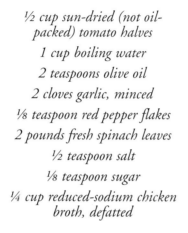

½ cup sun-dried (not oil-packed) tomato halves
1 cup boiling water
2 teaspoons olive oil
2 cloves garlic, minced
⅛ teaspoon red pepper flakes
2 pounds fresh spinach leaves
½ teaspoon salt
⅛ teaspoon sugar
¼ cup reduced-sodium chicken broth, defatted

1. In a small bowl, combine the sun-dried tomatoes and boiling water and let stand until the tomatoes have softened, about 15 minutes. Drain the tomatoes, reserving ¼ cup of the soaking liquid. Coarsely chop the tomatoes and set aside.

2. In a large nonstick skillet, heat the oil until hot but not smoking over medium heat. Add the garlic, red pepper flakes, spinach, salt, sugar, and broth and cook just until the garlic is fragrant, about 3 minutes. Add the sun-dried tomatoes and the reserved soaking liquid. Cover and cook just until the spinach is wilted, about 4 minutes. Spoon onto 4 plates and serve.

Helpful hint: Sand and grit will rinse out of spinach more quickly if you rinse the leaves in lukewarm, rather than ice-cold, tap water.

FAT: 3G/28%
CALORIES: 98
SATURATED FAT: .4G
CARBOHYDRATE: 14G
PROTEIN: 8G
CHOLESTEROL: 0MG
SODIUM: 501MG

CREAMY MASHED RUTABAGA

MAKES: 5 CUPS
WORKING TIME: 20 MINUTES
TOTAL TIME: 45 MINUTES

1¾ pounds rutabaga, peeled and thickly sliced

1 Granny Smith apple, peeled, cored, and thickly sliced

3 cloves garlic, slivered

¾ teaspoon dried marjoram or oregano

½ teaspoon salt

3 tablespoons evaporated low-fat milk

2 tablespoons grated Parmesan cheese

2 teaspoons unsalted butter

1. In a large saucepan, combine the rutabaga, apple, garlic, marjoram, and ¼ teaspoon of the salt. Add cold water to cover by 1 inch and bring to a boil. Reduce to a simmer, cover, and cook until the rutabaga is tender, about 25 minutes. Drain well and transfer the mixture to a large bowl.

2. Add the evaporated milk, Parmesan, butter, and remaining ¼ teaspoon salt and mash until the mixture is well blended but still chunky. Spoon the rutabaga mixture onto a platter and serve.

Helpful hints: This recipe can be prepared 1 day ahead through step 1 and refrigerated. To serve, gently reheat over low heat, stirring in the remaining ingredients. If you'd prefer a smooth vegetable purée, mash the mixture with a potato masher or an electric beater until no lumps remain.

VALUES ARE PER ½ CUP
FAT: 1G/24%
CALORIES: 48
SATURATED FAT: 0.7G
CARBOHYDRATE: 8G
PROTEIN: 2G
CHOLESTEROL: 4MG
SODIUM: 147MG

The apple adds a tangy sweetness to the already subtly sweet rutabaga. This is a natural with roast turkey or chicken.

ORANGE-GLAZED BAKED ACORN SQUASH

SERVES: 4
WORKING TIME: 15 MINUTES
TOTAL TIME: 55 MINUTES

This is so delicious you may want to double the recipe to have leftovers to enjoy the next day. Baking squash in a hot oven brings out its natural sweetness, while the orange-maple syrup glaze adds a wonderfully tangy flavor. These squash halves would look inviting on any dinner plate—for even more color, fill them with cooked peas.

2 small acorn squash (¾ pound each), halved lengthwise and seeded

½ teaspoon salt

¼ teaspoon freshly ground black pepper

¼ cup maple syrup

½ cup orange juice, preferably fresh

2 tablespoons orange marmalade

1 tablespoon fresh lemon juice

1. Preheat the oven to 450°. Sprinkle the cut sides of the squash with ¼ teaspoon of the salt and the pepper. Fill a large baking pan with 1 inch of water and place the squash, cut-sides up, in the pan. Brush 1 tablespoon of the maple syrup over the cut sides of the squash, cover with foil, and bake for 25 minutes, or until the squash is tender. Leave the oven on.

2. Meanwhile, in a small saucepan, combine the remaining 3 table-spoons maple syrup, the orange juice, marmalade, lemon juice, and remaining ¼ teaspoon salt and bring to a boil over medium heat. Cook until the mixture is reduced to a syrup thick enough to coat the back of a spoon, about 5 minutes.

3. Remove the squash from the baking pan and discard the water. Return the squash to the pan, cut-sides up. Brush the squash with the syrup and bake for 15 minutes longer, or until the syrup is slightly reduced and the squash is lightly browned around the edges. Place the squash on a platter and serve.

Helpful hints: Select acorn squash of equal size so the halves finish baking at the same time. If you'd like a bit of herb flavor, add a pinch of dried rosemary to the maple syrup mixture.

FAT: 0.2G/1%
CALORIES: 143
SATURATED FAT: 0G
CARBOHYDRATE: 37G
PROTEIN: 1G
CHOLESTEROL: 0MG
SODIUM: 285MG

HERBED PARMESAN OVEN FRIES

SERVES: 4
WORKING TIME: 15 MINUTES
TOTAL TIME: 55 MINUTES

1½ pounds baking potatoes, peeled

⅓ cup grated Parmesan cheese

½ teaspoon dried oregano

¼ teaspoon dried rosemary

¼ teaspoon freshly ground black pepper

¼ teaspoon salt

1. Preheat the oven to 400°. Cut the potatoes lengthwise into ¼-inch-thick slices, then cut the slices lengthwise into ¼-inch-wide sticks. Place the potatoes in a large bowl, lightly spray with nonstick cooking spray, and toss to coat. Add the Parmesan, oregano, rosemary, and pepper and toss again to coat thoroughly.

2. Transfer the potatoes to 2 baking sheets and bake for 40 minutes, turning every 10 minutes, or until the potatoes are golden brown and crisp. Place the fries on a platter, sprinkle with the salt, and serve.

Helpful hint: Be sure to spread out the fries on the baking sheets so there's plenty of room for them to bake to a nice crispness.

FAT: 3G/17%
CALORIES: 136
SATURATED FAT: 1.3G
CARBOHYDRATE: 24G
PROTEIN: 5G
CHOLESTEROL: 5MG
SODIUM: 267MG

These are every bit as good as the crunchy fries we all love. Spritzing the long potato sticks with nonstick cooking spray helps to create the crunch when they're baked, but without excessive fat, and also lets the Parmesan adhere. For our own zingy touch, we add a sprinkling of oregano, rosemary, and black pepper. Serve the fries with some hot mustard for dipping.

CAESAR SALAD

SERVES: 4
WORKING TIME: 15 MINUTES
TOTAL TIME: 15 MINUTES

The Italian chef Caesar Cardini devised this world-famous dish at his restaurant in Tijuana, Mexico, in the 1920s. In place of the traditional raw egg, we've used a little reduced-fat mayonnaise to add richness to the dressing. And to cut even more fat, the croutons are toasted instead of fried.

2 ounces Italian bread, cut into ½-inch cubes

3 tablespoons reduced-fat mayonnaise

2 tablespoons fresh lemon juice

2 tablespoons reduced-sodium chicken broth, defatted

1 teaspoon anchovy paste

½ teaspoon freshly ground black pepper

8 cups torn romaine lettuce

15½-ounce can red kidney beans, rinsed and drained

¼ cup grated Parmesan cheese

1. In a toaster oven or under the broiler, toast the bread cubes for about 1 minute, or until golden.

2. In a large bowl, combine the mayonnaise, lemon juice, broth, anchovy paste, and ¼ teaspoon of the pepper, whisking until smooth and blended.

3. Add the lettuce, beans, bread cubes, and Parmesan, tossing to coat thoroughly with the dressing. Sprinkle with the remaining ¼ teaspoon pepper and serve.

Helpful hint: You can make the dressing up to 12 hours in advance and store it in a covered jar. Shake or whisk the dressing again before pouring it over the salad.

FAT: 5G/23%
CALORIES: 193
SATURATED FAT: 1.5G
CARBOHYDRATE: 25G
PROTEIN: 11G
CHOLESTEROL: 5MG
SODIUM: 487MG

BAKED MUSHROOMS WITH PARMESAN AND BASIL

SERVES: 4
WORKING TIME: 20 MINUTES
TOTAL TIME: 30 MINUTES

Beefy portobellos topped with slivers of melted Parmesan make a tasty, hearty side dish for any meal.

⅓ cup balsamic vinegar

2 tablespoons no-salt-added tomato paste

1 teaspoon sugar

½ teaspoon salt

4 cloves garlic, crushed and peeled

½ cup chopped fresh basil

2½ pounds portobello mushrooms, or very large button mushrooms, cut into ¼-inch-thick slices

¼ cup shredded Parmesan cheese

1 teaspoon cornstarch mixed with 1 tablespoon water

1. In a large shallow baking dish, combine the vinegar, tomato paste, sugar, and salt. Add the garlic and 2 tablespoons of the basil, stirring to combine. Add the mushrooms, tossing to coat. Set aside.

2. Preheat the oven to 400°. With a slotted spoon, transfer the mushrooms and garlic to a 13-x-9-inch baking pan; reserve the marinade. Bake the mushrooms for 8 minutes, or until tender. Remove and discard the garlic. Sprinkle the cheese over the mushrooms and bake for 2 minutes, or just until the cheese has begun to melt.

3. Meanwhile, strain the reserved marinade into a small saucepan and bring to a boil over medium heat. Stir in the cornstarch mixture and cook, stirring, until slightly thickened, about 1 minute. Stir in the remaining 6 tablespoons basil. Spoon the sauce onto 4 plates and top with the mushrooms.

Helpful hint: Combining the cornstarch with cold water before adding it to the boiling marinade helps keep the cornstarch from lumping. To further ensure a lump-free sauce, stir or whisk the marinade constantly as you add the cornstarch mixture.

FAT: 2G/24%
CALORIES: 75
SATURATED FAT: 1G
CARBOHYDRATE: 11G
PROTEIN: 5G
CHOLESTEROL: 4MG
SODIUM: 375MG

CREAMED ONIONS

MAKES: 4 CUPS
WORKING TIME: 20 MINUTES
TOTAL TIME: 55 MINUTES

1½ pounds small white
onions, peeled
1 teaspoon unsalted butter
1 teaspoon sugar
2 tablespoons flour
2¼ cups low-fat (1%) milk
¾ teaspoon salt
½ teaspoon dried thyme
¼ teaspoon freshly ground
black pepper
¼ cup finely chopped fresh
parsley

1. In a large pot of boiling water, cook the onions for 2 minutes to blanch. Drain well.

2. In a large nonstick skillet, melt the butter over low heat. Add the onions, sprinkle the sugar over, and cook, shaking the pan frequently, until the onions are lightly golden and glazed, about 5 minutes.

3. Meanwhile, place the flour in a medium saucepan, and gradually whisk in the milk over medium heat until no lumps remain. Bring to a boil and whisk in the salt, thyme, and pepper. Reduce to a simmer and cook, whisking frequently, until the sauce is slightly thickened, about 5 minutes.

4. Pour the sauce over the onions, add the parsley, and stir well to combine. Return the pan to low heat, cover, and cook until the onions are tender, about 25 minutes. Spoon the creamed onions into a medium bowl and serve.

Helpful hint: The onions and white sauce can be prepared earlier in the day and stored separately in the refrigerator. To serve, proceed with step 4 of the recipe.

VALUES ARE PER ½ CUP
FAT: 1G/15%
CALORIES: 76
SATURATED FAT: 0.7G
CARBOHYDRATE: 13G
PROTEIN: 4G
CHOLESTEROL: 4MG
SODIUM: 250MG

N*o holiday buffet would be complete without this all-time favorite— made with a low-fat white sauce, not cream.*

CAULIFLOWER MILANESE

SERVES: 4
WORKING TIME: 15 MINUTES
TOTAL TIME: 40 MINUTES

The bread crumbs and Parmesan that top the cauliflower are what make this "Milanese." However, we've omitted one traditional Milanese ingredient—butter—and substituted a touch of olive oil for a more healthful dish. A deep-toned bowl, like the green one used here, displays the pale golden vegetable to good advantage.

5 cups cauliflower florets

½ cup reduced-sodium chicken broth, defatted

¾ teaspoon grated lemon zest

½ teaspoon salt

½ teaspoon dried marjoram

¼ teaspoon freshly ground black pepper

¼ cup plain dried bread crumbs

2 tablespoons grated Parmesan cheese

1 teaspoon olive oil

2 teaspoons fresh lemon juice

1. Preheat the oven to 400°. In a large pot of boiling water, cook the cauliflower for 4 minutes to blanch. Drain well.

2. Meanwhile, in a small bowl, combine the broth, lemon zest, salt, marjoram, and pepper. Set aside. In another small bowl, combine the bread crumbs and Parmesan. Set aside.

3. Spread the oil in a 13-x-9-inch baking dish and heat in the oven until hot, about 4 minutes. Add the cauliflower to the baking dish and bake, stirring occasionally, for 7 minutes, or until the cauliflower is golden. Pour the reserved broth mixture over the cauliflower and bake for 7 minutes, or until the cauliflower is tender. Sprinkle the bread crumb mixture over the cauliflower, drizzle with the lemon juice, and bake for 5 minutes, or until the topping is lightly crisped.

Helpful hint: When shopping for cauliflower, choose a firm head that's creamy white with crisp, green leaves at the base. Pass up heads that have dark speckles or soft spots.

FAT: 3G/22%
CALORIES: 82
SATURATED FAT: .7G
CARBOHYDRATE: 12G
PROTEIN: 5G
CHOLESTEROL: 2MG
SODIUM: 478MG

*S*avor all the creamy goodness of your favorite cole slaw recipe, but with substantially less fat—the secrets are nonfat yogurt and reduced-fat mayonnaise. We've also added some extra touches: tangy apples and fresh dill. This slaw would be terrific with a hearty onion tart, or spooned into a pita pocket with a slice of reduced-fat cheese.

RED CABBAGE SLAW

SERVES: 4
WORKING TIME: 20 MINUTES
TOTAL TIME: 20 MINUTES PLUS CHILLING TIME

⅔ cup plain nonfat yogurt

⅓ cup cider vinegar

3 tablespoons reduced-fat mayonnaise

1½ teaspoons sugar

¾ teaspoon salt

¼ teaspoon celery seed

6 cups shredded red cabbage (see tip)

4 carrots, shredded (see tip)

3 scallions, cut into 3-inch julienne strips

2 Granny Smith apples, cored, quartered, and cut into thin slices

¼ cup snipped fresh dill

1. In a large serving bowl, whisk together the yogurt, vinegar, mayonnaise, sugar, salt, and celery seed.

2. Add the cabbage, carrots, scallions, apples, and dill and toss well to combine. Cover with plastic wrap and refrigerate until well chilled, about 1 hour.

Helpful hints: You can prepare this cole slaw up to 1 day ahead. Green cabbage will work just as well as the red, but with less vivid color. You will need about 1 pound of cabbage (1 medium head) to make the slaw.

FAT: 3G/17%
CALORIES: 163
SATURATED FAT: 0.5G
CARBOHYDRATE: 33G
PROTEIN: 5G
CHOLESTEROL: 1MG
SODIUM: 571MG

TIP

You can use a food processor for shredding the vegetables, but we find it easier to use a hand grater—and there will be less to clean up. Quarter the cabbage, and then run each quarter across the coarse holes of the grater. Peel and then shred the carrots.

Brown and Wild Rice Pilaf

MAKES: 6 CUPS
WORKING TIME: 30 MINUTES
TOTAL TIME: 1 HOUR 5 MINUTES

½ cup wild rice

2 teaspoons olive oil

1 large onion, coarsely chopped

3 cloves garlic, minced

2 cups thickly sliced mushrooms

1 carrot, thinly sliced

1 green bell pepper, diced

2 cups reduced-sodium chicken broth, defatted

1 cup long-grain brown rice

½ teaspoon dried rosemary

½ teaspoon dried sage

¼ teaspoon salt

¼ teaspoon freshly ground black pepper

1. In a small bowl, combine the wild rice with cold water to cover. Let stand while you cook the vegetable mixture.

2. In a large saucepan, heat the oil until hot but not smoking over medium heat. Add the onion and garlic and cook, stirring frequently, until the onion is tender, about 7 minutes. Stir in the mushrooms, carrot, and bell pepper and cook, stirring frequently, until the vegetables are tender, about 5 minutes.

3. Drain the wild rice and add to the pan, stirring to coat. Stir in the broth, brown rice, 2 cups of water, the rosemary, sage, salt, and black pepper. Bring to a boil, reduce to a simmer, cover, and cook until the rice is tender, about 35 minutes.

Helpful hints: You may use all brown rice for this dish. Also, feel free to experiment with exotic fresh mushrooms, such as shiitake, portobello, or chanterelle. The pilaf can be prepared several hours ahead. To serve, gently reheat in the top of a steamer.

VALUES ARE PER ½ CUP
FAT: 1G/12%
CALORIES: 106
SATURATED FAT: 0.2G
CARBOHYDRATE: 21G
PROTEIN: 3G
CHOLESTEROL: 0MG
SODIUM: 157MG

Wild rice is actually the seed of a marsh grass native to the Great Lakes region, and not a rice at all. It tastes delicious in this nutty-sweet dish, which gets its woodsy flavor from mushrooms, rosemary, and sage. If you have attractive cookware, place the saucepan, with a trivet, directly on the holiday table. This pilaf is ideal alongside roast poultry, or inside as a stuffing.

VEGETABLES À LA GRECQUE

SERVES: 4
WORKING TIME: 25 MINUTES
TOTAL TIME: 40 MINUTES

1 cup reduced-sodium chicken broth

¾ teaspoon grated lemon zest

⅓ cup fresh lemon juice

½ teaspoon dried oregano

¼ teaspoon ground coriander

¼ teaspoon salt

2 carrots, halved lengthwise and cut into 2-inch pieces

2 cups small cauliflower florets

2 cups cut green beans (2-inch pieces)

3 cups quartered small mushrooms

1½ teaspoons cornstarch mixed with 1 tablespoon water

1. In a large skillet, combine the broth, ½ cup of water, the lemon zest, lemon juice, oregano, coriander, and salt. Bring to a boil over medium heat and add the carrots and cauliflower. Return to a boil, reduce to a simmer, cover, and cook for 5 minutes.

2. Add the green beans, return to a simmer, and cook, uncovered, until the vegetables are almost tender, about 4 minutes. Add the mushrooms and cook, stirring occasionally, until the vegetables are tender, about 5 minutes.

3. Return the mixture to a boil, stir in the cornstarch mixture, and cook, stirring constantly, until the mixture is slightly thickened, about 1 minute longer. Spoon the vegetables into a large bowl and serve.

Helpful hints: These vegetables are fine prepared up to 1 day ahead, and can be rewarmed or served at room temperature. Blanching in a flavorful liquid works with practically any vegetable, so try other favorites, adjusting the cooking times so everything remains crisp-tender.

The French term "à la Grecque" describes vegetables that are cooked in a seasoned oil and water mixture. We've replaced the olive oil with virtually fat-free chicken broth, and have pumped up the flavor with fresh lemon and oregano. This is the perfect refreshing side dish to offer with a bowl of sauced pasta. Or, serve the vegetables on their own as a crunchy snack.

FAT: 0.4G/6%
CALORIES: 72
SATURATED FAT: 0G
CARBOHYDRATE: 16G
PROTEIN: 4G
CHOLESTEROL: 0MG
SODIUM: 322MG

GARDEN-FRESH POTATO SALAD

SERVES: 4
WORKING TIME: 25 MINUTES
TOTAL TIME: 40 MINUTES

Lots of crunchy, sliced and diced vegetables show up in our version of this American favorite. For healthful eating, we've lightened up on the dressing: Nonfat yogurt and reduced-fat mayonnaise add the expected creaminess but little extra fat. For a nice presentation, line the serving bowl with crisp lettuce leaves and garnish with paprika.

1½ pounds small red potatoes, quartered

2 carrots, halved lengthwise and cut into thin slices

¼ cup distilled white vinegar

1 tablespoon Dijon mustard

¾ teaspoon salt

½ teaspoon freshly ground black pepper

6 radishes, thinly sliced

4 scallions, thinly sliced

1 red bell pepper, diced

1 rib celery, thinly sliced

¾ cup plain nonfat yogurt

2 tablespoons reduced-fat mayonnaise

1. In a large pot of boiling water, cook the potatoes for 18 minutes. Add the carrots and cook until the potatoes and carrots are tender, about 2 minutes longer. Drain well.

2. Meanwhile, in a large serving bowl, whisk together the vinegar, mustard, salt, and black pepper. Add the warm potatoes and carrots and toss well to coat.

3. Add the radishes, scallions, bell pepper, and celery and toss to combine. Add the yogurt and mayonnaise, stir gently to combine, and serve.

Helpful hint: We dress the salad while the potatoes are still warm so they will absorb more of the flavor as they cool.

FAT: 2G/8%
CALORIES: 215
SATURATED FAT: 0.3G
CARBOHYDRATE: 43G
PROTEIN: 7G
CHOLESTEROL: 1MG
SODIUM: 633MG

TOMATOES WITH HERBED CROUTON STUFFING

SERVES: 4
WORKING TIME: 20 MINUTES
TOTAL TIME: 40 MINUTES

4 ounces Italian bread, cut into ½-inch slices

2 cloves garlic, peeled and halved

¼ cup chopped fresh basil

¼ cup reduced-sodium chicken broth, defatted

2 tablespoons capers

2 teaspoons olive oil

¼ teaspoon salt

¼ teaspoon freshly ground black pepper

¼ teaspoon nutmeg

4 large tomatoes (8 ounces each)

1. Preheat the oven to 400°. Rub the bread with the cut sides of the garlic and then cut the bread into small cubes. Bake, turning once, for 6 minutes, or until lightly toasted. Transfer the bread cubes to a large bowl. Add the basil, 2 tablespoons of the broth, the capers, oil, salt, pepper, and nutmeg.

2. With a serrated knife, cut a ½-inch slice from the stem end of each tomato. With a small spoon, scoop the seeds and a little of the pulp out of the tomatoes (leaving a ½-inch-thick wall inside each tomato) and discard. Place the tomato shells in a shallow baking dish, spoon the bread mixture into the tomatoes, sprinkle with the remaining 2 tablespoons broth, and bake for 15 minutes, or until piping hot.

Helpful hint: If you have a little extra time, place the seeded tomatoes upside down on paper towels and let stand for 15 minutes or so to drain off any excess liquid.

Arrange these plump stuffed tomatoes on a platter with grilled steaks, chops, or chicken breasts for an instantly festive meal. The garlicky croutons that fill the tomatoes are oven-toasted, not fried like traditional croutons.

FAT: 4G/26%
CALORIES: 140
SATURATED FAT: .7G
CARBOHYDRATE: 24G
PROTEIN: 4G
CHOLESTEROL: 0MG
SODIUM: 467MG

ONIONS AGRODOLCE

SERVES: 4
WORKING TIME: 15 MINUTES
TOTAL TIME: 20 MINUTES

Here's a unique and easy accompaniment for roast pork or poultry. The classic recipe for onions in "agrodolce" (sweet-and-sour sauce) is not quite so quick and easy: Small whole onions need to be braised for as long as two hours to become completely tender. The frozen pearl onions we've used cook in about ten minutes— and of course you don't have to peel them, either.

1 teaspoon olive oil

1 pound frozen pearl onions, thawed

2 tablespoons sugar

½ teaspoon salt

½ cup reduced-sodium chicken broth, defatted

⅓ cup red wine vinegar

1 teaspoon unsalted butter

2 tablespoons chopped fresh parsley

2 tablespoons chopped fresh mint

1. In a large nonstick skillet, heat the oil until hot but not smoking over medium heat. Add the pearl onions and cook, shaking the pan, until the onions are nicely coated, about 2 minutes. Sprinkle the sugar and salt over the onions and continue cooking and shaking the pan until the sugar is melted and bubbly, about 3 minutes.

2. Add the broth and vinegar, reduce the heat to a simmer, and cook until the sauce is slightly syrupy and the onions are tender, about 4 minutes. Remove from the heat, stir in the butter, parsley, and mint and serve.

Helpful hint: You can serve the onions chilled if you like; but if you do so, leave out the butter, which will solidify when cool and give the dish an unappealing texture.

FAT: 2G/20%
CALORIES: 89
SATURATED FAT: .7G
CARBOHYDRATE: 17G
PROTEIN: 2G
CHOLESTEROL: 3MG
SODIUM: 366MG

CUCUMBER SALAD

SERVES: 4
WORKING TIME: 30 MINUTES
TOTAL TIME: 30 MINUTES PLUS CHILLING TIME

½ cup plain nonfat yogurt

2 tablespoons reduced-fat sour cream

½ teaspoon grated lime zest

1 tablespoon fresh lime juice

½ teaspoon salt

¼ teaspoon freshly ground black pepper

2½ pounds cucumbers (about 5), peeled and thinly sliced

½ cup julienne-cut radishes

½ cup thinly sliced scallions

3 tablespoons chopped fresh mint

1. In a large serving bowl, whisk together the yogurt, sour cream, lime zest, lime juice, salt, and pepper.

2. Add the cucumbers, radishes, scallions, and mint and toss gently to combine. Cover with plastic wrap and refrigerate until well chilled, about 1 hour.

Helpful hints: This salad can be made and chilled up to 8 hours in advance, but no longer—further chilling may result in a watery mixture as the cucumbers release their moisture. If fresh mint is unavailable, substitute chopped fresh parsley—not the same flavor but refreshing nonetheless.

FAT: 1G/18%
CALORIES: 70
SATURATED FAT: 0.5G
CARBOHYDRATE: 12G
PROTEIN: 4G
CHOLESTEROL: 3MG
SODIUM: 319MG

This is our version of tzatziki, the yogurty cucumber salad that's a standard in Greece. We've substituted nonfat yogurt for the full-fat variety, and have added some richness while softening the flavor with a little reduced-fat sour cream. Strongly accented with lime and mint, this salad can hold its own with spicy entrées of all sorts. It's also great served as a snack with a slice of crusty bread.

DESSERTS

Left, Strawberry-Topped Lemon Cheesecake (p. 428).
Above, Mocha Pudding Cake (p. 437).

STRAWBERRY CHEESECAKE MOUSSE

SERVES: 4
WORKING TIME: 20 MINUTES
TOTAL TIME: 20 MINUTES PLUS CHILLING TIME

Compare this recipe to one for a baked cheesecake and you'll notice that both the ingredient list and the preparation time have been dramatically shortened. Of course this isn't a cake— instead of baking the filling in a crust, we've spooned it into dessert bowls. The "cheesecake" mixture has a touch of tartness, and the flavor of the strawberries is underscored with a swirl of strawberry spreadable fruit.

½ teaspoon unflavored gelatin
2 pints fresh strawberries
2 tablespoons strawberry spreadable fruit
8 ounces nonfat cream cheese
¼ cup reduced-fat sour cream
½ cup granulated sugar
½ cup evaporated milk, chilled

1. Place ¼ cup of cold water in a small bowl, sprinkle the gelatin over, and let stand until softened, about 4 minutes. Set the bowl over a small saucepan of simmering water and stir until the gelatin dissolves, about 3 minutes. Set aside to cool.

2. Meanwhile, reserving 4 whole berries for a garnish, halve the strawberries. In a medium bowl, combine the halved fresh strawberries and the spreadable fruit, tossing until well coated.

3. In a food processor, combine the cream cheese, 2 tablespoons of the sour cream, and ¼ cup of the sugar and process until smooth. In a medium bowl, with an electric mixer, beat the evaporated milk with the remaining 2 tablespoons sour cream and remaining ¼ cup sugar until soft peaks form. Gradually beat in the cooled gelatin mixture.

4. Fold the cream cheese mixture into the evaporated milk mixture. Divide the strawberry mixture among 4 goblets or dessert bowls. Top with the "cheesecake" mixture and garnish with the reserved strawberries. Chill until set, about 1 hour, and serve.

Helpful hint: Spreadable fruit is like jam, but it is sweetened with fruit juice rather than sugar. It is used in this recipe because it is soft enough, even at room temperature, to coat the strawberries.

FAT: 5G/16%
CALORIES: 282
SATURATED FAT: 2.5G
CARBOHYDRATE: 49G
PROTEIN: 12G
CHOLESTEROL: 20MG
SODIUM: 314MG

NECTARINE-PEACH CRUMBLE

SERVES: 8
WORKING TIME: 20 MINUTES
TOTAL TIME: 55 MINUTES

A nectarine is not simply a fuzzless peach: Although the two fruits are closely related, nectarines are generally sweeter. We've used both in this luscious warm dessert (you could use all of one or the other), seasoning them with allspice and black pepper and spiking them with a shot of bourbon. A dollop of vanilla yogurt or ice milk would be delicious with the crumble.

1 pound nectarines, cut into ½-inch thick wedges

1⅓ cups firmly packed light brown sugar

¼ cup cornstarch

1 pound peaches, cut into ½-inch thick wedges

3 tablespoons bourbon, Scotch, or brandy

1 teaspoon grated lemon zest

2 tablespoons fresh lemon juice

⅛ teaspoon allspice

⅛ teaspoon freshly ground black pepper

⅓ cup old-fashioned rolled oats

⅓ cup flour

3 tablespoons unsalted butter, cut into small pieces

2 tablespoons reduced-fat sour cream

1. Preheat the oven to 375°. Spray a 6-cup glass or ceramic baking dish with nonstick cooking spray.

2. In a medium saucepan, combine half of the nectarines, 1 cup of the brown sugar, the cornstarch, and 1 tablespoon of water. Bring to a boil over medium heat. Remove from the heat and stir in the remaining nectarines, the peaches, bourbon, lemon zest, lemon juice, allspice, and pepper. Pour the mixture into the prepared baking dish.

3. In a medium bowl, stir together the oats, flour, and the remaining ⅓ cup brown sugar. With a pastry blender or 2 knives, cut in the butter and sour cream until the mixture resembles coarse crumbs. Spread the mixture over the fruit and bake for 30 minutes, or until browned and bubbly.

4. Serve warm or at room temperature.

Helpful hint: Old-fashioned rolled oats are whole, so they make a nice crisp crumble topping. You can substitute quick-cooking oats if necessary; however, because they are cut into pieces before rolling, they tend to get mushy. Instant oatmeal, which is cut even finer, should not be used.

FAT: 6G/20%
CALORIES: 275
SATURATED FAT: 3G
CARBOHYDRATE: 57G
PROTEIN: 2G
CHOLESTEROL: 13MG
SODIUM: 18MG

RASPBERRY-FILLED CHOCOLATE CUPCAKES

MAKES: 1 DOZEN
WORKING TIME: 30 MINUTES
TOTAL TIME: 50 MINUTES PLUS COOLING TIME

The cream-filled cupcakes of our childhoods now have a grown-up counterpart: petite chocolate cakes with hearts of raspberry jam (which you can flavor with raspberry liqueur for a truly adult treat).

The cupcakes are decorated with a swirl of semisweet chocolate and a few fresh berries. Red paper cups add a note of sophistication; look for them in kitchenware shops.

⅓ cup raspberry spreadable fruit

¾ teaspoon raspberry-flavored liqueur (optional)

1¼ cups flour

3 tablespoons unsweetened cocoa powder

½ teaspoon baking soda

⅛ teaspoon salt

¼ cup unsalted butter, at room temperature

½ cup granulated sugar

1 large egg

⅔ cup low-fat (1%) milk

½ ounce chocolate chips (about 1 tablespoon), melted

1 cup fresh raspberries

1. Preheat the oven to 375°. Line twelve 2½-inch muffin-tin cups with paper liners or spray with nonstick cooking spray; set aside. In a small bowl, combine the raspberry spreadable fruit and the raspberry liqueur; set aside.

2. In a medium bowl, combine the flour, cocoa powder, baking soda, and salt. In a large bowl, with an electric mixer, beat the butter and sugar until light and fluffy. Add the egg and beat until well combined. Alternately beat in the flour mixture and the milk, beginning and ending with the flour mixture.

3. Spoon about 1 tablespoon of batter into each muffin cup. Make a small indentation in the batter. Dividing evenly, spoon the raspberry spreadable fruit mixture into each indentation (using about 1¼ teaspoon per cupcake). Spoon the remaining batter evenly over the raspberry mixture. Bake for 20 minutes, or until the tops of the cupcakes spring back when lightly touched. Turn the cupcakes out onto a wire rack to cool completely.

4. Spoon the melted chocolate into a small plastic bag, then snip off the very tip of one corner of the bag. Pipe the melted chocolate on top of each cupcake. Top with fresh raspberries before serving.

Helpful hint: If you like, cherry-flavored kirsch can be substituted for the raspberry-flavored liqueur.

VALUES ARE PER CUPCAKE
FAT: 5G/29%
CALORIES: 158
SATURATED FAT: 2.9G
CARBOHYDRATE: 26G
PROTEIN: 3G
CHOLESTEROL: 29MG
SODIUM: 89MG

LEMON POPPY SEED CAKE

SERVES: 12
WORKING TIME: 20 MINUTES
TOTAL TIME: 1 HOUR PLUS COOLING TIME

This is one of those moist cakes that tastes better a day after baking. Delicately textured, it makes a wonderful indulgence for a special brunch or dinner, or a quiet tea break in the afternoon. Keep this recipe in mind when you need a hostess offering for a holiday party—it will always be welcomed.

3 tablespoons poppy seeds
2½ cups cake flour
1½ teaspoons baking powder
½ teaspoon baking soda
¼ teaspoon salt
¼ teaspoon ground allspice
2 whole eggs
1 egg white
6 tablespoons unsalted butter
1¾ cups sugar
1 tablespoon grated lemon zest
1½ cups low-fat (1.5%) buttermilk
¼ cup fresh lemon juice

1. Preheat the oven to 350°. Spray a 10-inch angel food or tube cake pan with nonstick cooking spray. Dust with flour, shaking off the excess. Spread the poppy seeds on a baking sheet with sides and bake for 4 minutes, or until lightly crisped. Set aside to cool.

2. On a sheet of wax paper, combine the flour, baking powder, baking soda, salt, allspice, and poppy seeds. In a small bowl, whisk together the eggs and egg white. In a large bowl, with an electric mixer, beat the butter, 1½ cups of the sugar, and the lemon zest until creamy. Gradually beat in the egg mixture, 1 teaspoon at a time, until light in texture. With a rubber spatula, alternately fold in the flour mixture and buttermilk, beginning and ending with the flour mixture, until just blended. Scrape the batter into the prepared pan, smoothing the top. Bake for 35 minutes, or until a toothpick inserted in the center comes out clean. Transfer to a wire rack.

3. In a small saucepan, stir together the lemon juice and remaining ¼ cup sugar. Bring to a boil over medium heat and cook, stirring constantly, until the sugar dissolves, about 2 minutes. With a fork, prick holes in the top of the cake and pour the hot syrup over the cake. Transfer to a wire rack and cool the cake in the pan for 10 minutes. Transfer to the rack and cool completely.

Helpful hint: For homemade buttermilk, combine 1½ tablespoons lemon juice and 1½ cups low-fat milk; let stand for 5 minutes to sour.

FAT: 8G/26%
CALORIES: 290
SATURATED FAT: 4.3G
CARBOHYDRATE: 50G
PROTEIN: 5G
CHOLESTEROL: 53MG
SODIUM: 191MG

The
seductive, silky texture
of this chiffon pie
is rendered even more
irresistible with a
lacing of heady
hazelnut liqueur.
The secret to the
remarkably low-fat
profile is the faux
whipped cream, made
with powdered milk.
Toast the pecans (this
brings out the flavor)
in a 350° oven on a
baking sheet with sides
for about ten minutes,
stirring occasionally.

PUMPKIN CHIFFON PIE WITH PECANS

SERVES: 8
WORKING TIME: 30 MINUTES
TOTAL TIME: 3 HOURS (INCLUDES CHILLING TIME)

1 cup instant nonfat powdered milk

½ cup ice water

1 cup zwieback crumbs (about 12 zwieback)

1 cup graham cracker crumbs

3 tablespoons honey

2 tablespoons canola oil

2 envelopes unflavored gelatin

6 ounces nonfat cream cheese

1 cup firmly packed dark brown sugar

1¼ teaspoons cinnamon

1 teaspoon vanilla

2 cups canned solid-pack pumpkin purée

2 tablespoons hazelnut liqueur (optional)

¼ cup coarsely chopped pecans or hazelnuts, toasted

1. Preheat the oven to 350°. Place a small mixing bowl and beaters, the powdered milk, and ice water in the freezer to chill while you prepare the crust and filling. Spray a 9-inch pie plate with nonstick cooking spray. In a food processor, combine all the crumbs, the honey, and oil and process until blended. Scrape the mixture into the prepared pie plate and press firmly into the bottom and up the sides. Bake in the lower third of the oven for 8 to 10 minutes, or until the crust is just set. Transfer to a wire rack to cool.

2. Meanwhile, place ½ cup of cold water in a small bowl, and sprinkle the gelatin on top. Set the bowl over a small saucepan of simmering water and stir until the gelatin dissolves, about 3 minutes. Remove from the heat. In a food processor, combine the cream cheese, brown sugar, cinnamon, and vanilla and process until creamy. Add the pumpkin and liqueur and process until smooth. Add the dissolved gelatin and process until combined. Transfer to a medium bowl and refrigerate until the mixture is just beginning to set and is the texture of raw egg whites, about 45 minutes.

3. In the chilled mixing bowl, combine the powdered milk and ice water. With the chilled beaters, beat until very soft peaks form (see tip). With a rubber spatula, fold the milk mixture into the pumpkin mixture. Scrape the mixture into the crust and refrigerate until set, at least 1½ hours. Sprinkle the pecans on top and serve.

FAT: 8G/20%
CALORIES: 364
SATURATED FAT: 1G
CARBOHYDRATE: 64G
PROTEIN: 10G
CHOLESTEROL: 6MG
SODIUM: 280MG

TIP

Ice water and well-chilled powdered milk whip up to very soft peaks of "whipped cream." Folding this into the pie filling lightens the mixture without adding fat. If you normally use beaten egg whites for a chiffon-type pie, this does the job without the safety problems associated with using uncooked eggs.

DOUBLE CHOCOLATE CHEWS

MAKES: 2 DOZEN
WORKING TIME: 20 MINUTES
TOTAL TIME: 30 MINUTES PLUS COOLING TIME

I*t may be hard to believe, but both "double chocolate" and "low in fat" are phrases that describe this big, beautiful cookie.*

1 cup flour

½ cup unsweetened cocoa powder

¼ teaspoon salt

3 tablespoons unsalted butter

2½ ounces nonfat cream cheese

⅓ cup granulated sugar

½ cup firmly packed dark brown sugar

1 teaspoon vanilla extract

1½ ounces mini chocolate chips (about 3 tablespoons)

1. Preheat the oven to 350°. Spray 2 cookie sheets with nonstick cooking spray.

2. On a sheet of waxed paper, sift together the flour, cocoa powder, and salt. In a large bowl, with an electric mixer, beat the butter, cream cheese, granulated sugar, and brown sugar until creamy. Beat in the vanilla. Beat the flour mixture into the butter mixture. With your fingers, knead in the chocolate chips.

3. Divide the dough into quarters. Divide each quarter into 6 equal pieces. Roll each piece of dough into a ball and place on the prepared cookie sheets. Repeat to form 24 balls. Using the bottom of a glass, press the balls into 2-inch rounds.

4. Bake the cookies, in two batches, for 8 minutes, or until slightly puffed and very soft to the touch. Let cool on the pans for 1 minute, then transfer to wire racks to cool before serving.

Helpful hint: To prevent the glass from sticking when you flatten the balls of dough, coat the bottom of the glass with granulated sugar. Dip the glass in water, then into a saucer of sugar. After you've flattened the first cookie, the glass will become sticky and the sugar will adhere to it.

VALUES ARE PER COOKIE
FAT: 2G/24%
CALORIES: 76
SATURATED FAT: 1.3G
CARBOHYDRATE: 14G
PROTEIN: 1G
CHOLESTEROL: 4MG
SODIUM: 39MG

BUTTERSCOTCH PUDDING

SERVES: 4
WORKING TIME: 15 MINUTES
TOTAL TIME: 15 MINUTES PLUS CHILLING TIME

¼ cup cornstarch
⅔ cup firmly packed light brown sugar
3 cups low-fat (1%) milk
¼ teaspoon salt
1 large egg
1 tablespoon unsalted butter
1 teaspoon vanilla extract
3 tablespoons whipped cream

1. In a small bowl, whisk together the cornstarch, ⅓ cup of the brown sugar, and ½ cup of the milk. In a medium saucepan, combine the remaining 2½ cups milk, the remaining ⅓ cup brown sugar, and the salt. Bring to a boil over medium heat. Stir the cornstarch mixture into the boiling milk mixture and cook, stirring, until thickened, about 4 minutes.

2. In a small bowl, lightly beat the egg. Gradually whisk some of the hot milk mixture into the egg, then whisk the warmed egg mixture back into the saucepan. Return to the heat and cook, whisking constantly, for about 1 minute. Remove from the heat and stir in the butter and vanilla. Spoon into 4 dessert bowls and refrigerate until chilled, about 1 hour. With a #21 star tip and a pastry bag, pipe the whipped cream on top of the pudding (or, use a spoon to form small dollops) and serve.

Helpful hint: Mixing the cornstarch with a small amount of milk (in step 1) helps prevent the cornstarch from forming lumps when it's added to the hot milk.

FAT: 8G/23%
CALORIES: 310
SATURATED FAT: 4G
CARBOHYDRATE: 53G
PROTEIN: 8G
CHOLESTEROL: 74MG
SODIUM: 260MG

A *modest amount of butter is added at the last possible moment here so that its pure flavor shines through.*

Decadently fudgy and moist, this cake, spiked with a touch of rum, will elicit murmurs of delight from the most demanding dessert connoisseurs. And as the name implies, a slightly concave top is to be expected. Garnish with whole strawberries and arrange the cake as the centerpiece for a holiday dessert buffet.

Fallen Chocolate Mousse Cake

SERVES: 8
WORKING TIME: 20 MINUTES
TOTAL TIME: 45 MINUTES PLUS COOLING TIME

1 cup plain nonfat yogurt

¾ cup granulated sugar

½ cup unsweetened cocoa powder, preferably Dutch process

¼ cup firmly packed light brown sugar

1 teaspoon cinnamon

¼ teaspoon ground nutmeg

1 tablespoon dark rum

2 ounces semisweet chocolate, coarsely chopped and melted (see tip)

2 eggs, separated

6 tablespoons flour

2 egg whites

¼ teaspoon cream of tartar

¼ teaspoon salt

2 teaspoons confectioners' sugar

1. Preheat the oven to 375°. Spray an 8½-inch springform pan with nonstick cooking spray. Line the bottom of the pan with a circle of wax paper. In a small bowl, stir together the yogurt and 2 tablespoons of the granulated sugar. Refrigerate until serving time.

2. In a medium bowl, stir together ½ cup of the granulated sugar, the cocoa powder, brown sugar, cinnamon, and nutmeg. Stir in ⅓ cup of hot water, the rum, and half of the melted chocolate. In a small bowl, with a fork, lightly beat the egg yolks. Stir in one-quarter of the warm cocoa mixture, then stir the yolk mixture back into the cocoa mixture. With a rubber spatula, stir in the flour.

3. In a large bowl, with an electric mixer, beat the 4 egg whites until foamy. Add the cream of tartar and salt and beat until soft peaks form. Gradually beat in the remaining 2 tablespoons granulated sugar until stiff peaks form. Stir ½ cup of the egg whites into the batter to lighten, then gently fold in the remaining whites. Scrape the batter into the prepared pan, smoothing the top. Bake for 25 minutes, or until a toothpick inserted in the center comes out just clean. Transfer to a wire rack to cool completely.

4. With a metal spatula, loosen the cake from the side of the pan and remove the pan side. Place the cake on a plate, dust with the confectioners' sugar, and drizzle the remaining melted chocolate on top. Serve the sweetened yogurt on the side.

FAT: 4G/18%
CALORIES: 213
SATURATED FAT: 2.1G
CARBOHYDRATE: 41G
PROTEIN: 6G
CHOLESTEROL: 54MG
SODIUM: 124MG

TIP

Melting chocolate in a homemade "double boiler" helps prevent separation or graininess. Coarsely chop the chocolate, and then gently melt it in a bowl set over, not in, a pan of simmering water. Use half of the melted chocolate in the batter, and then remove the entire double boiler from the heat. The warmth of the hot water will hold the remaining melted chocolate for the final garnish.

DEEP-DISH APPLE COBBLER

SERVES: 8
WORKING TIME: 30 MINUTES
TOTAL TIME: 1 HOUR 10 MINUTES

1 cup plus 1 tablespoon flour

3 tablespoons plus ¾ cup sugar

1 teaspoon grated lemon zest

⅜ teaspoon salt

¼ teaspoon baking powder

*3 tablespoons plus 2 teaspoons
unsalted butter, cut up*

¼ cup reduced-fat sour cream

*6 Granny Smith apples, peeled,
cored, and thinly sliced*

2 teaspoons fresh lemon juice

¾ teaspoon cinnamon

⅛ teaspoon ground nutmeg

1. In a large bowl, stir together 1 cup of the flour, 3 tablespoons of the sugar, the lemon zest, ¼ teaspoon of the salt, and the baking powder. With a pastry blender or 2 knives, cut in 3 tablespoons of the butter until the mixture resembles coarse meal. Stir in the sour cream and 2 tablespoons of cold water. Add up to 1 tablespoon more water, 1 teaspoon at a time, until the dough just comes together. Pat into a disk, wrap in plastic wrap, and chill for 30 minutes.

2. Meanwhile, in a large bowl, combine the apples, remaining ¾ cup sugar, and remaining 1 tablespoon flour and toss well to coat. Add the lemon juice, cinnamon, nutmeg, and remaining ⅛ teaspoon salt and toss to combine. Spoon the mixture into a 9-inch deep-dish pie plate and dot the top with the remaining 2 teaspoons butter.

3. Preheat the oven to 425°. On a lightly floured board, pat the chilled dough into an 8-inch circle. Gently lift the dough and place on top of the filling. Place the cobbler on a baking sheet and bake for 15 minutes. Reduce the oven to 350° and bake for 25 minutes longer, or until the crust is golden brown. Transfer to a wire rack and cool the cobbler for 10 minutes, then serve.

Helpful hint: For a freshly baked dessert without fuss, assemble the filling in the pie plate and refrigerate it for up to 8 hours, then pat the top crust into a circle and refrigerate that as well. Just before you sit down to dinner, place the crust on top of the filling and pop it in the oven.

FAT: 7G/21%
CALORIES: 294
SATURATED FAT: 3.9G
CARBOHYDRATE: 58G
PROTEIN: 2G
CHOLESTEROL: 17MG
SODIUM: 120MG

This farmhouse favorite is a boon during the busy holiday season since it's easy to prepare, and can be served warm or at room temperature, depending on your timetable. The rich-tasting crust, made surprisingly low in fat with reduced-fat sour cream, is accented with a little lemon zest. Try serving the cobbler topped with vanilla nonfat yogurt, along with mugs of hot mulled cider.

*T*hough
only a modest amount
of butter is used in this
cake, the buttery flavor
is quite prominent.
That's because the top
of the cake is glazed
with a mixture of
butter and brown
sugar (these ingredients
go into the pan first, so
they end up as a
topping when the cake
is turned out). Be sure
to try a slice of this
cake while it's still
warm.

PINEAPPLE UPSIDE-DOWN CAKE

SERVES: 12
WORKING TIME: 25 MINUTES
TOTAL TIME: 1 HOUR 20 MINUTES PLUS COOLING TIME

¼ cup plus 1 tablespoon
unsalted butter

½ cup firmly packed light brown
sugar

Two 8-ounce cans juice-packed
pineapple rings, drained and
juice reserved

8 dried cherries or raisins

2¼ cups sifted cake flour

2½ teaspoons baking powder

½ teaspoon baking soda

¼ teaspoon salt

¼ cup reduced-fat sour cream

1 cup granulated sugar

1 whole large egg

4 large egg whites

2 teaspoons vanilla extract

⅔ cup low-fat (1%) milk

1. Preheat the oven to 325°. In a 10-inch ovenproof skillet, preferably cast iron, melt 1 tablespoon of the butter over low heat. Stir in the brown sugar and 2 tablespoons of the reserved pineapple juice. Cook until the sugar is dissolved and the mixture is smooth, about 1 minute. Remove from the heat. Arrange the pineapple rings in a single layer on top of the brown sugar mixture. Place a dried cherry in the center of each pineapple ring; set aside.

2. On a sheet of waxed paper, sift together the flour, baking powder, baking soda, and salt. In a large bowl, with an electric mixer, beat the remaining ¼ cup butter, the sour cream, and sugar until light and fluffy. Beat in the whole egg and egg whites, one at a time, beating well after each addition. Beat in the vanilla. With a wooden spoon, alternately stir in the flour mixture and the milk, beginning and ending with the flour mixture, until just combined.

3. Carefully spoon the batter over the pineapple slices. Bake for 50 to 55 minutes, or until a toothpick inserted in the center comes out clean. Transfer to a wire rack and cool the cake in the skillet for 5 minutes. Run a knife around the edges of the skillet and invert the cake onto a heatproof plate (see tip).

Helpful hint: If your skillet doesn't have an ovenproof handle, wrap the handle in a double thickness of foil so that it does not scorch.

FAT: 6G/21%
CALORIES: 260
SATURATED FAT: 3.5G
CARBOHYDRATE: 48G
PROTEIN: 4G
CHOLESTEROL: 33MG
SODIUM: 237MG

TIP

When the cake has cooled slightly, place a heatproof serving plate over the skillet, then invert the skillet and plate. Then carefully lift the skillet; the cake should slip out onto the plate.

To capture the lovely flavor of hazelnuts in a low-fat mousse, we've flavored this mixture with Frangelico, a hazelnut-flavored liqueur, and we use just one ounce of nuts as a topping. Be careful, when chopping the nuts, not to run the machine too long, or you'll end up with hazelnut butter.

FROZEN HAZELNUT MOUSSE

SERVES: 4
WORKING TIME: 15 MINUTES
TOTAL TIME: 35 MINUTES PLUS FREEZING TIME

1 ounce hazelnuts
½ cup granulated sugar
3 tablespoons flour
2¼ cups low-fat (1%) milk
1 tablespoon light corn syrup
¼ teaspoon salt
1 large egg
2 tablespoons reduced-fat sour cream
3 tablespoons Frangelico
¼ teaspoon almond extract

1. Preheat the oven to 375°. Toast the hazelnuts until they are fragrant and the skins begin to pop, about 7 minutes (see tip, top photo). Rub the nuts in a cloth to remove the skin (bottom photo), then transfer to a food processor and pulse until coarsely chopped.

2. In a small bowl, stir together ¼ cup of the sugar and the flour. In a medium saucepan, combine the milk, the remaining ¼ cup sugar, the corn syrup, and salt. Bring to a boil over medium heat. Whisk the flour mixture into the milk mixture and cook, stirring constantly, until thickened, about 5 minutes.

3. In a small bowl, lightly beat the egg. Gradually whisk some of the hot milk mixture into the egg, then whisk the warmed egg mixture back into the saucepan. Return to the heat and cook, whisking constantly, for 2 minutes. Remove from the heat and cool to room temperature. Stir in the sour cream, Frangelico, and almond extract. Spoon into four 6- to 8-ounce goblets and freeze until solid. Let sit at room temperature for 20 minutes, top with the hazelnuts, and serve.

Helpful hint: Corn syrup prevents sugar from crystallizing, thereby assuring a silky texture in frozen desserts.

FAT: 8G/24%
CALORIES: 298
SATURATED FAT: 2.1G
CARBOHYDRATE: 45G
PROTEIN: 8G
CHOLESTEROL: 61MG
SODIUM: 230MG

TIP

To remove the inner skin from shelled hazelnuts, first spread the nuts in a shallow pan and toast them in a 375° oven. Turn the toasted nuts onto a kitchen towel and rub them in the towel; don't worry if flecks of the skin remain here and there on the nuts.

BERRY CAKE

SERVES: 8
WORKING TIME: 15 MINUTES
TOTAL TIME: 50 MINUTES PLUS COOLING TIME

*1½ cups assorted whole berries
(such as blackberries, blueberries,
and raspberries)*

1 cup flour

*¾ cup plus 1 tablespoon
granulated sugar*

½ teaspoon baking soda

½ teaspoon ground ginger

¼ teaspoon salt

*½ cup low-fat (1.5%)
buttermilk*

2 tablespoons vegetable oil

2 large eggs, lightly beaten

1. Preheat the oven to 375°. Spray an 8-inch round cake pan with nonstick cooking spray. In a small bowl, combine the berries; set aside.

2. In a medium bowl, combine the flour, ¾ cup of the sugar, the baking soda, ginger, and salt. Make a well in the center and pour in the buttermilk, oil, and eggs. Stir until no dry flour is visible.

3. Scrape the batter into the prepared pan. Spoon the berries on top and sprinkle with the remaining 1 tablespoon sugar. Bake for 35 to 40 minutes, or until a toothpick inserted in the center comes out clean. Cool in the pan on a wire rack. Remove from the pan, transfer to a plate, and serve.

Helpful hints: You can use any small berries for this recipe, except strawberries, which will add too much moisture. It's important to stir the dry ingredients thoroughly to mix them, and, conversely, to go easy on the mixing once you've added the liquid ingredients so that the cake turns out nice and tender.

FAT: 5G/22%
CALORIES: 207
SATURATED FAT: 1G
CARBOHYDRATE: 37G
PROTEIN: 4G
CHOLESTEROL: 54MG
SODIUM: 171MG

This irresistible buttermilk cake is a snap to make, and it comes with its own garnish to boot; fresh berries peeking out from a crispy, glossy top. It's perfect for a convivial morning coffee klatch, a gracious afternoon tea, or a casual dinner with friends. Try it in the summer, when berries are cheap and plentiful.

CAPPUCCINO CHEESECAKE

SERVES: 12
WORKING TIME: 20 MINUTES
TOTAL TIME: 2 HOURS 15 MINUTES PLUS CHILLING TIME

While cheesecake may be the original "oh no, there goes my diet" dessert, nobody can blame this cake for dietary downfall. It's made with low-fat cottage cheese and reduced-fat and nonfat cream cheeses, and has only a bottom crust, made with about a quarter the usual quantity of oil. The result: Our rich coffee-infused cake has a fraction of the fat of regular cheesecake.

10 chocolate wafer cookies (about 2½ ounces)

1 tablespoon vegetable oil

1 cup plus 1 tablespoon granulated sugar

3 tablespoons instant espresso powder

3 tablespoons coffee liqueur

1 quart low-fat (1%) cottage cheese

8 ounces reduced-fat cream cheese (Neufchâtel), at room temperature

4 ounces nonfat cream cheese, at room temperature

2 tablespoons flour

2 whole large eggs

2 large egg whites

¼ teaspoon salt

⅛ teaspoon cinnamon

12 chocolate-covered coffee beans (optional)

1. Preheat the oven to 300°. Spray a 9-inch springform pan with nonstick cooking spray. In a food processor, process the chocolate wafers until fine crumbs form. Remove ½ teaspoon of the crumbs and set aside. Add the oil and 1 tablespoon of the sugar and process until the crumbs are evenly moistened. Place the crumb mixture in the prepared pan and press onto the bottom of the pan.

2. In a small bowl, dissolve the espresso powder in the coffee liqueur; set aside. In a food processor, process the cottage cheese until it is very smooth, about 2 minutes. Add the reduced-fat cream cheese, nonfat cream cheese, the remaining 1 cup sugar, the flour, whole eggs, egg whites, salt, cinnamon, and reserved coffee liqueur mixture. Process until smooth.

3. Scrape the batter into the prepared pan and bake for 1 hour and 25 minutes, or until firm around the edges but still wobbly in the center. Turn off the oven and leave the cheesecake in the oven with the door closed for 30 minutes. Transfer to a wire rack to cool completely. Cover and refrigerate until chilled, at least 4 hours. Sprinkle the reserved crumbs around the edge of the cheesecake and decorate with the coffee beans. Remove the springform ring and serve.

Helpful hint: If you don't want to buy a large bottle of coffee liqueur for this recipe, look for the little bottles, called "nips" or "tasters," that are sold in liquor stores; they contain just the amount called for here.

FAT: 7G/27%
CALORIES: 237
SATURATED FAT: 3.1G
CARBOHYDRATE: 28G
PROTEIN: 15G
CHOLESTEROL: 48MG
SODIUM: 534MG

417

Apple Bread Pudding

SERVES: 6
WORKING TIME: 20 MINUTES
TOTAL TIME: 45 MINUTES

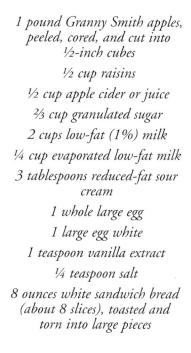

Apples are simmered in cider here to intensify their flavor, and are then combined with bread and bathed in a vanilla egg custard.

1 pound Granny Smith apples, peeled, cored, and cut into ½-inch cubes

½ cup raisins

½ cup apple cider or juice

⅔ cup granulated sugar

2 cups low-fat (1%) milk

¼ cup evaporated low-fat milk

3 tablespoons reduced-fat sour cream

1 whole large egg

1 large egg white

1 teaspoon vanilla extract

¼ teaspoon salt

8 ounces white sandwich bread (about 8 slices), toasted and torn into large pieces

1. Preheat the oven to 350°. Spray an 8-cup glass or ceramic baking dish with nonstick cooking spray.

2. In a large nonstick skillet, combine the apples, raisins, and cider. Bring to a boil over medium heat, reduce to a simmer, cover, and cook until the apples are softened, about 5 minutes.

3. Meanwhile, in a large bowl, whisk together the sugar, low-fat milk, evaporated milk, sour cream, whole egg, egg white, vanilla, and salt. Place the toast pieces in the prepared baking dish along with the apple mixture. Pour the milk mixture on top and bake for 25 minutes, or until the custard is just set and the top is golden brown. Serve warm or at room temperature.

Helpful hints: If you like, Cortland or McIntosh apples can be used instead of the Granny Smiths. If you can't find evaporated low-fat milk, you can use evaporated skimmed milk instead.

FAT: 5G/13%
CALORIES: 345
SATURATED FAT: 1.6G
CARBOHYDRATE: 68G
PROTEIN: 9G
CHOLESTEROL: 43MG
SODIUM: 371MG

Zesty Lemon Squares

MAKES: 16 SQUARES
WORKING TIME: 15 MINUTES
TOTAL TIME: 1 HOUR 20 MINUTES PLUS COOLING TIME

¼ cup unsalted butter

2 ounces nonfat cream cheese

1¼ cups granulated sugar

¾ cup plus 3 tablespoons flour

¼ teaspoon salt

1 whole large egg

3 large egg whites

1 tablespoon grated lemon zest

¼ cup plus 2 tablespoons fresh lemon juice

½ teaspoon baking powder

1 teaspoon confectioners' sugar

1. Preheat the oven to 350°. In a medium bowl, with an electric mixer, beat the butter, cream cheese, and ¼ cup of the granulated sugar until creamy. Blend in ¾ cup of the flour and the salt on low speed until the mixture resembles fine crumbs. Press the mixture evenly over the bottom of an 8-inch square baking pan. Bake for 20 minutes.

2. Meanwhile, in a medium bowl, with an electric mixer, beat the whole egg, egg whites, and remaining 1 cup granulated sugar until thick, about 2 minutes. Beat in the lemon zest, lemon juice, remaining 3 tablespoons flour, and the baking powder and beat for 2 minutes.

3. Pour the filling over the baked crust and return to the oven for about 25 minutes, or until the topping is firm in the center and golden brown around the edges. Cool in the pan on a wire rack. Cut into 2-inch squares and transfer to a plate. Just before serving, dust with the confectioners' sugar.

Helpful hints: The crust for these cookies (step 1) can be baked up to a day in advance and kept covered in the refrigerator until you're ready to use it. You'll need 2 medium lemons for the 6 tablespoons of juice called for.

VALUES ARE PER SQUARE
FAT: 3G/21%
CALORIES: 126
SATURATED FAT: 1.9G
CARBOHYDRATE: 22G
PROTEIN: 2G
CHOLESTEROL: 21MG
SODIUM: 81MG

These delicate lemon bars are perfect for afternoon tea. We've cut half a stick of butter from the classic recipe.

PEAR AND CRANBERRY SHORTCAKES

SERVES: 8
WORKING TIME: 25 MINUTES
TOTAL TIME: 1 HOUR PLUS COOLING TIME

This winter spin on a summer specialty is a delicious study in sweet and tart—cranberries and pears are bathed in a brandy-spiked sauce. We brush the tops of the buttermilk biscuits before baking with a little low-fat milk for a soft sheen. When the table is cleared, let guests retire to comfortable easy chairs in the living room, and serve the shortcakes with nut-flavored coffee.

1 teaspoon active dry yeast
¼ cup granulated sugar
2 cups all-purpose flour
1 tablespoon baking powder
½ teaspoon baking soda
½ teaspoon salt
3 tablespoons unsalted butter, cut up
¾ cup low-fat (1.5%) buttermilk
2 Bartlett pears, peeled, cored, and cut into 1-inch chunks
3 tablespoons brandy
12-ounce package fresh or frozen cranberries
¾ cup firmly packed light brown sugar
¼ teaspoon ground allspice
1 teaspoon cornstarch mixed with 1 tablespoon water
1 teaspoon vanilla
2 tablespoons low-fat (1%) milk
¼ cup reduced-fat sour cream

1. Place ¼ cup of warm water in a small bowl. Sprinkle the yeast and ½ teaspoon of the granulated sugar over and let stand until foamy, about 5 minutes. In a large bowl, combine the flour, all but 1 tablespoon of the granulated sugar, baking powder, baking soda, and salt. With a pastry blender or 2 knives, cut in 2 tablespoons plus 2 teaspoons of the butter until the mixture resembles coarse meal. Stir the buttermilk into the yeast mixture, then stir into the dry ingredients until just blended. Cover; let rise in a warm place for 20 minutes.

2. Meanwhile, in a large nonstick skillet, cook the pears in the remaining 1 teaspoon butter over medium heat until lightly colored, about 2 minutes. Add the brandy and cook for 1 minute. Transfer to a bowl. Add the cranberries, brown sugar, allspice, and ½ cup of water to the pan and cook, stirring, until the berries pop, about 7 minutes. Stir in the cornstarch mixture and pears and bring to a boil. Cook, stirring, for 1 minute. Remove from the heat and stir in the vanilla.

3. Preheat the oven to 450°. On a lightly floured board, pat the dough into a rectangle about ½ inch thick. With a 3-inch biscuit cutter, cut out biscuits. Gather scraps, pat out, and cut out more biscuits. Transfer to a nonstick baking sheet, brush with the milk, sprinkle the remaining 1 tablespoon granulated sugar over, and bake for 14 minutes, or until crisp. Transfer to a wire rack to cool. Split the biscuits, place on 8 plates, fill with the fruit and sour cream, and serve.

FAT: 6G/16%
CALORIES: 347
SATURATED FAT: 3.5G
CARBOHYDRATE: 66G
PROTEIN: 5G
CHOLESTEROL: 16MG
SODIUM: 422MG

WINTER FRUIT COMPOTE

SERVES: 6
WORKING TIME: 20 MINUTES
TOTAL TIME: 35 MINUTES

½ cup granulated sugar

1-inch piece of fresh ginger, peeled and very thinly slivered

2 Granny Smith apples, peeled, cored, and cut into wedges

1 firm-ripe pear, peeled, cored, and cut into ¾-inch chunks

½ cup dried apricots

2 cups fresh or frozen cranberries

2 oranges, peeled and sectioned

1. In a large saucepan, combine the sugar, 1½ cups of water, and the ginger. Bring to a boil over high heat. Add the apples, pear, and apricots. Reduce the heat to low and simmer, uncovered, until the fruit is softened, about 5 minutes.

2. Add the cranberries and cook, stirring occasionally, until the cranberries pop, about 5 minutes. Stir in the orange sections and remove from the heat. Transfer the compote to a bowl and serve warm or at room temperature.

Helpful hint: You can use any flavorful apple in this recipe. Some less familiar ones to try are Empires, Ida Reds, Macouns, Jonathans, Cortlands, and Winesaps. If you don't find them at the supermarket, visit a farmers' market, orchard, or roadside fruit stand.

FAT: 1G/5%
CALORIES: 172
SATURATED FAT: 0G
CARBOHYDRATE: 44G
PROTEIN: 1G
CHOLESTEROL: 0MG
SODIUM: 2MG

Warm fruit compote, redolent of ginger, is a lovely cold weather dessert; you might offer vanilla yogurt or sour cream with the compote, and pass a plate of crisp, simple cookies. The colorful fruit mixture would also be perfect at a brunch, served with warm muffins or biscuits. Stock up on cranberries at holiday time, when they're widely available, and keep them in the freezer.

GINGERBREAD WITH LEMON SAUCE

SERVES: 8
WORKING TIME: 20 MINUTES
TOTAL TIME: 50 MINUTES PLUS COOLING TIME

There's nothing like the aroma of gingerbread baking to bring on the holiday spirit—crystallized ginger gives this version a tasty twist.

1¼ cups cake flour

1¼ teaspoons ground ginger

1 teaspoon baking powder

½ teaspoon baking soda

½ teaspoon cinnamon

¼ teaspoon dry mustard

¼ teaspoon salt

3 tablespoons unsalted butter

½ cup firmly packed dark brown sugar

1 egg

2 tablespoons finely chopped crystallized ginger

2 teaspoons grated lemon zest

½ cup low-fat (1.5%) buttermilk

3 tablespoons molasses

3 tablespoons freshly brewed coffee

⅓ cup fresh lemon juice

¼ cup granulated sugar

¼ teaspoon ground nutmeg

1 teaspoon cornstarch mixed with 1 tablespoon water

1 tablespoon confectioners' sugar

1. Preheat the oven to 350°. Spray an 8-inch square cake pan with nonstick cooking spray. Dust the pan with flour, shaking off the excess. Line the bottom of the pan with a square of wax paper. On a sheet of wax paper, combine the flour, ground ginger, baking powder, baking soda, cinnamon, mustard, and salt.

2. In a large bowl, with an electric mixer, beat the butter and brown sugar until creamy. Beat in the egg, crystallized ginger, and zest. In a small bowl, mix the buttermilk, molasses, and coffee. With a rubber spatula, alternately fold the flour mixture and buttermilk mixture into the butter mixture, beginning and ending with the flour mixture, until just blended. Scrape into the prepared pan and smooth the top. Bake for 25 minutes, or until a toothpick inserted in the center comes out clean. Transfer to a wire rack and cool in the pan for 10 minutes. Turn out onto the rack; cool completely.

3. In a small saucepan, stir together the lemon juice, granulated sugar, 2 tablespoons of water, and nutmeg. Bring to a boil, reduce to a simmer, and cook until the sugar dissolves, about 2 minutes. Return to a boil, stir in the cornstarch mixture, and cook, stirring, until slightly thickened, about 1 minute. Place the cake on a plate, dust with the confectioners' sugar, and serve with the sauce.

Helpful hint: To garnish, place 2 ferns or a paper doily on the cake, dust with confectioners' sugar, then carefully lift off the pattern-maker.

FAT: 5G/20%
CALORIES: 237
SATURATED FAT: 3G
CARBOHYDRATE: 45G
PROTEIN: 3G
CHOLESTEROL: 39MG
SODIUM: 235MG

FREEFORM APRICOT SOUFFLÉ

SERVES: 8
WORKING TIME: 20 MINUTES
TOTAL TIME: 35 MINUTES

¾ cup reduced-fat sour cream

½ cup low-fat (1%) cottage cheese

4 large egg yolks

2 tablespoons flour

1 cup apricot jam

¼ cup granulated sugar

2 tablespoons apricot brandy

1 teaspoon grated lemon zest

6 large egg whites, at room temperature

1. Preheat the oven to 425°. Spray a 10-inch nonstick skillet with an ovenproof handle with nonstick cooking spray.

2. In a food processor, combine the sour cream, cottage cheese, egg yolks, and flour and process until smooth, about 1 minute. Transfer the mixture to a large bowl and whisk in the jam, sugar, brandy, and lemon zest.

3. In a large bowl, with an electric mixer, beat the egg whites until stiff peaks form. Stir one-fourth of the egg whites into the cottage cheese mixture to lighten, then gently fold in the remaining whites. Scrape the mixture into the prepared skillet. Bake for about 15 minutes, or until golden brown and puffed.

Helpful hints: Egg whites separate more easily when they're cold, but they beat up to greater volume when they're at room temperature. Separate the eggs as soon as you take them out of the refrigerator, then set them aside in a covered bowl to come to room temperature before beating. (Refrigerate the yolks.) If the skillet you are using doesn't have an ovenproof handle, you can ovenproof it yourself by wrapping the handle in several layers of foil.

FAT: 6G/24%
CALORIES: 229
SATURATED FAT: 2.4G
CARBOHYDRATE: 37G
PROTEIN: 8G
CHOLESTEROL: 114MG
SODIUM: 130MG

This simplest of soufflés is made in a skillet for an unpretentious presentation. It bakes in just 15 minutes.

OLD-FASHIONED ORANGE BUTTERMILK CAKE

SERVES: 8
WORKING TIME: 25 MINUTES
TOTAL TIME: 50 MINUTES PLUS COOLING TIME

This sunny-flavored single-layer cake, tangy with low-fat buttermilk and orange juice, will brighten any holiday table. For a simple garnish, we add orange slices, strips of orange zest, and fresh mint sprigs. Serve as a light finale for a lavish holiday dinner, or partner with cappuccino for a weekend open house.

1¼ cups cake flour

¾ teaspoon baking powder

¼ teaspoon baking soda

¼ teaspoon salt

¼ teaspoon ground ginger

1 whole egg

1 egg white

3 tablespoons unsalted butter

½ cup granulated sugar

⅓ cup firmly packed light brown sugar

2 teaspoons grated orange zest

2 tablespoons plus 2 teaspoons orange juice

⅔ cup low-fat (1.5%) buttermilk

½ cup confectioners' sugar

1. Preheat the oven to 350°. Spray an 8-inch round cake pan with nonstick cooking spray. Dust with flour, shaking off the excess. Line the bottom of the pan with a circle of wax paper. On a sheet of wax paper, stir together the flour, baking powder, baking soda, salt, and ginger. In a small bowl, whisk together the whole egg and egg white until well combined.

2. In a large bowl, with an electric mixer, beat the butter, granulated sugar, brown sugar, and orange zest until creamy. Gradually beat in the egg mixture, 1 teaspoon at a time, until light in texture, about 2 minutes. Beat in 2 tablespoons of the orange juice. With a rubber spatula, alternately fold in the flour mixture and the buttermilk, beginning and ending with the flour mixture, until just combined. Scrape the batter into the prepared pan, smoothing the top. Bake for 23 to 25 minutes, or until a toothpick inserted in the center comes out clean. Transfer to a wire rack and cool the cake in the pan for 10 minutes. Turn out onto the rack and cool completely.

3. In a small bowl, stir together the confectioners' sugar and remaining 2 teaspoons orange juice until smooth. Place the cake on a serving plate, spoon the glaze over, letting it drip down the sides, and serve.

Helpful hints: Substitute lemon zest and juice for the orange. This cake can be made 1 month ahead through step 2, wrapped tightly in plastic wrap, and frozen. Thaw in the refrigerator overnight, then glaze.

FAT: 6G/21%
CALORIES: 237
SATURATED FAT: 3.1G
CARBOHYDRATE: 44G
PROTEIN: 3G
CHOLESTEROL: 39MG
SODIUM: 182MG

STRAWBERRY-TOPPED LEMON CHEESECAKE

SERVES: 12
WORKING TIME: 25 MINUTES
TOTAL TIME: 1 HOUR 35 MINUTES PLUS COOLING TIME

1 cup zweiback crumbs (about 12 zweiback)

1 cup graham cracker crumbs

2 tablespoons honey

1 tablespoon canola oil

2½ cups low-fat (1%) cottage cheese

11 ounces reduced-fat cream cheese (Neufchâtel)

3 tablespoons flour

1 tablespoon grated lemon zest

2 teaspoons vanilla

1¼ cups sugar

2 whole eggs

2 egg whites

1 cup halved strawberries, stems left on if desired

2 tablespoons strawberry jelly

1. Preheat the oven to 350°. In a medium bowl, stir together all the crumbs, the honey, and oil. Firmly press the mixture into the bottom and halfway up the sides of a 9-inch springform pan.

2. In a food processor or blender, combine the cottage cheese, cream cheese, flour, lemon zest, and vanilla and purée until smooth. Add the sugar, whole eggs, and egg whites and process until just combined. Scrape the batter into the crust and bake for 50 minutes, or until the cheesecake is still a little jiggly in the center but set around the edges. Turn off the oven, prop the oven door open, and let the cheesecake cool in the oven for 30 minutes. Transfer to a wire rack to cool completely.

3. With a metal spatula, loosen the cheesecake from the side of the pan and remove the pan side. Place the cake on a plate and arrange the strawberries in the center. In a small saucepan, warm the jelly over low heat until melted, brush over the strawberries, and serve.

Helpful hints: Other berries—such as raspberries or blueberries—could be nicely substituted for the strawberries. The cheesecake can be prepared up to 1 day ahead and refrigerated.

G*randly finish a holiday dinner with this spectacular cheesecake, and do so confidently, knowing its appearance and taste belie its low-fat nature—the tricks are using low-fat cottage cheese and reduced-fat cream cheese.*

FAT: 10G/29%
CALORIES: 310
SATURATED FAT: 4.7G
CARBOHYDRATE: 43G
PROTEIN: 12G
CHOLESTEROL: 58MG
SODIUM: 392MG

BANANA PUDDING

SERVES: 4
WORKING TIME: 15 MINUTES
TOTAL TIME: 15 MINUTES PLUS COOLING AND CHILLING TIME

3 cups low-fat (1%) milk
⅔ cup granulated sugar
¼ teaspoon nutmeg
¼ teaspoon ground ginger
¼ teaspoon salt
¼ cup flour
1 large egg
1 teaspoon unsalted butter
¾ pound ripe bananas, cut into
½-inch slices
8 chocolate wafer cookies
(2 ounces)

1. In a medium saucepan, combine the milk, ⅓ cup of the sugar, the nutmeg, ginger, and salt. Bring to a boil over medium heat. In a small bowl, whisk together the remaining ⅓ cup sugar and the flour. Stir into the milk mixture and cook, whisking, until thickened, about 1 minute.

2. In a small bowl, lightly beat the egg. Gradually whisk some of the hot milk mixture into the egg, then whisk the warmed egg mixture back into the saucepan. Return to the heat and cook, whisking, for 1 minute. Remove from the heat and stir in the butter. Set aside to cool to room temperature, then fold in all but 4 slices of the bananas.

3. Break the chocolate wafers into small pieces. Spoon half of the pudding into 4 bowls and top with a layer of cookies. Spoon in the remaining pudding. Chill at least 1 hour or as long as 8 hours. Before serving top each pudding with the remaining cookies and 1 of the reserved banana slices.

Helpful hint: To speed the ripening of green bananas, place them in a brown paper bag with half an apple and leave at room temperature.

Grown-up Southerners tend to be nostalgic about the "nanner" pudding they grew up with: vanilla pudding layered with sliced bananas and vanilla wafers. For our tempting update, the bananas are folded into a lightly spiced pudding and layered with crushed chocolate wafer cookies.

FAT: 7G/17%
CALORIES: 376
SATURATED FAT: 2.8G
CARBOHYDRATE: 72G
PROTEIN: 10G
CHOLESTEROL: 63MG
SODIUM: 326MG

POACHED PEARS WITH CARAMEL SAUCE

SERVES: 4
WORKING TIME: 15 MINUTES
TOTAL TIME: 40 MINUTES PLUS CHILLING TIME

These pears, infused with a spicy flavor, are lusciously teamed with a caramel sauce made with evaporated low-fat milk—not cream.

1¼ cups dry white wine
⅓ cup granulated sugar
1 bay leaf
8 black peppercorns
½ teaspoon ground ginger
¼ teaspoon cinnamon
⅛ teaspoon ground allspice
4 ripe Bartlett pears, stems left on, peeled and cored
3 tablespoons firmly packed light brown sugar
1 tablespoon light corn syrup
½ cup evaporated low-fat milk

1. In a medium saucepan just large enough to hold the pears lying on their sides, combine the wine, granulated sugar, ½ cup of water, the bay leaf, peppercorns, ginger, cinnamon, and allspice. Bring to a boil over medium heat, reduce to a simmer, and add the pears. Place a sheet of wax paper on top and poach, turning occasionally, until the pears are tender, about 20 minutes. (The poaching time will vary depending on the ripeness of the pears.) Transfer the pears and poaching liquid to a bowl and refrigerate until well chilled, at least 1 hour.

2. In a small saucepan, stir together the brown sugar and corn syrup. Stir in the evaporated milk. Bring to a boil over medium heat, reduce to a simmer, and cook until the sauce is just slightly thickened, about 5 minutes. Let cool to room temperature.

3. Spoon about half of the caramel sauce into 4 dessert dishes, dividing evenly. With a slotted spoon, place 1 pear in each dish, discarding the poaching liquid in the bowl. Spoon the remaining caramel sauce on top and serve.

Helpful hint: Both the pears and the sauce can be prepared 1 day ahead and refrigerated separately. Let the sauce stand at room temperature for about 1 hour before serving, or very gently rewarm.

FAT: 1G/4%
CALORIES: 266
SATURATED FAT: 0G
CARBOHYDRATE: 60G
PROTEIN: 3G
CHOLESTEROL: 5MG
SODIUM: 47MG

BROWNIES

MAKES: 16 BROWNIES
WORKING TIME: 15 MINUTES
TOTAL TIME: 50 MINUTES PLUS COOLING TIME

1 cup pitted prunes

⅓ cup hot water

¾ cup flour

¾ cup plus 2 tablespoons firmly packed light brown sugar

⅓ cup unsweetened cocoa powder

¾ teaspoon baking powder

⅛ teaspoon salt

¼ cup vegetable oil

2 ounces chocolate chips (about ¼ cup), melted and cooled

¼ cup light corn syrup

1 whole large egg

1 large egg white

2 teaspoons vanilla extract

1 tablespoon plus 1½ teaspoons chopped walnuts

1. Preheat the oven to 350°. Spray an 8-inch square baking pan with nonstick cooking spray. Line the bottom with waxed paper. In a food processor, process the prunes and hot water to a smooth purée.

2. In a large bowl, combine the flour, brown sugar, cocoa powder, baking powder, salt, oil, melted chocolate, corn syrup, whole egg, and egg white. Stir in the prune purée and vanilla.

3. Scrape the batter into the prepared pan and smooth the top. Sprinkle the walnuts over and bake for about 35 minutes, or until a toothpick inserted in the center comes out clean. Cool the brownies in the pan on a wire rack before cutting and serving.

Helpful hint: If you want to freeze the brownies, turn out the whole uncut "cake" onto a sheet of foil, wrap, and freeze: They'll stay fresher if you don't cut them until you're ready to serve.

VALUES ARE PER BROWNIE
FAT: 6G/29%
CALORIES: 170
SATURATED FAT: 1.3G
CARBOHYDRATE: 31G
PROTEIN: 2G
CHOLESTEROL: 13MG
SODIUM: 59MG

Good news! America's favorite bar cookie has been slimmed down—with no loss of fudgy flavor.

SPIKED STRAWBERRY-RASPBERRY SORBET

SERVES: 4
WORKING TIME: 10 MINUTES
TOTAL TIME: 10 MINUTES PLUS FREEZING TIME

Sorbets capture the pure flavor of fruit in all its delicious intensity; this one has the added double punch of tequila and orange liqueur, making it a sort of frozen berry margarita. We've used frozen raspberries and strawberries, so you can serve this splendid dessert at any time of year. Garnish the sorbet with a few fresh berries, or top it with thin strips of orange and lime zest.

12-ounce package unsweetened frozen raspberries, thawed
12-ounce package unsweetened frozen strawberries, thawed
¾ cup granulated sugar
¼ cup fresh lime juice
3 tablespoons honey
2 tablespoons tequila or vodka
2 tablespoons orange liqueur (such as Triple Sec) or orange juice

1. In a food processor, combine the raspberries, strawberries, sugar, lime juice, honey, tequila, and orange liqueur and process to a smooth purée. Push the purée through a strainer to remove the seeds.

2. Transfer the fruit purée to the canister of an ice cream maker and freeze according to the manufacturer's directions. Divide among 4 bowls and serve.

Helpful hint: Use exactly the amounts of tequila and liqueur called for in the recipe: Alcohol lowers the freezing point of the mixture, and if you add too much alcohol, the sorbet may not freeze to the right consistency.

FAT: 1G/3%
CALORIES: 313
SATURATED FAT: 0G
CARBOHYDRATE: 74G
PROTEIN: 1G
CHOLESTEROL: 0MG
SODIUM: 3MG

MOCHA PUDDING CAKE

SERVES: 8
WORKING TIME: 25 MINUTES
TOTAL TIME: 55 MINUTES

*I*f you find that the whole process of baking seems magical, this recipe will be even more astonishing than most. You mix the batter, sprinkle it with a mixture of cocoa powder and sugar, and pour hot water over it; forty minutes later you're swooning over a luscious, brownie-like chocolate cake with a thick, hot, fudgy sauce. Even more amazing: It's low in fat, too.

¾ cup firmly packed dark brown sugar

6 tablespoons plus 1½ teaspoons unsweetened cocoa powder

1 cup granulated sugar

2 tablespoons plus 1 teaspoon instant espresso powder

1 cup flour

2 teaspoons baking powder

¼ teaspoon cinnamon

¼ teaspoon salt

½ cup low-fat (1%) milk

¼ cup unsalted butter, melted

1 teaspoon vanilla extract

1¾ cups very hot water

1½ cups nonfat coffee frozen yogurt

1. Preheat the oven to 350°. In a small bowl, combine the brown sugar, ¼ cup of the cocoa powder, ¼ cup of the granulated sugar, and 1 teaspoon of the espresso powder. Set aside.

2. In a medium bowl, combine the flour, baking powder, cinnamon, salt, the remaining 2 tablespoons plus 1½ teaspoons cocoa powder, the remaining ¾ cup granulated sugar, and the remaining 2 tablespoons espresso powder. In a small bowl, combine the milk, butter, and vanilla. Stir the milk mixture into the flour mixture until well combined.

3. Scrape the batter into an ungreased 9-inch square baking pan. Sprinkle the reserved brown sugar mixture over the batter. Pour the hot water over and bake for 40 minutes, or until the top is set and the mixture is bubbly.

4. Divide the mocha pudding cake among 8 plates. Serve warm or at room temperature with a scoop of frozen yogurt alongside.

Helpful hint: You can substitute regular instant coffee if espresso powder is not available; use the powdered kind rather than freeze-dried crystals, which will not readily combine with the other dry ingredients.

FAT: 7G/19%
CALORIES: 341
SATURATED FAT: 4G
CARBOHYDRATE: 69G
PROTEIN: 4G
CHOLESTEROL: 16MG
SODIUM: 225MG

GLOSSARY

Allspice—A dark, round, dried berry about the size of a peppercorn, called allspice because it tastes like a blend of cloves, cinnamon, and nutmeg. Usually sold in ground form, allspice is often mistakenly thought to be a mix of several spices.

Balsamic vinegar—A dark red vinegar made from the unfermented juice of pressed grapes, most commonly the white Trebbiano, and aged in wooden casks. The authentic version is produced in a small region in Northern Italy, around Modena, and tastes richly sweet with a slight sour edge. Because this vinegar is so mild, you can make dressings and marinades with less oil.

Basil—A highly fragrant herb with a flavor somewhere between licorice and cloves. Like many fresh herbs, basil will retain more of its taste if added at the end of cooking; dried basil is quite flavorful and can stand up to longer cooking. Store fresh basil by placing the stems in a container of water and covering the leaves loosely with a plastic bag.

Beans, cannellini—Large white kidney beans often used in Italian cooking. Cannellini are sold both dried and canned. Like all canned beans, cannellini should be rinsed and drained before use; this removes much of the sodium present in the canning liquid and also gives the beans a fresher flavor. Look for cannellini in the canned vegetable or Italian foods section of your supermarket.

Buttermilk—A tart, tangy milk product made by adding a special bacterial culture to nonfat or low-fat milk. Buttermilk's acidity inhibits the development of gluten (a tough protein in flour), so baked goods made with it turn out tender. Our recipes call for 1.5% buttermilk. In a pinch, make your own "buttermilk" by combining 1 tablespoon lemon juice or vinegar with enough 1% milk to measure 1 cup.

Canadian bacon—A lean smoked meat, similar to ham. This bacon is precooked, so it can be used as is. (For extra flavor, cook it in a skillet until the edges are lightly crisped.) Just a small amount adds big flavor to soups and stews, but with much less fat than regular bacon.

Chili powder—A commercially prepared seasoning mixture made from ground dried chilies, oregano, cumin, coriander, salt, and dehydrated garlic, and sometimes cloves and allspice. Use in chilis, sauces, and spice rubs for a Southwestern punch. Chili powders can range in strength from mild to very hot; for proper potency, use within 6 months of purchase. Pure ground chili powder, without any added spices, is also available.

Chives—A member of the onion family distinguished by long, green shoots. Because their subtle flavor is lost when heated, it is best to add chives to a cooked dish at the last minute. Snip rather than chop chives to avoid crushing the delicate herb.

Chutney—A sweet, spicy condiment ranging from smooth to chunky, generally made of fruit or vegetables, vinegar, sweeteners, and spices. Chutney is most often used in Indian cuisine, especially as an accompaniment to curries, but it's also a lively addition to sauces.

Cilantro/Coriander—A lacy-leaved green herb (called by both names). The plant's seeds are dried and used as a spice (known as coriander). The fresh herb, much used in Mexican and Asian cooking, looks like pale flat-leaf parsley and is strongly aromatic. Store fresh cilantro by placing the stems in a container of water and covering the leaves loosely with a plastic bag. Coriander seeds are important in Mexican and Indian cuisines; sold whole or ground, they have a somewhat citrusy flavor that complements both sweet and savory dishes.

Couscous—Fine granules of pasta made from semolina flour. Of North African origin, couscous is traditionally cooked by steaming it over boiling water or a pot of stew. The couscous sold in boxes in American markets is quick cooking ("instant"): It requires only a few minutes of steeping in boiling water or broth. Couscous can be served as a side dish, like rice, or used as the basis for a hearty main dish.

Cumin—A pungent, peppery-tasting spice essential to many Middle Eastern, Asian, Mexican, and Mediterranean dishes. Available ground or as whole seeds; the spice can be toasted in a dry skillet to bring out its flavor.

Currants, dried—Tiny raisins made from a small variety of grape. Use interchangeably with raisins for baking or in sauces or rice dishes, keeping in mind that currants are smaller and will disperse more flavor and sweetness because you get more currants in every bite.

Curry powder—Not one spice but a mix of spices, commonly used in Indian cooking to flavor a dish with sweet heat and add a characteristic yellow-orange color. While curry blends vary (consisting of as many as 20 herbs and spices), they typically include turmeric (for its vivid yellow color), fenugreek, ginger, cardamom, cloves, cumin, coriander, and cayenne pepper. Commercially available Madras curry is hotter than other store-bought types.

Dill—A name given to both the fresh herb and the small, hard seeds that are used as a spice. Add the light, lemony, fresh dill leaves (also called dillweed) toward the end of cooking. Dill seeds provide a pleasantly distinctive bitter taste and marry beautifully with sour cream- or yogurt-based sauces.

Fennel, fresh—A vegetable resembling a flattened head of celery, with a subtle licorice flavor. The feathery fronds that top the stalks are used as an herb, and the bulb is used raw and cooked, like celery. Choose firm, unblemished fennel bulbs with fresh green fronds. Store in the refrigerator in a plastic bag for three to four days. Fennel seeds, which come from a slightly different plant, have an almost sweet, licorice-like taste; they are often used in Italian dishes and with fish.

Fennel seeds—The seeds of the common fennel plant, which have a slightly sweet, licorice-like taste. Fennel seeds are often used to season Italian sausages, and are also used in pasta sauces and with seafood.

Feta cheese—A soft, crumbly, cured Greek cheese, traditionally made from sheep's or goat's milk. White and rindless, feta is usually available as a square block packed in brine; it's best to rinse it before using to eliminate some of the sodium. Use feta in casseroles and salads for bold flavor.

Garlic—The bulb of a plant closely related to onions. Garlic can be assertive or sweetly mild, depending on how it is prepared: Minced or crushed garlic yields a more powerful flavor than whole or halved cloves. Whereas sautéing turns garlic rich and savory, slow simmering or roasting produces a mild, mellow flavor. Select firm, plump heads with dry skins; avoid heads that have begun to sprout. Store in an open or loosely covered container in a cool, dark place for up to 2 months.

Ginger—A thin-skinned root used as a seasoning. Fresh ginger adds sweet pungency to Asian and Indian dishes. Tightly wrapped, unpeeled fresh ginger can be refrigerated for 1 week or frozen for up to 6 months. Ground ginger is not a true substitute for fresh, but it will lend a warming flavor to soups, stews, and sauces.

Green chilies, canned—The pungent, pod-shaped fruit of various chili pepper plants, ranging from exceptionally hot to quite mild. Many varieties are available fresh, but canned chilies tend to be either jalapeños (see below) or those simply labeled "mild." Use the mild green chilies—which come whole or chopped—to add a subtly piquant green chili flavor to soups, stews, and casseroles.

Hot pepper sauce—A highly incendiary sauce made from a variety of hot peppers flavored with vinegar and salt. This sauce comes into play in Caribbean and Tex-Mex dishes as well as Creole and Cajun cuisines. Use sparingly, drop by drop, to introduce a hot edge to any dish.

Jalapeño peppers—Hot green chili peppers about two inches long and an inch in diameter, with rounded tips. Most of the heat resides in the membranes (ribs) of the pepper, so remove them for a milder effect—wear gloves to protect your hands from the volatile oils. Jalapeños are also sold whole or chopped in small cans, although the canned version is not nearly as arresting as the fresh. Toss a little jalapeño into soups, sautés, baked dishes, or anywhere you want to create some fire

Julienne—Thin, uniform, matchstick-size pieces of an ingredient, usually a vegetable, typically 2 inches long. To form julienne, cut the food into long, thin slices; stack the slices and cut lengthwise into sticks, then crosswise into the desired length.

Leek—A mild-flavored member of the onion family that resembles a giant scallion. Buy leeks with firm bottoms and fresh-looking tops; store them, loosely wrapped in plastic, in the refrigerator. To prepare, trim the root end and any blemished dark green ends. Split the leek lengthwise, then rinse thoroughly to remove any dirt trapped between the leaves.

Mango—A yellow-skinned fruit with vivid orange flesh and an unmistakable sweet-tart flavor. Although they originated in India, mangoes are now cultivated in other parts of the world. Mangoes can range from about 10 ounces to about four pounds in weight; all have a large, flat seed from which the flesh must be cut away. An unripe mango can be placed in a brown paper bag at room temperature to ripen. When ripe, the fruit will give to slight pressure and will have a rich, flowery fragrance.

Marjoram—A member of the mint family that tastes like mildly sweet oregano. Fresh marjoram should be added at the end of the cooking so the flavor doesn't vanish. Dried marjoram, sold in leaf and ground form (the more intense leaf being preferable), stands up to longer cooking.

Mayonnaise, reduced-fat—A form of mayonnaise in which other thickeners, such as food starch, take the place of some of the oil. Reduced-fat mayonnaise is not quite as rich-tasting as regular, but it has a light, tangy flavor. Don't substitute fat-free mayonnaise, which usually has water as its first ingredient, and is quite tasteless.

Mozzarella cheese—A very mild-flavored Italian cheese with exceptional melting properties. Mozzarella was originally made from water buffalo's milk, but is now more commonly made from cow's milk; it is available in whole-milk, part-skim, and fat-free varieties. The part-skim variety is the best option for cooking, as it is relatively low in fat but still has a nice texture and good melting properties. The rubbery texture of nonfat mozzarella makes it unsuitable for most recipes.

Nutmeg—The hard, brown, nutlike seed of the nutmeg tree. Although mainly used in sweet dishes, nutmeg also complements green vegetables such as broccoli and spinach. Ground nutmeg is convenient, but the flavor of freshly grated nutmeg is far superior. This whole spice keeps almost indefinitely, and you can grate it freshly as needed on a special nutmeg grater or an ordinary box grater.

Olive, Calamata—A ripe, purple-black, brine-cured Greek olive that adds a distinctive earthy bite to salads, pasta sauces, and other savory dishes. But use sparingly, since all olives contain fat and salt, the latter a result of processing.

Olive oil—A fragrant oil pressed from olives. Olive oil is one of the signature ingredients of Italian cuisine. This oil is rich in monounsaturated fats, which make it more healthful than butter and other solid shortenings. Olive oil comes in different grades, reflecting the method used to refine the oil and the resulting level of acidity. The finest, most expensive oil is cold-pressed extra-virgin, which should be reserved for flavoring salad dressings and other uncooked or lightly cooked foods. "Virgin" and "pure" olive oils are slightly more acidic with less olive flavor, and are fine for most types of cooking.

Orzo—A small pasta shape that resembles large grains of rice. Orzo is popular in Greece and makes a delicious alternative to rice, especially with Mediterranean-inspired meals.

Paprika—A spice ground from a variety of red peppers and used in many traditional Hungarian and Spanish dishes. Paprika colors foods a characteristic brick-red and flavors dishes from sweet to spicy-hot, depending on the pepper potency. Like all pepper-based spices, paprika loses its color and flavor with time; check your supply and replace it if necessary.

Parmesan—An intensely flavored, hard grating cheese. Genuine Italian Parmesan, stamped "Parmigiano-Reggiano" on the rind, is produced in the Emilia-Romagna region, and tastes richly nutty with a slight sweetness. Buy Parmesan in blocks and grate it as needed for best flavor and freshness. For a fine, fluffy texture that melts into hot foods, grate the cheese in a hand-cranked grater.

Pine nuts—The seeds of certain pine trees that grow in several parts of the world, including Italy. Called pignoli or pinoli in Italian, they are best known for their role in pesto, the classic basil sauce for pasta; they're also used in cookies and other desserts. Use pine nuts sparingly, since they are high in fat. Look for them in the nuts or Italian foods section of your market. Store the nuts in a tightly closed jar in the freezer for up to six months. Toast pine nuts briefly before using to bring out their full flavor.

Potatoes, small red—Diminutive versions of the waxy round red boiling potato, usually no larger than 1½ inches in diameter. These are sometimes mistakenly called "new potatoes"—which they may or may not be, depending on the season (the term "new" refers to any type of potato that has been freshly dug and has not been stored). Small white potatoes can be used instead.

Rice vinegar—A pale vinegar made from fermented rice, it is milder than most other types of vinegar. Its light, clean flavor is much favored in Asian cooking. Japanese rice vinegar is widely available; be sure to buy the unseasoned type.

Ricotta cheese—A fresh, creamy white, Italian cheese with a grainier texture than cottage cheese and a slightly sweet flavor. Available in whole-milk and part-skim versions, it is often used in stuffed and baked pastas, and a little part-skim ricotta can be stirred into a sauce for added richness as well as creamy body.

Romano cheese—A hard grating cheese similar to Parmesan but with a saltier, more robust flavor. Italian Romano cheese is traditionally made from sheep's milk and is called pecorino Romano; the American version is most often made from cow's milk (or a blend of cow's and goat's or sheep's milk). Grate Romano as you would Parmesan and use it in assertively flavored dishes; Romano can overpower more delicate foods.

Rosemary—An aromatic herb with needle-like leaves and a sharp pine-citrus flavor. Rosemary's robust flavor complements lamb particularly well, and it stands up to long cooking better than most herbs. If you can't get fresh rosemary, use whole dried leaves, which retain the flavor of the fresh herb quite well. Crush or chop rosemary leaves with a mortar and pestle or a chef's knife.

Rutabaga—A larger, rounder relative of the turnip, with a thick skin and deep-yellow flesh. Rutabagas can be used interchangeably with turnips, but their flesh is rich in beta carotene (turnips have none), so there is an advantage to seeking them out. The purplish-tan skin of rutabagas is almost always heavily waxed, so this vegetable should be pared with a sharp knife before using. Rutabagas will keep in the refrigerator for two weeks or more.

Sage—An intensely fragrant herb with grayish-green leaves. Sage will infuse a dish with a pleasant, musty mint taste; it's especially good with poultry. In its dried form, sage is sold as whole leaves, ground, and in a fluffy "rubbed" version. For the best flavor from the dried herb, buy whole leaves and crush them yourself.

Sesame oil, Oriental—A dark, polyunsaturated oil, pressed from toasted sesame seeds, used as a flavor enhancer in many Asian and Indian dishes. Do not confuse the Oriental oil with its lighter colored counterpart, which is cold-pressed from untoasted sesame seeds and imparts a much milder flavor. Store either version in the refrigerator for up to 6 months.

Shallot—A member of the onion family, looking rather like large cloves of garlic. Shallots are used to infuse savory dishes with a mild, delicate onion flavor. Refrigerate for no more than 1 week to maintain maximum flavor.

Shiitake mushroom—A meaty, Oriental variety of mushroom with an almost steak-like flavor, used in pasta sauces and salads for depth. Choose fresh shiitakes that are plump and unblemished, and avoid broken or shriveled caps, a

sign of age. Remove the tough part of the stem before slicing. Dried shiitakes, which must be reconstituted in warm water before using, are also available.

Snow pea—A flat pea pod that is fully edible, even uncooked. Slightly sweet and very tender, snow peas need only quick cooking and add both crunch and color. Select crisp, bright green pods, and refrigerate in a plastic bag for up to 3 days. String the peas and remove the tips before using.

Sour cream—A soured dairy product, resulting from treating sweet cream with a lactic acid culture. Regular sour cream contains at least 18 percent milk fat by volume; reduced-fat sour cream contains 4 percent fat; nonfat sour cream is, of course, fat-free. In cooking, the reduced-fat version can be substituted for regular sour cream; use the nonfat cautiously since it behaves differently, especially in baking. To avoid curdling, do not subject sour cream to high heat.

Soy sauce, reduced-sodium—A condiment made from fermented soybeans, wheat, and salt used to add a salty, slightly sweet flavor to food. Soy sauce is especially at home in Asian-style preparations. Keep in mind that reduced-sodium sauces add the same flavor but much less sodium.

Sun-dried tomato—Plum tomatoes that have been dried slowly to produce a chewy, intensely flavorful sauce ingredient. Although oil-packed tomatoes are widely available, the dry-packed type are preferred for their lower fat content. For many recipes, the dried tomatoes must be soaked in hot water to soften them before using.

Tarragon—A potent, sweet herb with a licorice- or anise-like taste; often used with chicken or fish. Dried tarragon loses its flavor quickly; check its potency by crushing a little between your fingers and sniffing for the strong aroma. As with most herbs, you may substitute 1 teaspoon dried for each tablespoon of fresh.

Turmeric—A root used in Indian cooking as well as in preparing curry powder. When dried and ground, this spice is valued more for its ability to color dishes a vivid yellow-orange than for its bitter, pungent flavor. It's a sensible coloring substitute for the more extravagantly expensive saffron.

Watercress—A slightly peppery-tasting aquatic herb that adds zip to salads and cooked dishes. The assertive flavor of watercress provides a peppery counterpoint to savory or sweet flavors. To prepare, rinse the bunch of watercress under cold water and blot dry with paper towels. Remove the tough stalks and use just the tender stems, or, for a more delicate flavor, use only the leaves.

Yogurt, low-fat and nonfat—Delicately tart cultured milk products made from low-fat or skim milk. Plain yogurt makes a healthful base for marinades, and its acidity tenderizes the meat a bit and helps seasonings to penetrate (tandoori chicken is marinated in a yogurt-based sauce). Be careful when cooking with yogurt, as it will curdle if boiled or stirred too vigorously: Adding flour or cornstarch to the yogurt before adding it to a hot sauce helps stabilize it.

Zest, citrus—The thin, outermost colored part of the rind of citrus fruits that contains strongly flavored oils. Zest imparts an intense flavor that makes a refreshing contrast to the richness of meat, poultry, or fish. Remove the zest with a grater, citrus zester, or vegetable peeler; be careful to remove only the colored layer, not the bitter white pith beneath it.

INDEX

Time-Life Books is a division of Time Life Inc.

TIME LIFE INC.

PRESIDENT and CEO: George Artandi

TIME-LIFE CUSTOM PUBLISHING

VICE PRESIDENT and PUBLISHER: Terry Newell
ASSOCIATE PUBLISHER: Teresa Hartnett

Vice President of Sales and Marketing: Neil Levin
Director of Special Markets: Liz Ziehl
Managing Editor: Donia Steele
Production Manager: Carolyn Clark
Quality Assurance Manager: Miriam P. Newton

Design for *Great Taste-Low Fat* by David Fridberg
  of Miles Fridberg Molinaroli, Inc.
Cover design by Christopher M. Register

TIME-LIFE BOOKS

PRESIDENT: John D. Hall
PUBLISHER/MANAGING EDITOR: Neil Kagan

Vice President, Director of Finance: Christopher Hearing
Vice President, Book Production: Marjann Caldwell
Director of Publishing Technology: Betsi McGrath
Director of Photography and Research: John Conrad Weiser
Director of Editorial Administration (Acting): Barbara Levitt
Library: Louise D. Forstall

 REBUS, INC.

PUBLISHER: Rodney M. Friedman
EDITORIAL DIRECTOR: Charles L. Mee

Editorial Staff for *Great Taste-Low Fat*
Director, Recipe Development and Photography:
  Grace Young
Editorial Director: Kate Slate
Senior Recipe Developer: Sandra Rose Gluck
Recipe Developers: Helen Jones, Paul Piccuito,
  Marianne Zanzarella
Managing Editor: Julee Binder Shapiro
Writers: Bonnie J. Slotnick, David J. Ricketts
Editorial Assistant: James W. Brown, Jr.
Nutritionists: Hill Nutrition Associates

Art Director: Timothy Jeffs
Photographers: Lisa Koenig, Vincent Lee
Photographers' Assistants: Alix Berenberg, Eugene DeLucie,
  Katie Bleacher Everard, Petra Liebetanz,
  Rainer Fehringer, Robert Presciutti
Food Stylists: A.J. Battifarano, Helen Jones, Karen Pickus,
  Roberta Rall, Andrea B. Swenson, Karen J.M. Tack
Assistant Food Stylists: Mako Antonishek,
  Catherine Chatham, Charles Davis, Amy Lord, Ellie Ritt
Prop Stylists: Sara Abalan, Debra Donahue
Prop Coordinator: Karin Martin

Books produced by Time-Life Custom Publishing are
available at special bulk discount for promotional and
premium use. Custom adaptations can also be created to
meet your specific marketing goals.
Call 1-800-323-5255